INSIDE THE AMERICAN

INSIDE THE AMERICAN

ANTON CORBIJN

SCHIRMER/MOSEL

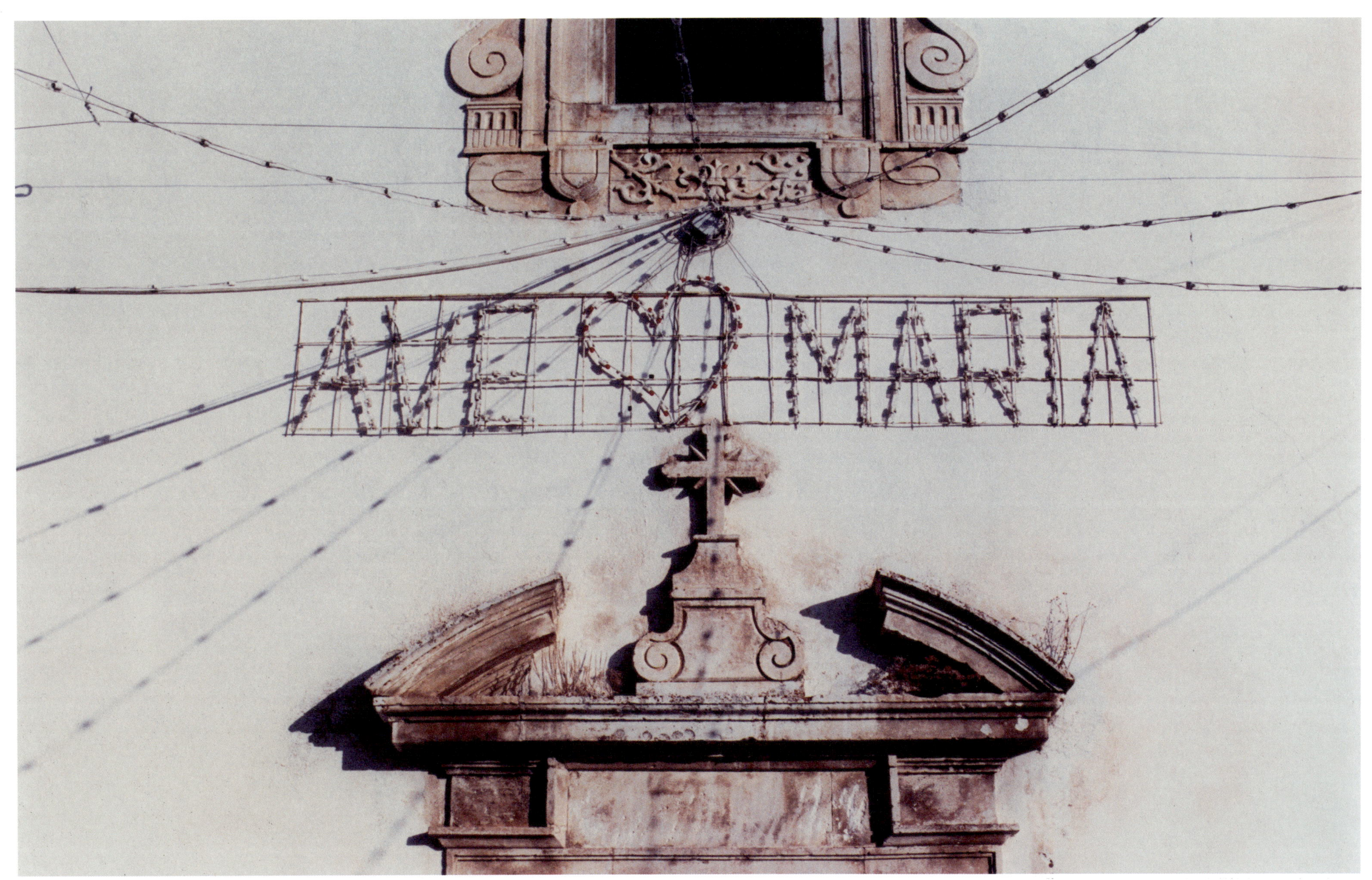

Front of the church from where the procession in Castel del Monte starts.

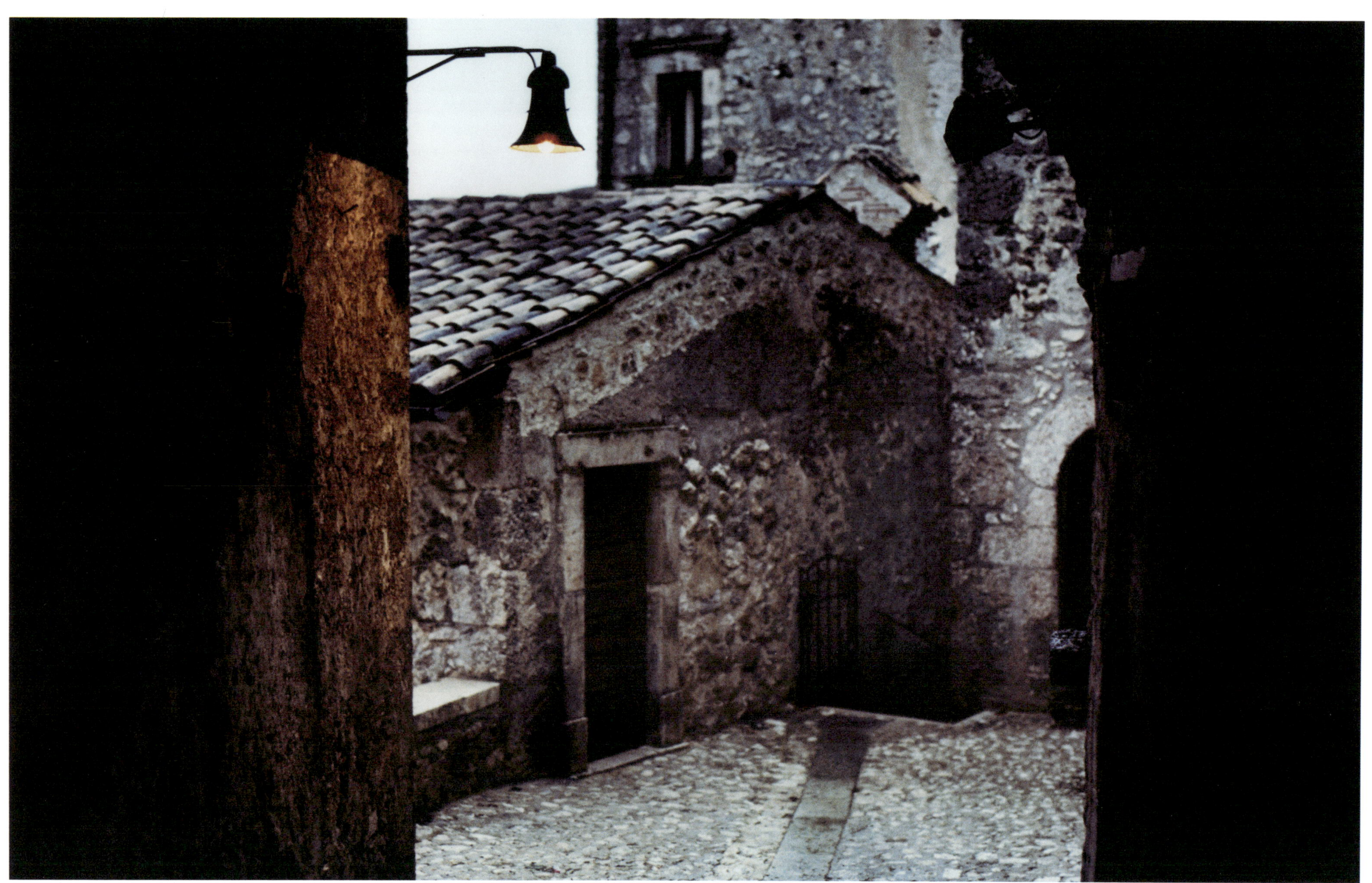

The entrance to my room in Santo Stefano di Sessanio where i stayed for a month while filming in Castel del Monte and surroundings.

PRODUCTION

Starting on a filmproject is kind of daunting. It's like waking up a young abandoned wild animal from a deep sleep and taking care of it till it can take care of itself and let it go back into the wild. You don't know really what it is you've just taken on.

After finishing and releasing the lifechanging experience that was CONTROL, i set out to do the promotour for it. I found this to be so souldestroying that i went back to my life as a still photographer for a while. However i soon realised that i was bitten by the filmbug so went in search of another adventure, another story.

Wanting to avoid the obvious, i rejected all scripts sent to me dealing with England in the 70's or with deceased musicians.

My surprise entry into the filmworld had been at a relatively late stage in my life and i was, still am, determined to get as many varied experiences as i can in that world. I went searching for a different genre, something fictional and contemporary. I came across a script based on 'A Very Private

In every town in Abruzzo were no-go areas after the earthquake which is why i couldn't use all the locations i found in january 2009 for the film. This is taken in Santo Stefano, which like Castel del Monte, had a damaged tower.

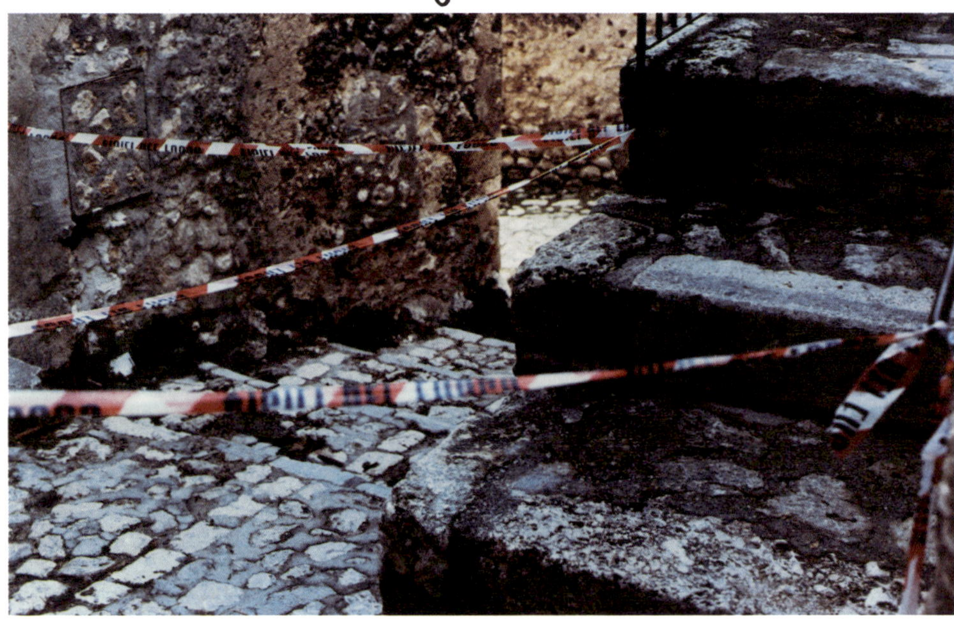

Testing film and looks with Thekla Reuten with a wig we ended up not using.

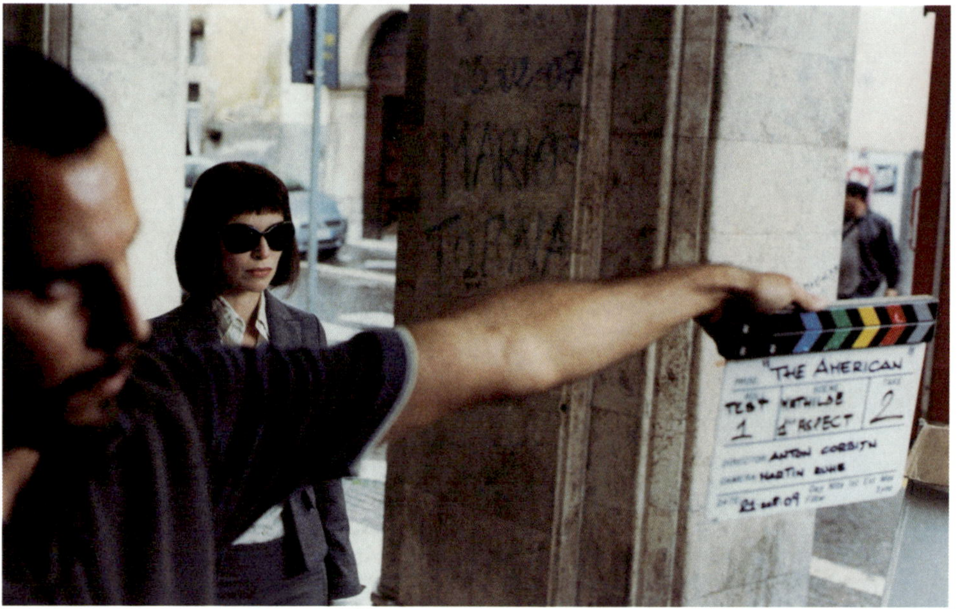

Gentleman' by an english author named Martin Booth. After reading that script, i read the novel and realised the way i saw a film based on this book would require a fresh start. I met up with Rowan Joffe and together we set off to Italy for inspiration, locations and ideas for the script in the area the book describes: Abruzzo.

My love for Westerns made me want to install a story of morality as well as a kind of western structure to the story. You know, the one where a guy kills someone, becomes a fugitive and hides in another small western town. Being the outsider there, he'll hook up with the priest (spiritual)

The market place in Sulmona as seen from my balcony. I stayed there for about 3 weeks. The scene where Jack meets Mathilde for the first time is on the right side of this picture but in better weather.

At home with Ennio Morricone in Rome. We talked thru an interpreter about westerns and his music, and ended up with a short bit of 'once upon a time' music in a bar scene. I gave Rowan Joffe a bunch of his cd's to listen to while writing the screenplay, although i might be the only one to spot a connection between the film and a western.

9

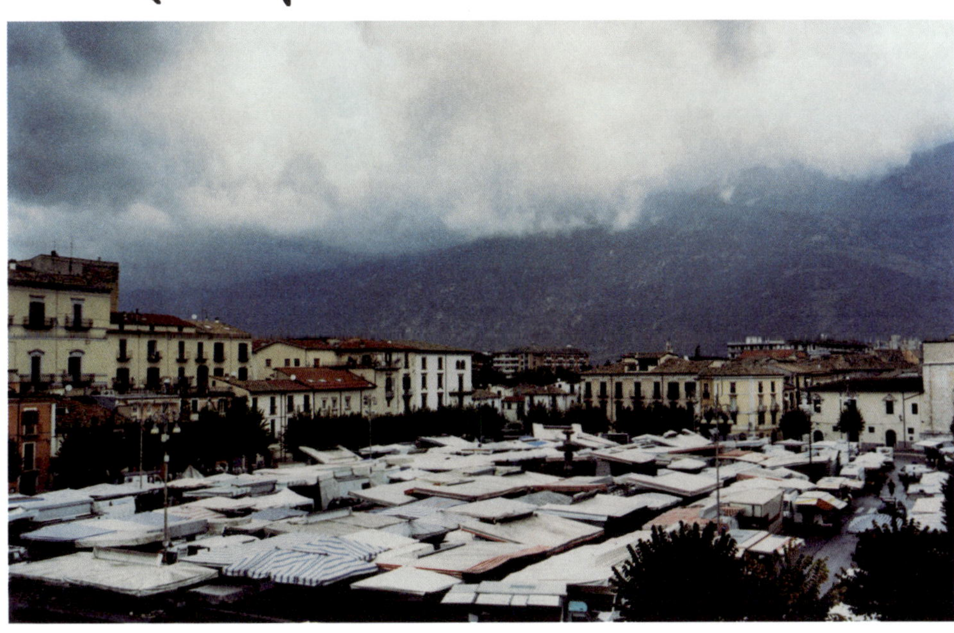

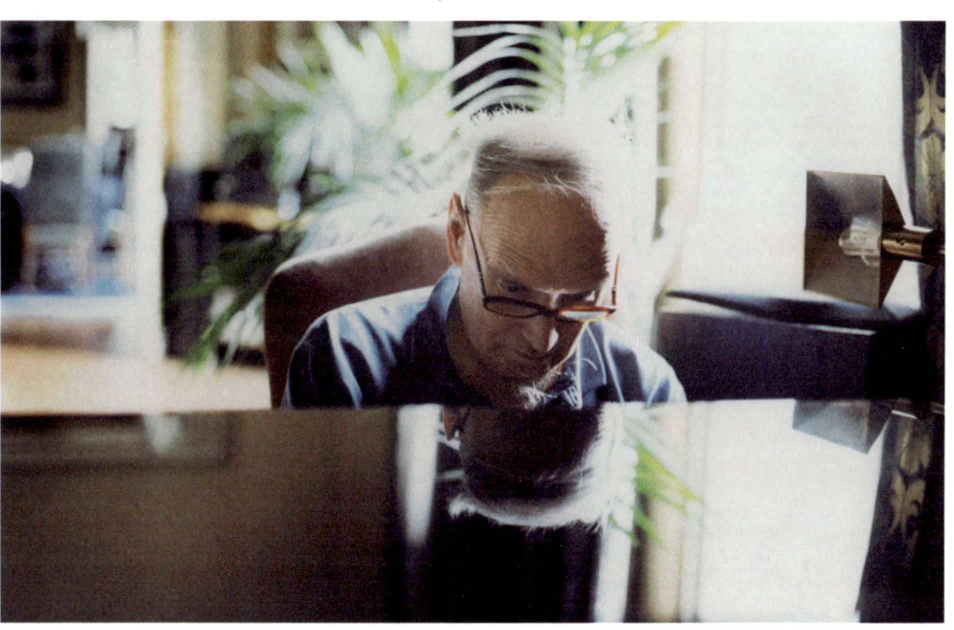

and the hooker (physical). The past catches up with him, there's a shoot-out and he leaves town again. Classic.

Abruzzo is also home to some fantastic Western like locations such as Campo Imperatore which is pictured elsewhere in this book. After locating some stunning visual settings we returned home. Three months later, script in hand, i was meeting up with George Clooney. It was a day I'll never forget – april 6 2009. I woke up in St. Louis, Missouri, to the news of a disaster: L'Aquila, our main location for the film, looked all but destroyed by a terrible earthquake. I was a technical scout at the river which we heavily 'greened' up a week prior to the shooting and we had a security guard at night after a group of wild boars tore into our 'paradise' one night.

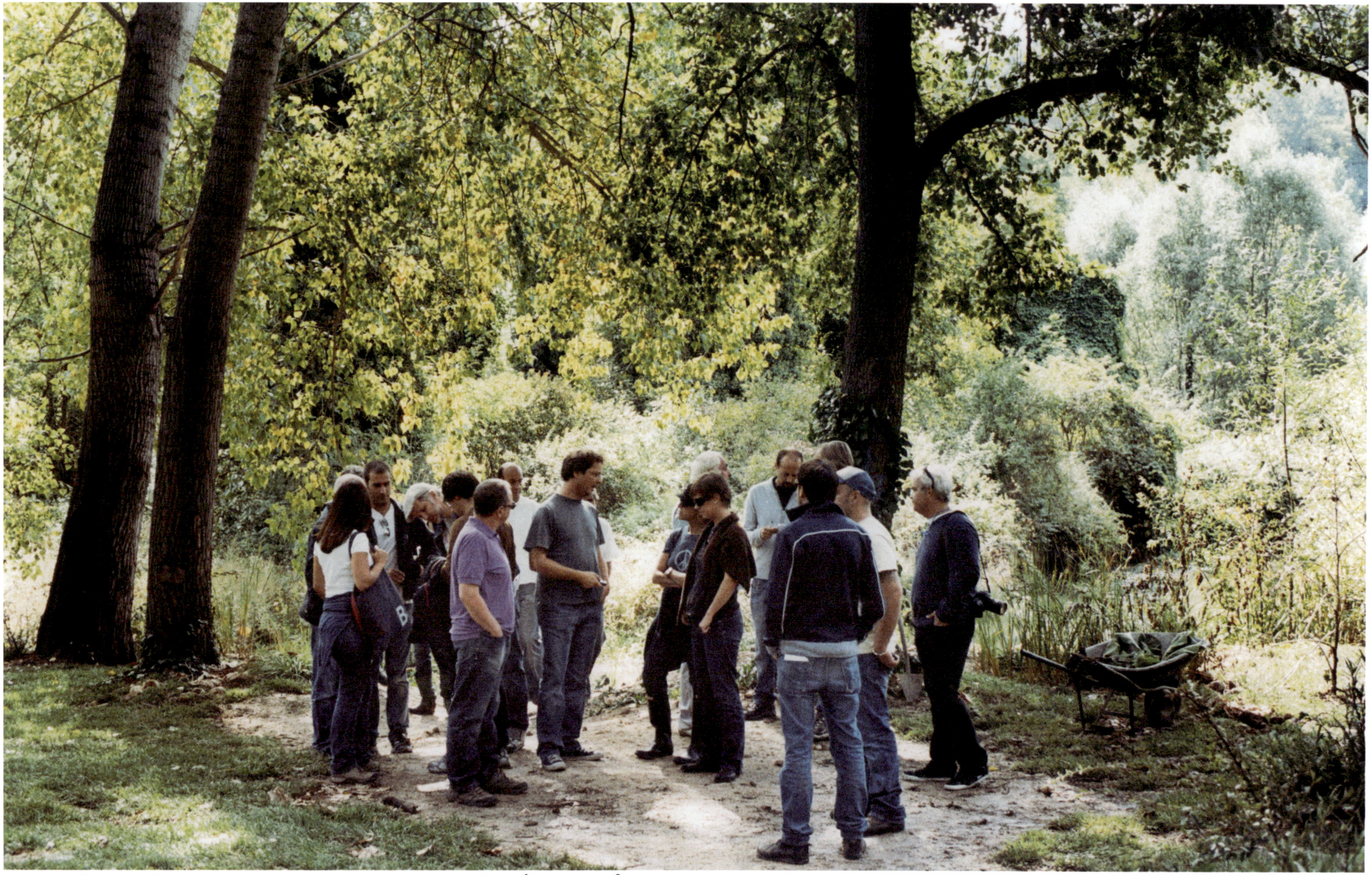

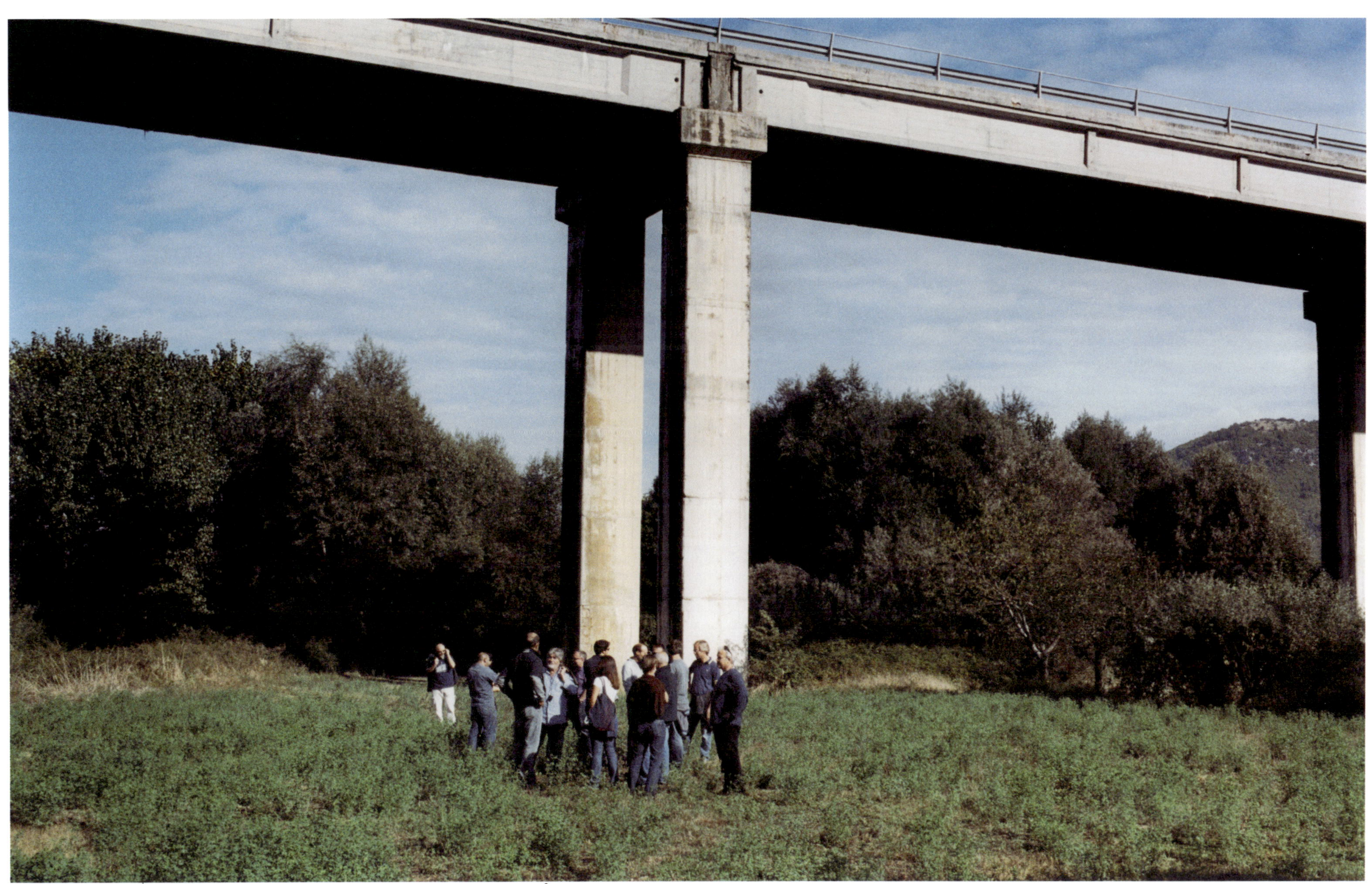

again, a tec scout for a scene where George throws his phone from the car when on a viaduct

our humble offices during the pre-production on the grounds of Cinecitta Studios. Legendary place and you couldn't help feeling special walking around there. in the 60's and 70's so many memorable films + names were connected to this studio.

think of Fellini, Antonioni, Visconti, Bertolucci, Pasolini, Sergio Leone etc. i loved this huge head that i encountered on my daily walk to the canteen.

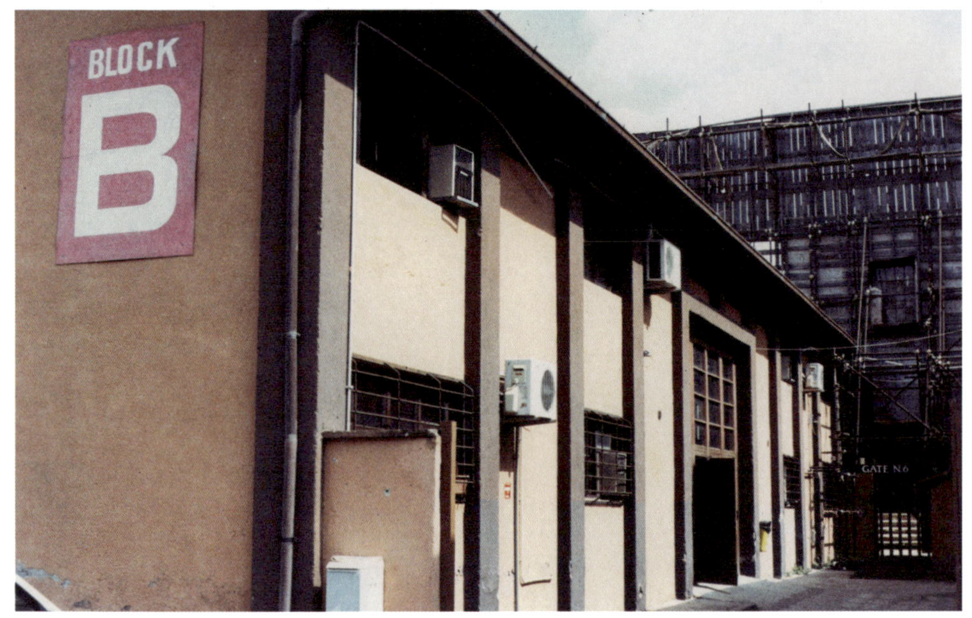

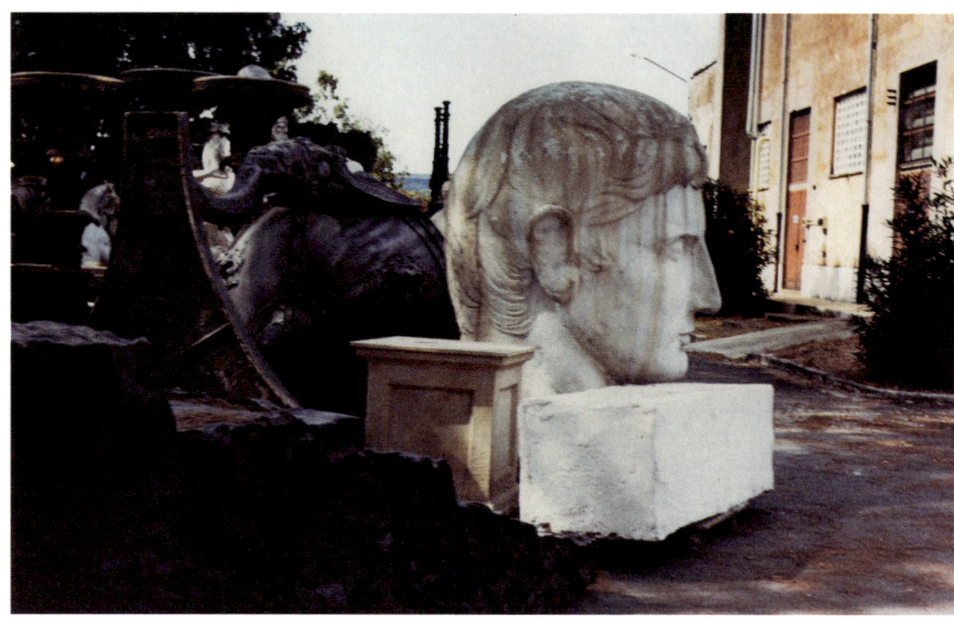

convinced that despite me meeting George that day, the movie was not going to happen. The destruction was immense, people lost their lives, their homes, their family. Surely, the movie would be collapsing too. In the end George liked the script and (i guess) my work enough to commit to this film, we managed where needed to find alternative locations in Abruzzo to replace those we lost, with Sulmona taking L'Aquila's place.

The original novel deals with an eccentric English guy, part hit-man, part gunsmith, whose idea to lay low is to hide in a small town in the Abruzzan mountains under the guise of a butterfly lover and -painter.

our gun expert, jon baker, had a large selection of guns for us to choose from. it is an area where i know very little about, growing up in a pacifist household.

the art department seemed more fun, researching images for the poster in the brothel. in the end we went with a more graphic illustration. in the garage of Fabio we needed a typical car/nudity associated calendar which we found easily.

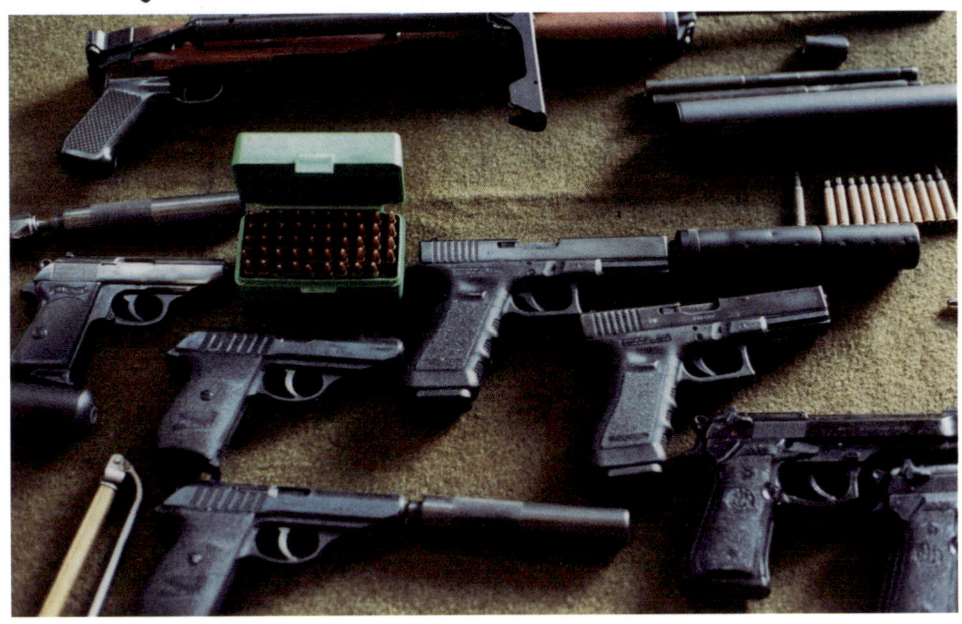

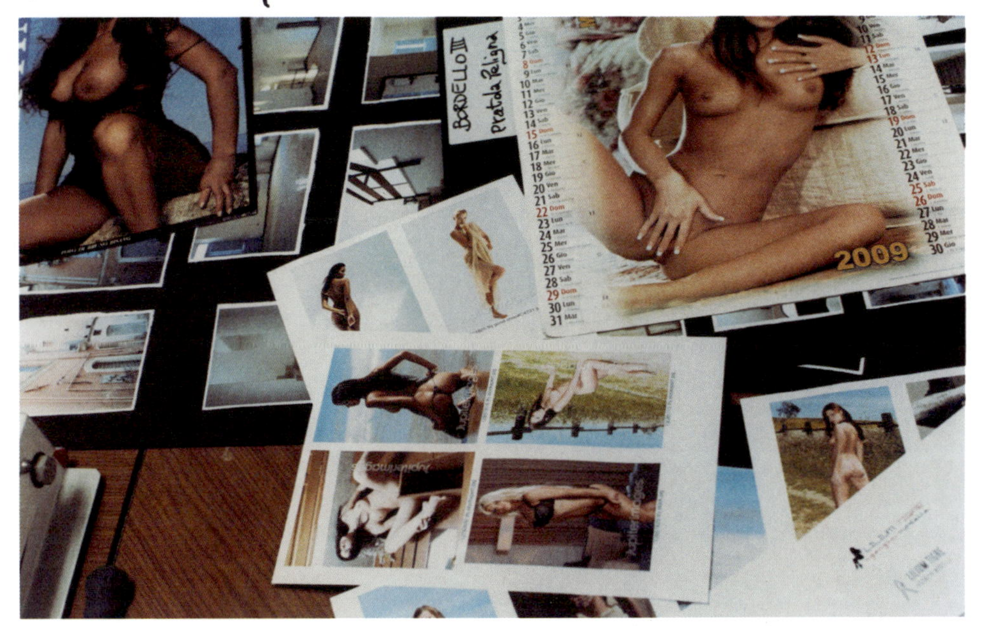

Since i made the protagonist American, that kind of eccentricity seemed implausible. the butterfly, and there are many in Abruzzo, is now used as a metaphor for freedom and for the change in him that was triggered off by him killing his girlfriend.

My initial title was 'Il Americano' – incorrect italian for The American. It relates to Westerns in my thinking and to an american not completely successfully blending in. The title had to become 'The American' but for me the film is still living under that original moniker.

I found it hard to give up on my hobby, photography, so i always had a camera with me on set.

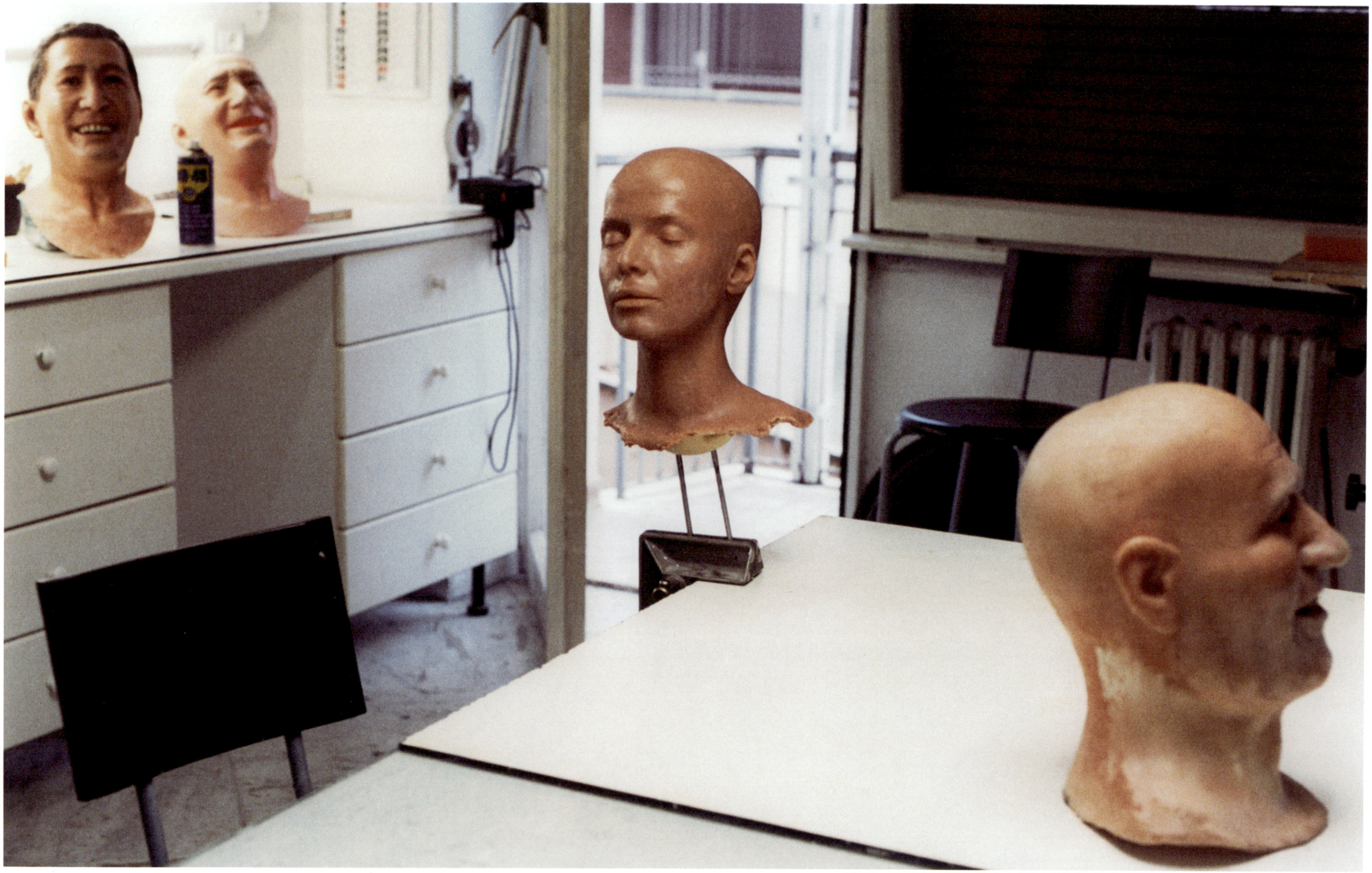

a magnificent cast of thekla's head, ready for action in manlio rocchetti's studio. we didn't use it in the end but i'm glad we got it made.

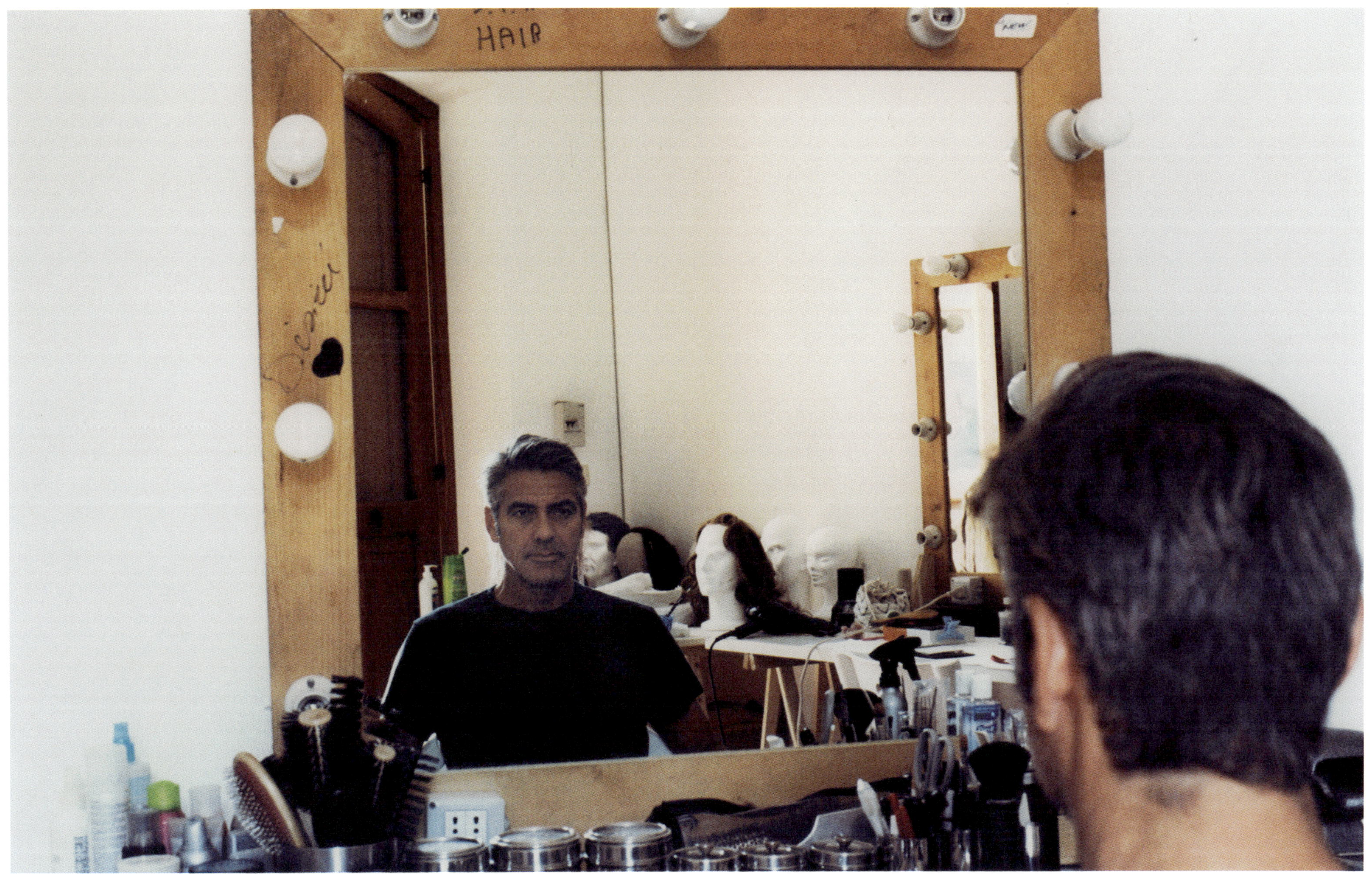

George waiting to get his hair cut on his first day in Sulmona, a few days prior to the shoot.

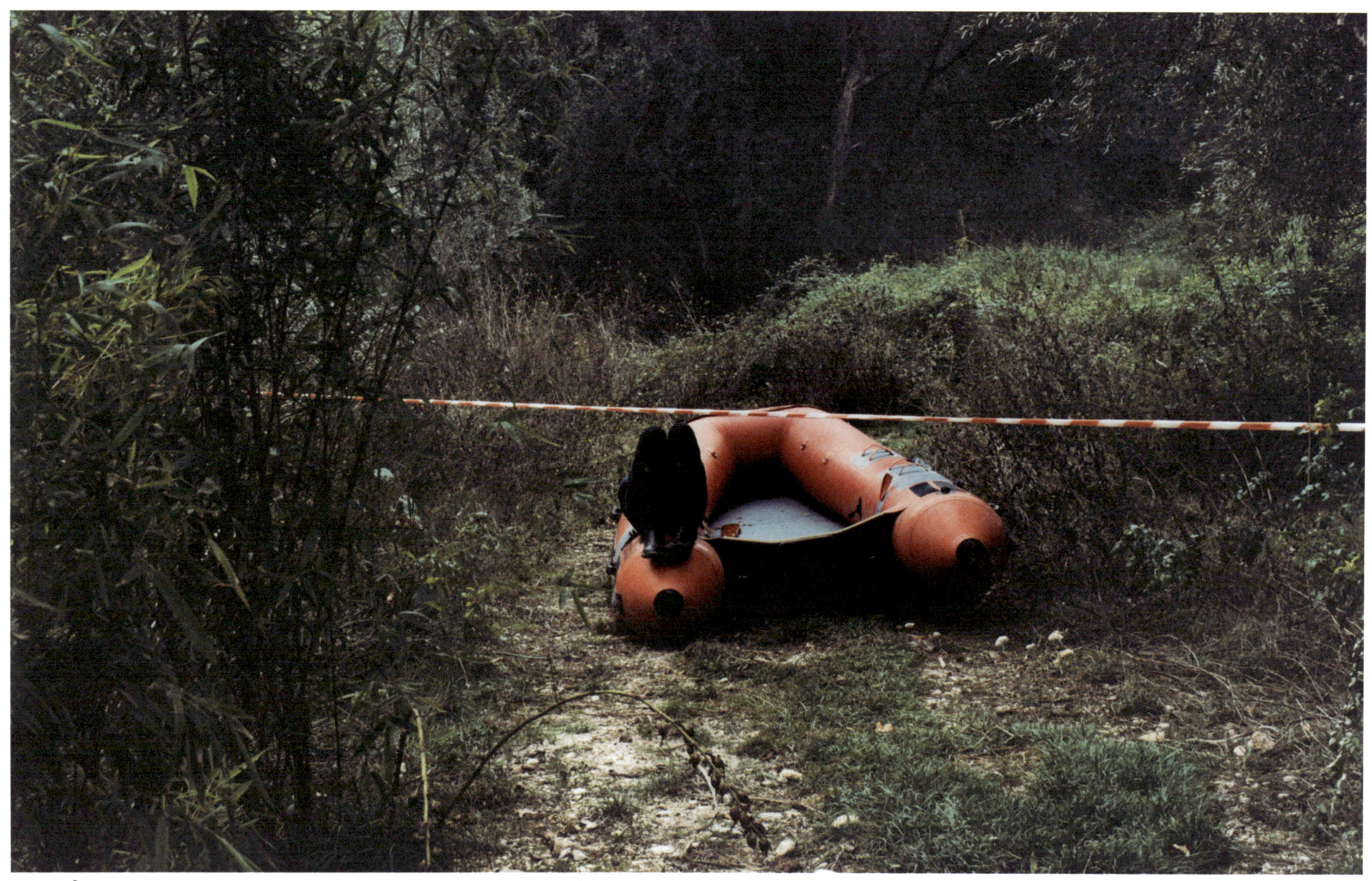

thekla having a break, or a re-think, near the river. this was a week prior to the shoot.

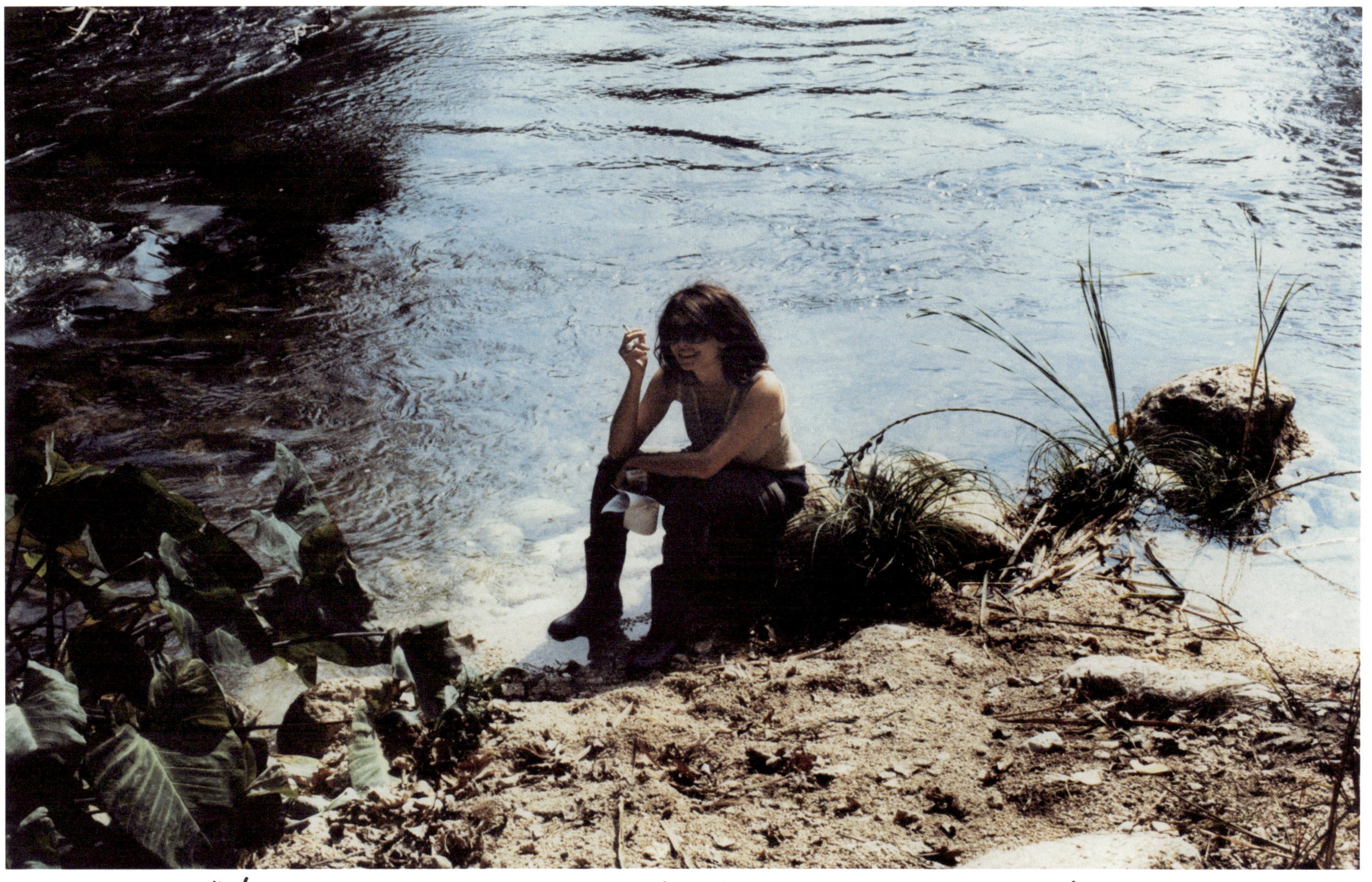

while nearby Violante is testing the water. in the mountains rivers and streams are always cold.

thekla testing the gun at the building in Sulmona where the art department was located.

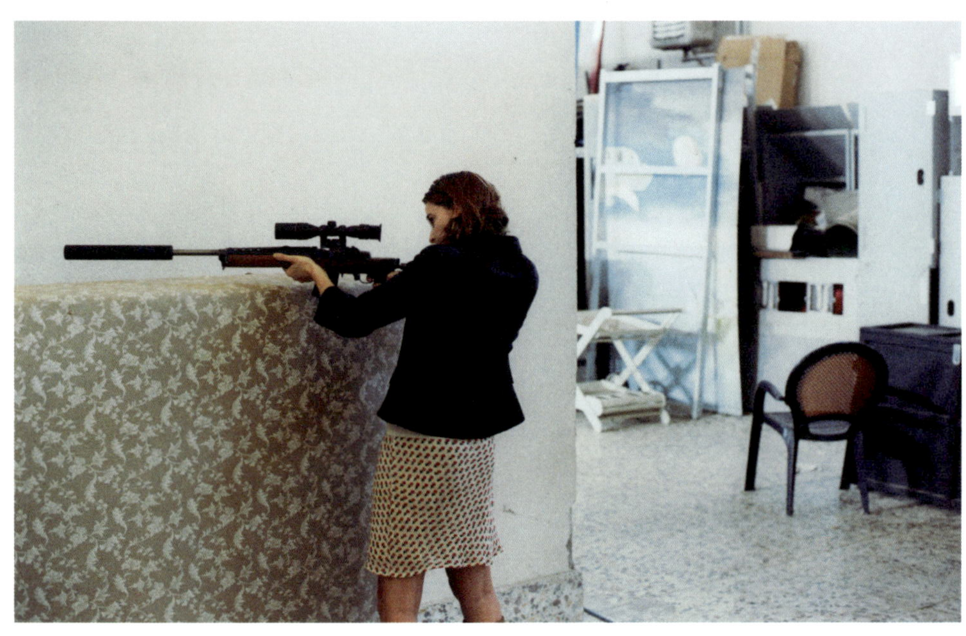

the picnic scene near the river required Thekla to assemble the gun in no time. she mastered it after a good few days practising and was competing with time and herself.

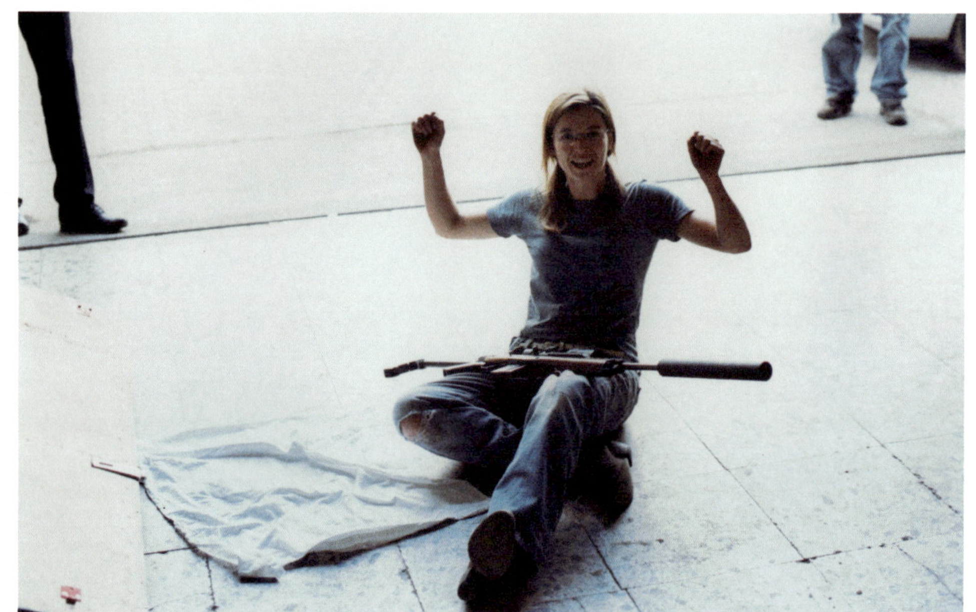

I intended to take a daily snapshot of the proceedings but obviously there were days when i had no time whatsoever to even think of taking a photograph (shot on film by the way, not digitally)
The book shows some reproduction of the work, stuff needed doing prior to a film starting to shoot.
I'm not the set photographer so my photos are of people, sets, places i enjoy looking at. Sometimes my camera is used as a way to take attention away from the filming itself.
The photo order in this book is more or less the order in which we shot the film, so yes, the beginning was shot last.

testing small explosions to be used for the gun practising scenes with George and Thekla.

George testing some pistols prior to settling on a Walther PPK.

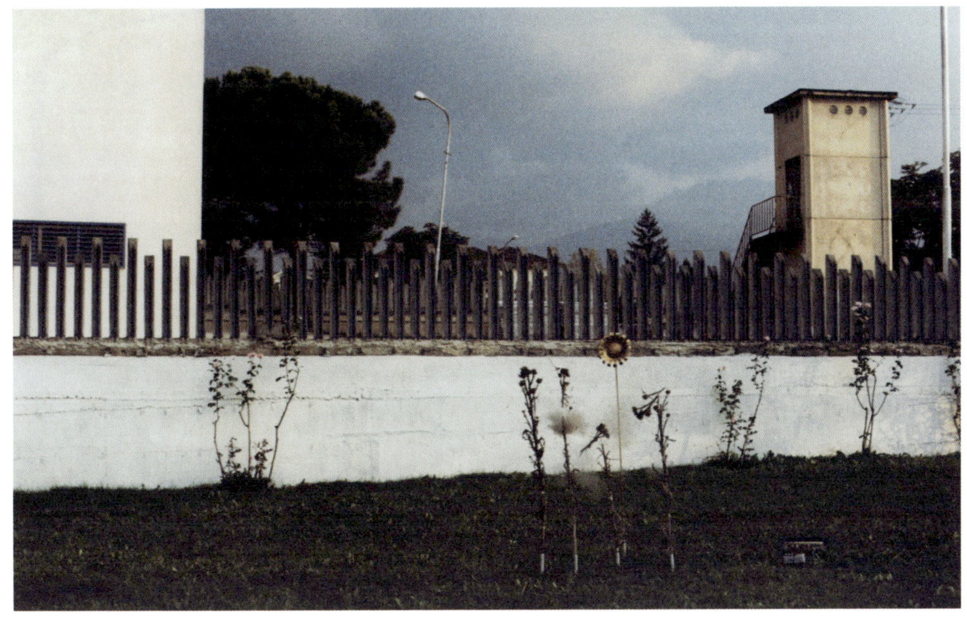

19

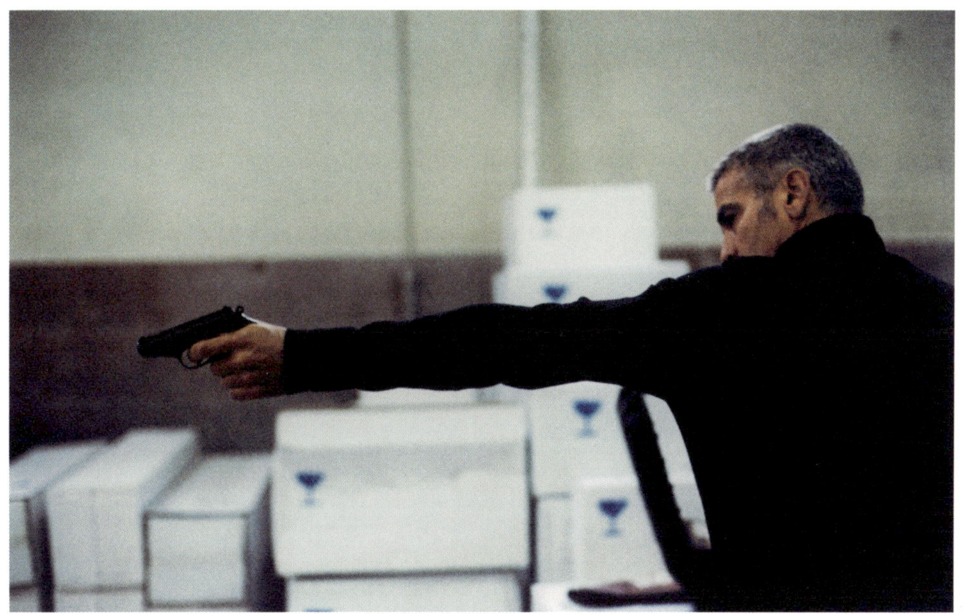

Some photographs are accompanied by rather abstract drawings: these are my drawings for specific scenes or places, indicating camera angles. Possible pretty un-intelligible stuff but that's how magic happens sometimes. or confusion. Probably in equal measure, you'll be the judge of that.

anton corbijn
London 6/'10

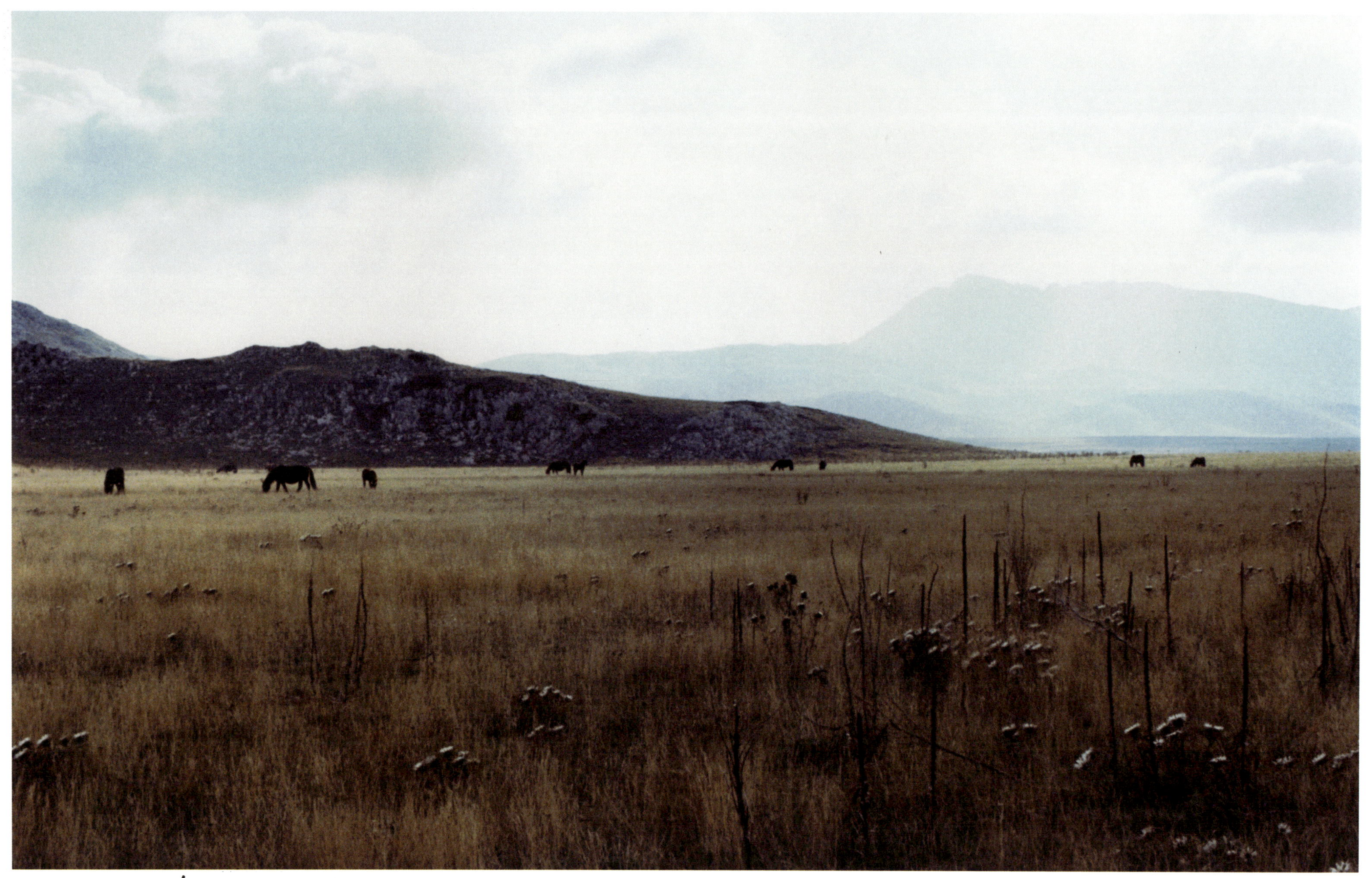

semi-wild horses on the Campo Imperatore, an alpine meadow at roughly 1500 meters height.

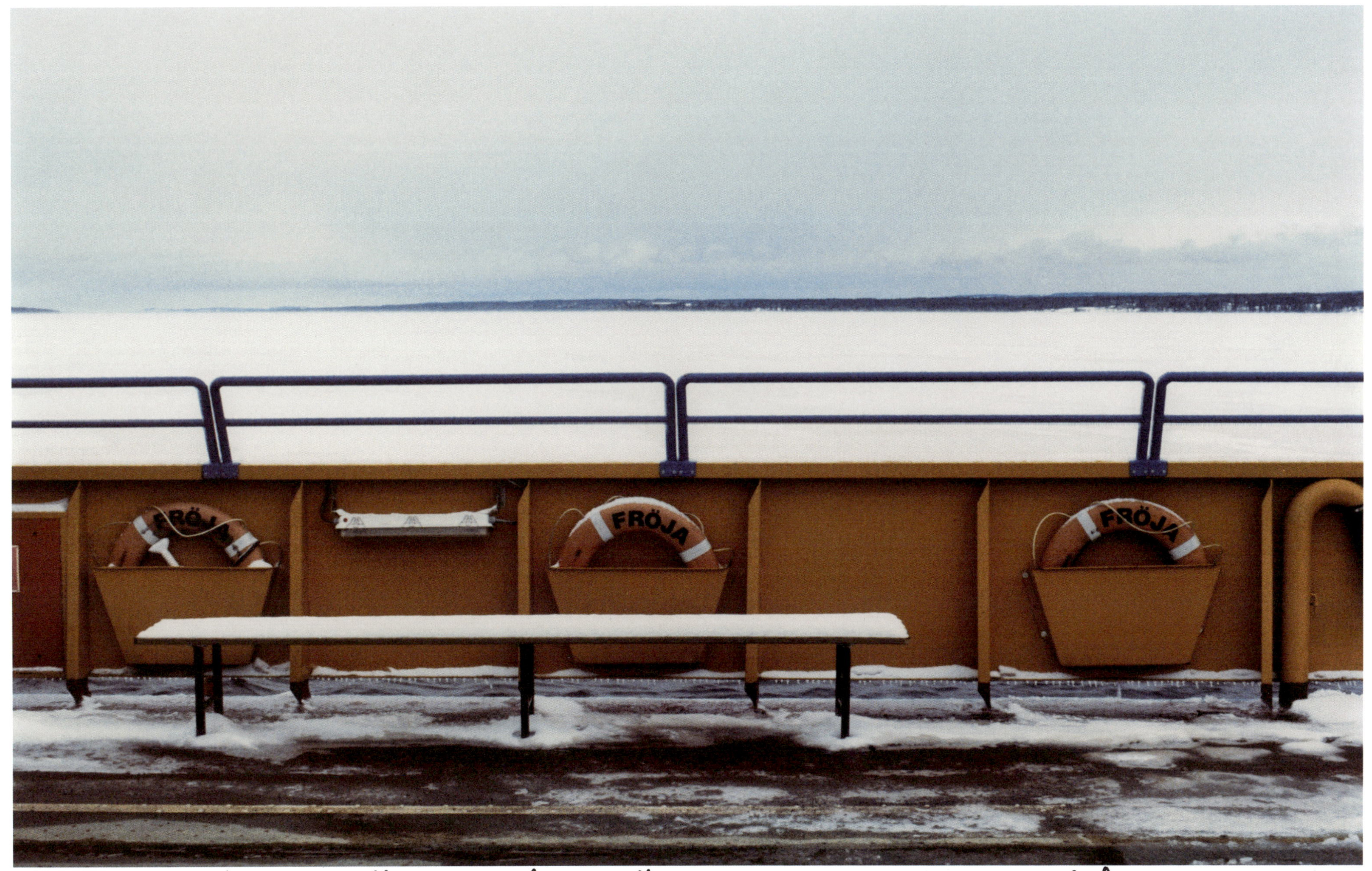

on board of a ferry near Östersund, the middle of Sweden. Most ferries are taken out during the winter and cars cross the water by driving over the ice at specific places.

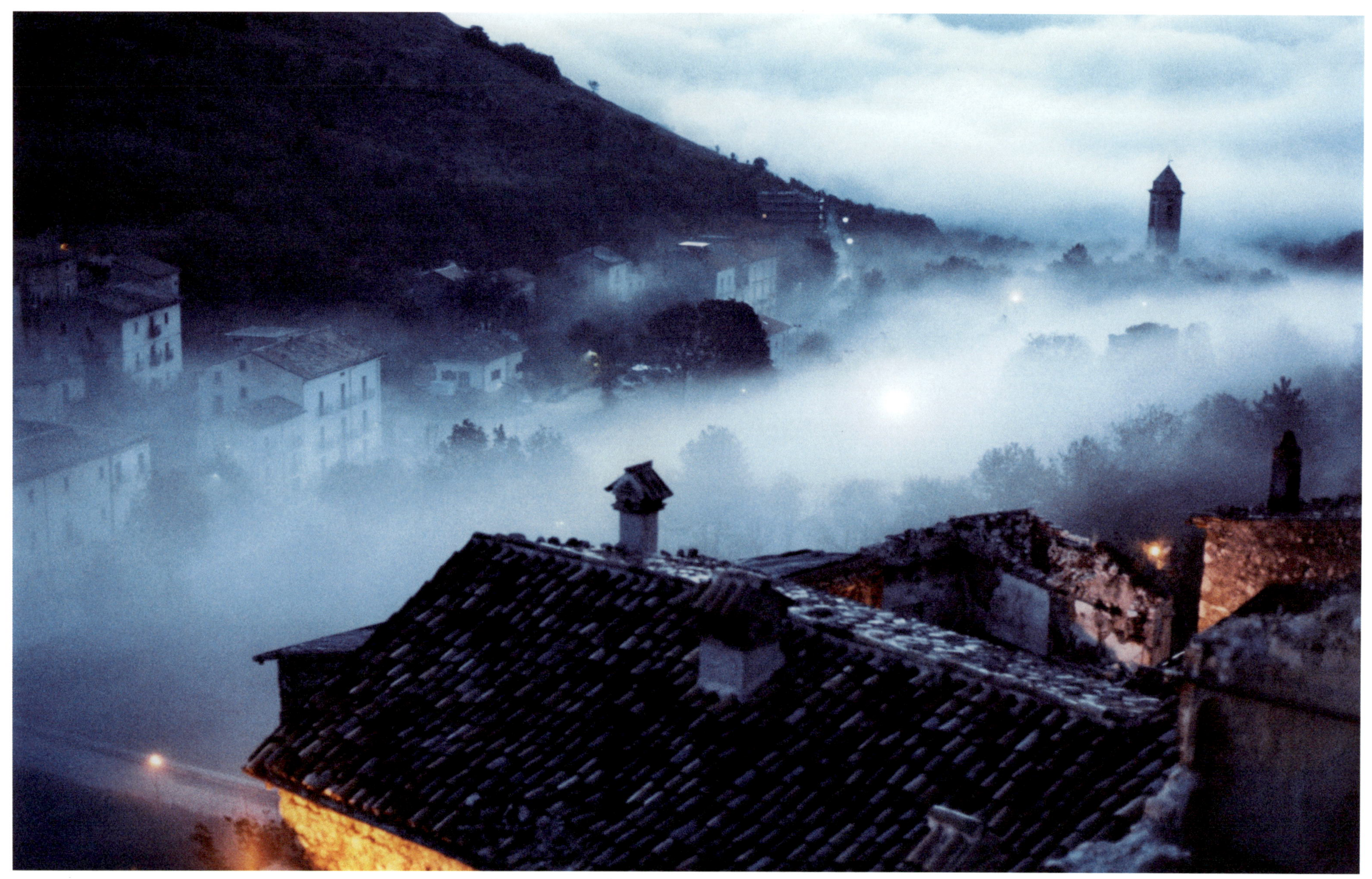

early morning view from my window in Santo Stefano. Great way to start the day with a view.

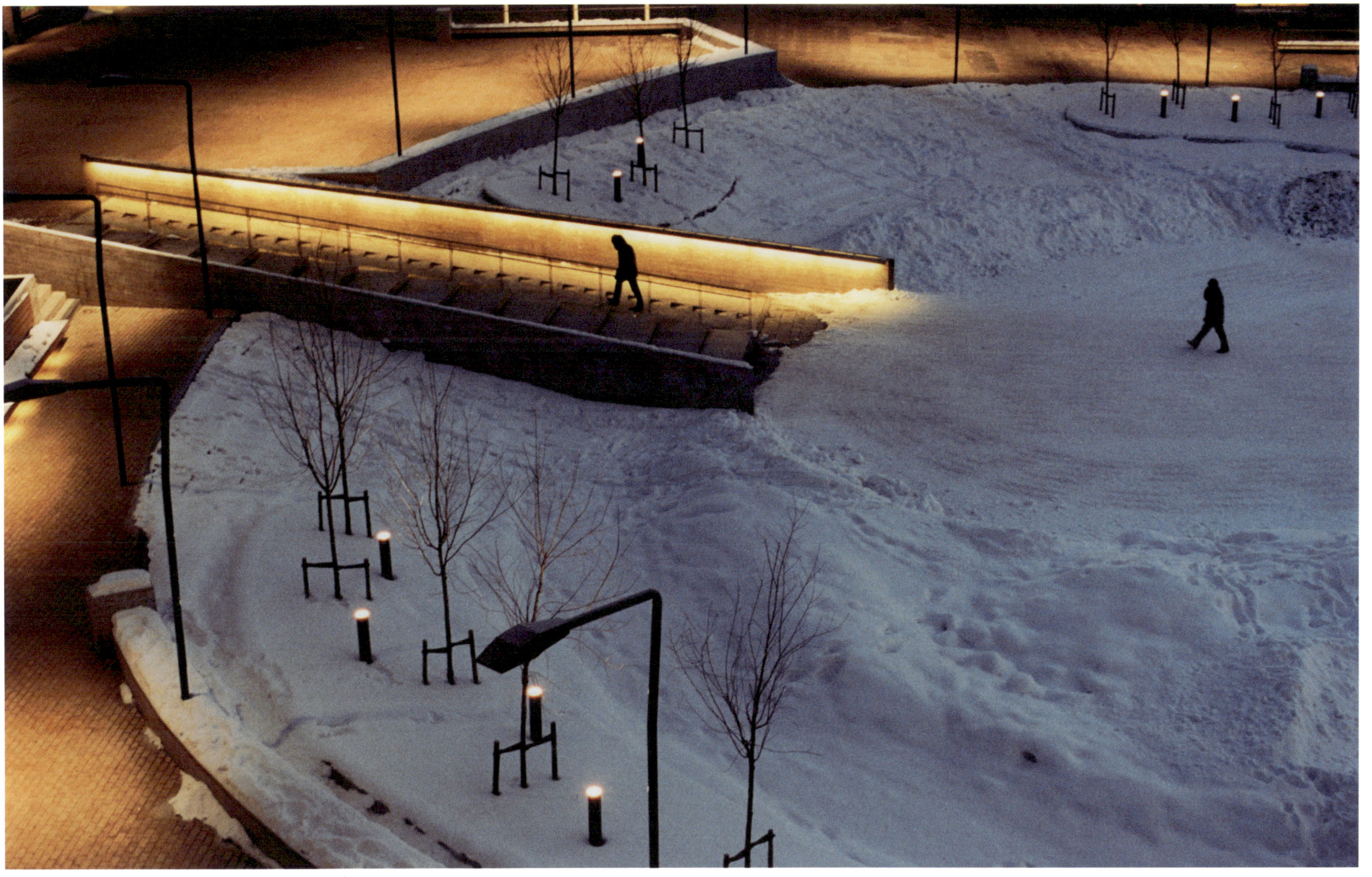

late evening view from my hotelroom in Östersund. I always look out of my window(s).

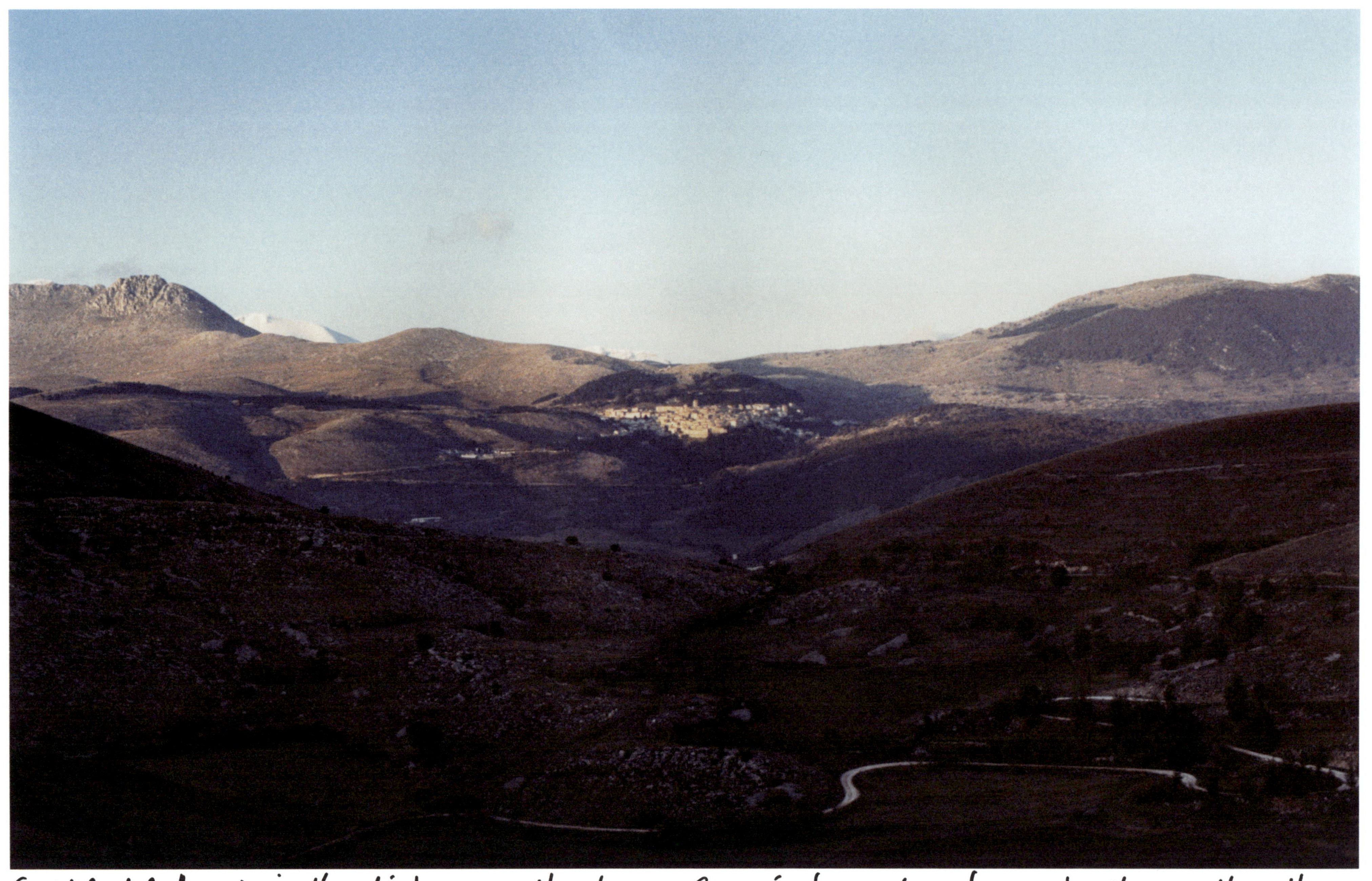

24

Castel del Monte in the distance. The town George's character chooses to stay rather than the suggested nearby town of Castelvecchio.

FILM

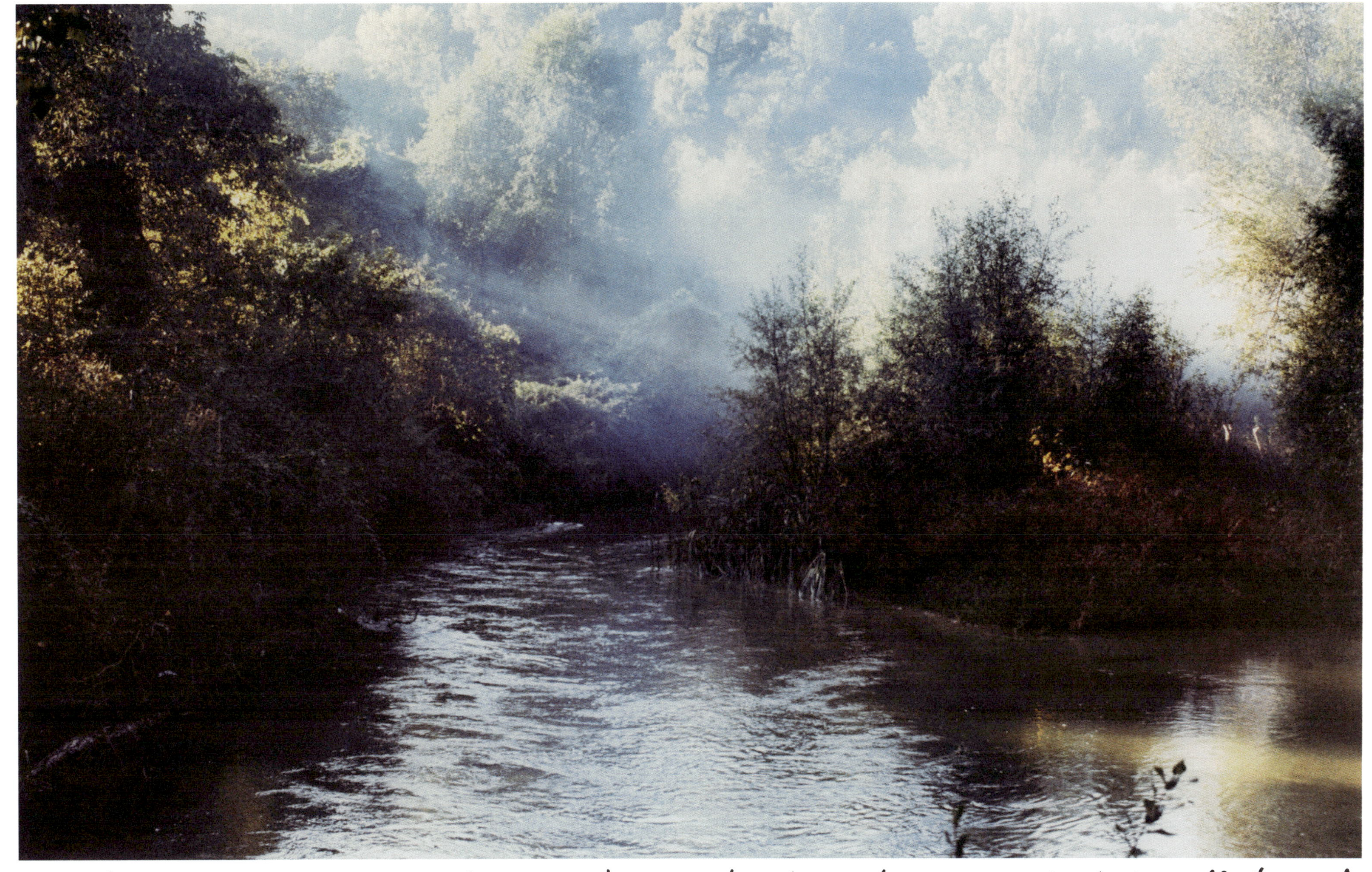

arriving early morning in late september at the river, the scenery is doing all the work.

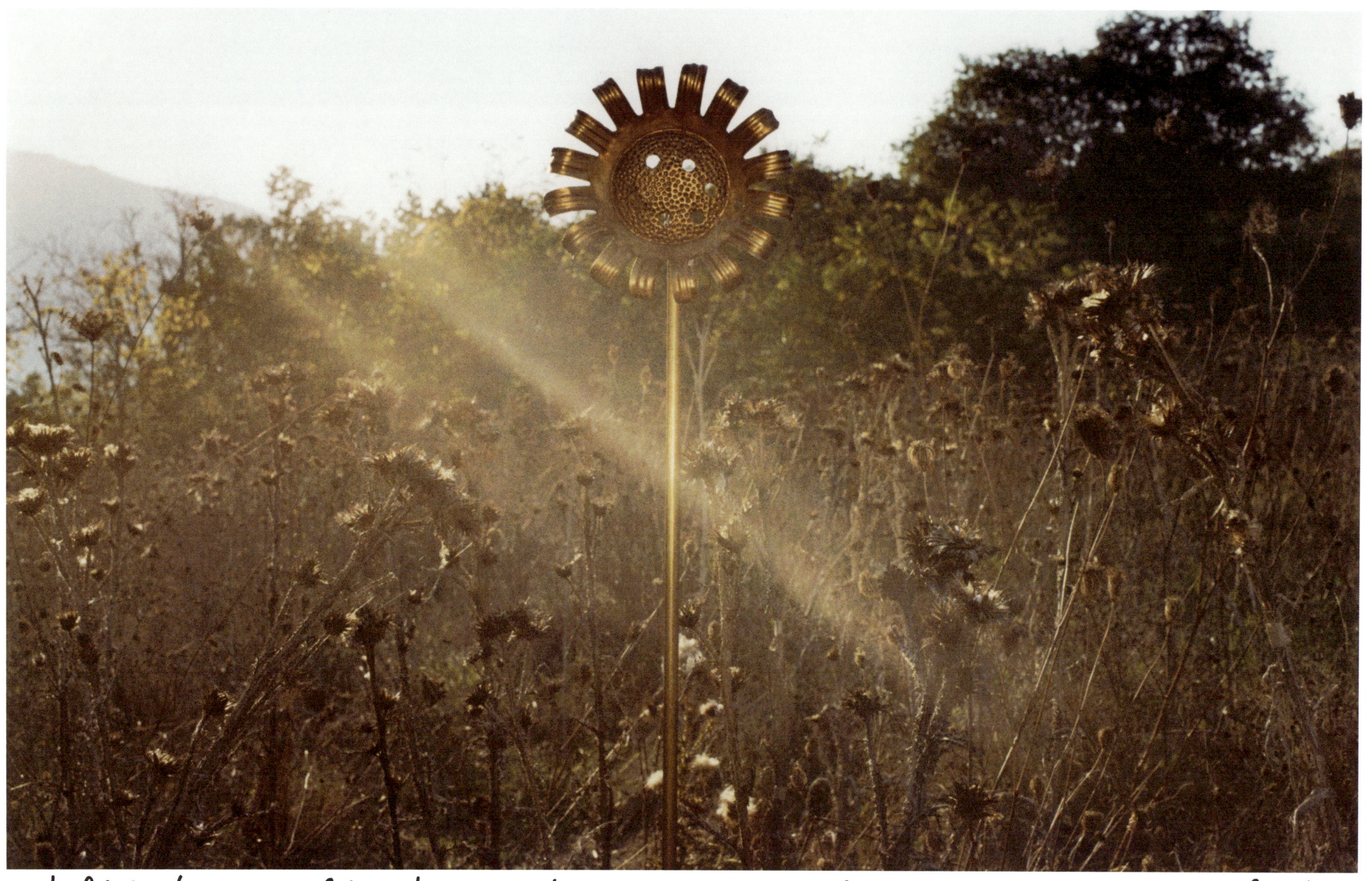

Thekla's character brings her own target – a copper sunflower. I wanted something kind of poetic to stand in this field. The book told of a cut-out airplane with someone in the doorway.

28

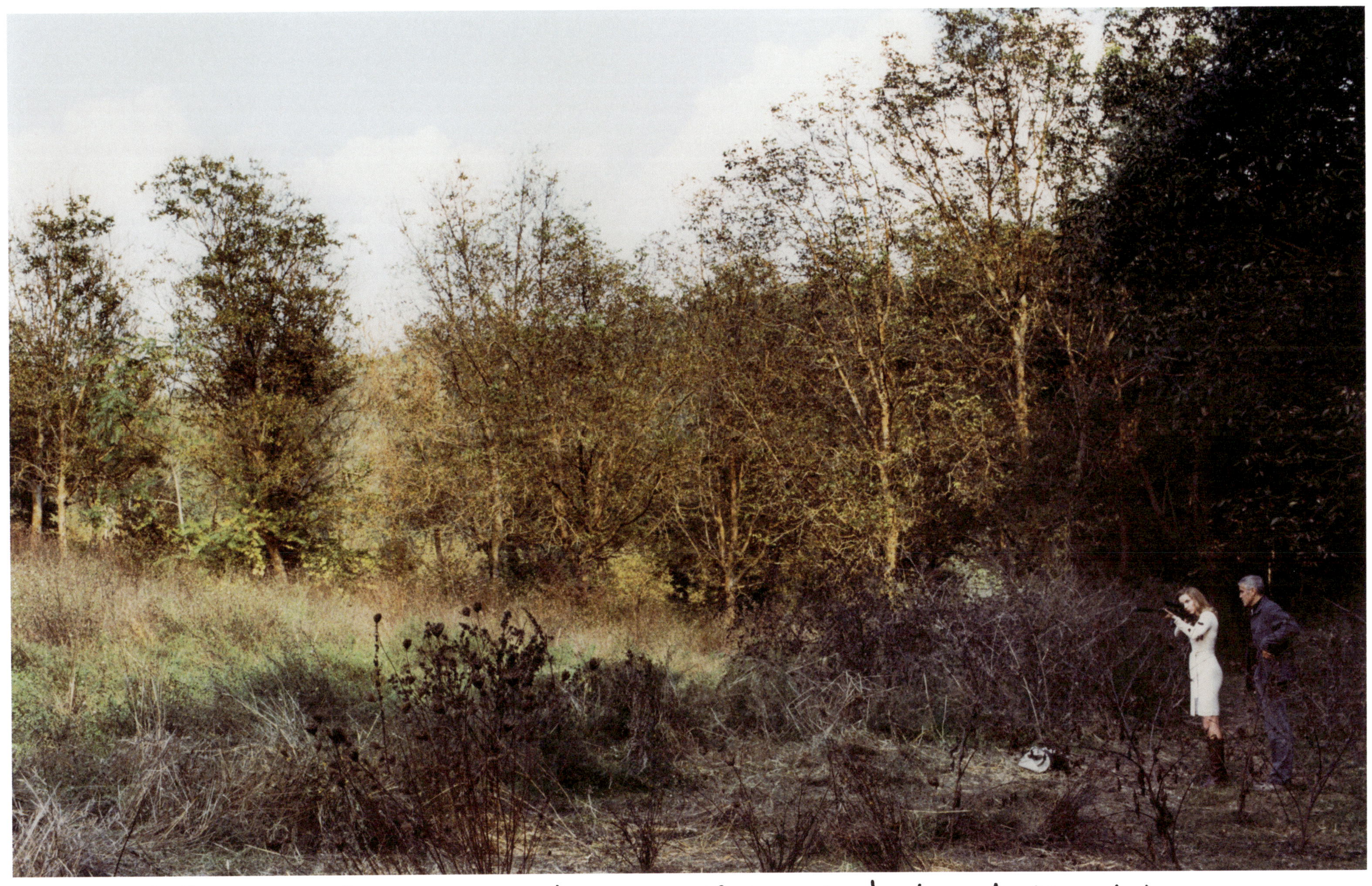

We found this wonderful area near the river filled with shrubs and old apple trees.

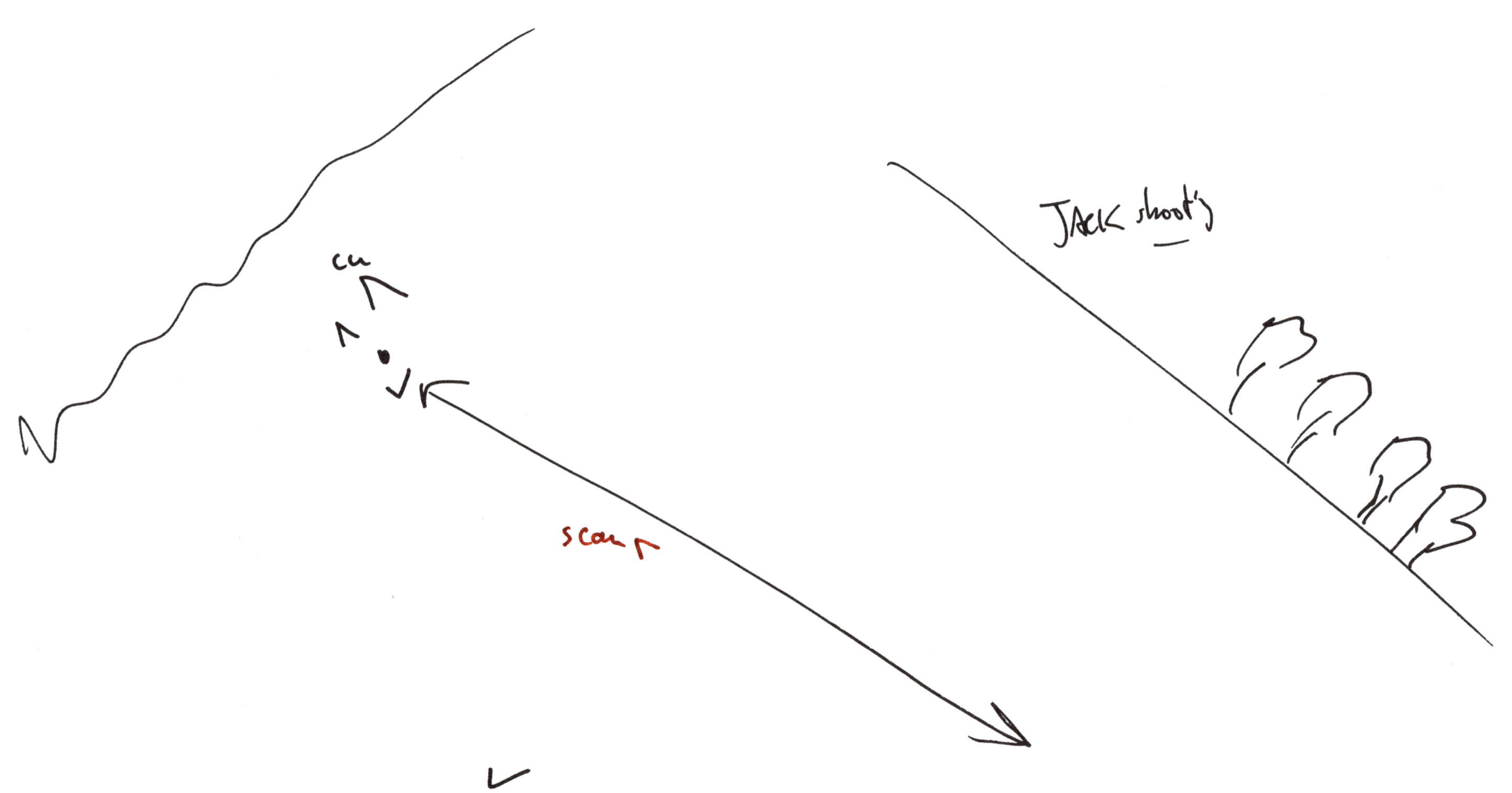
JACK shoot'g
cu
scan

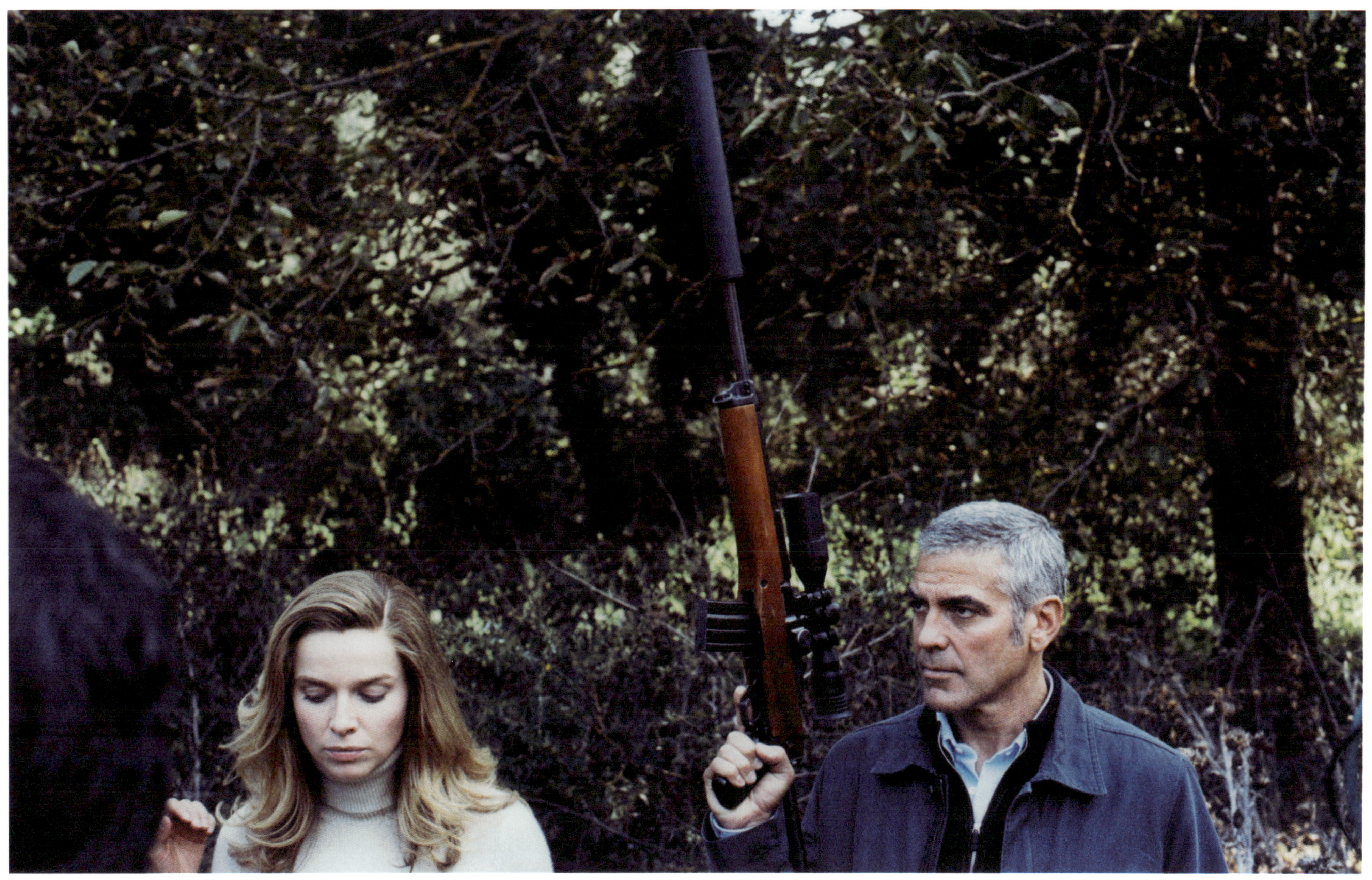

Thekla and George and a very large gun.

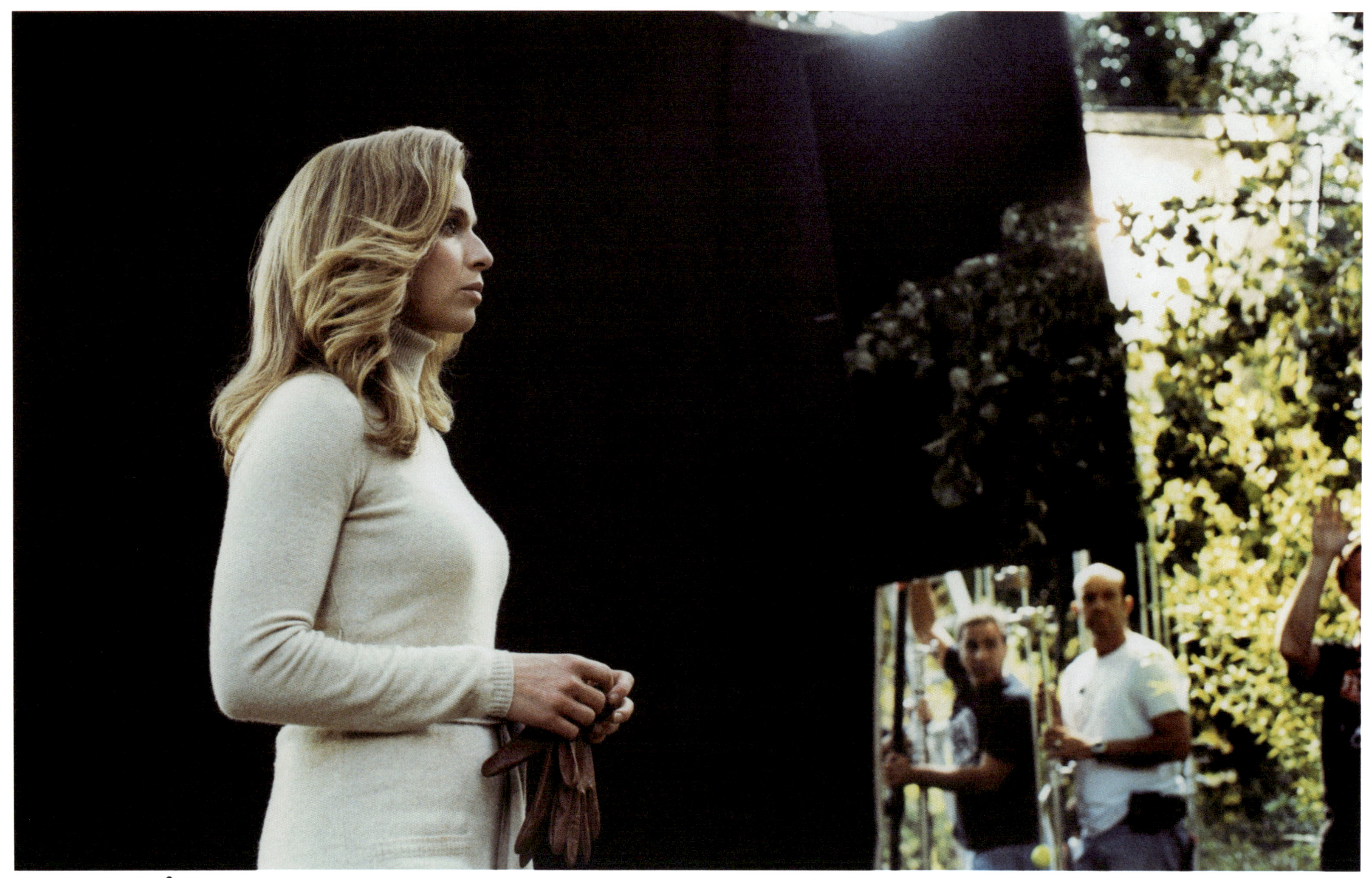

this is Thekla's second 'look' in the film. She looks completely different every time she meets JACK.

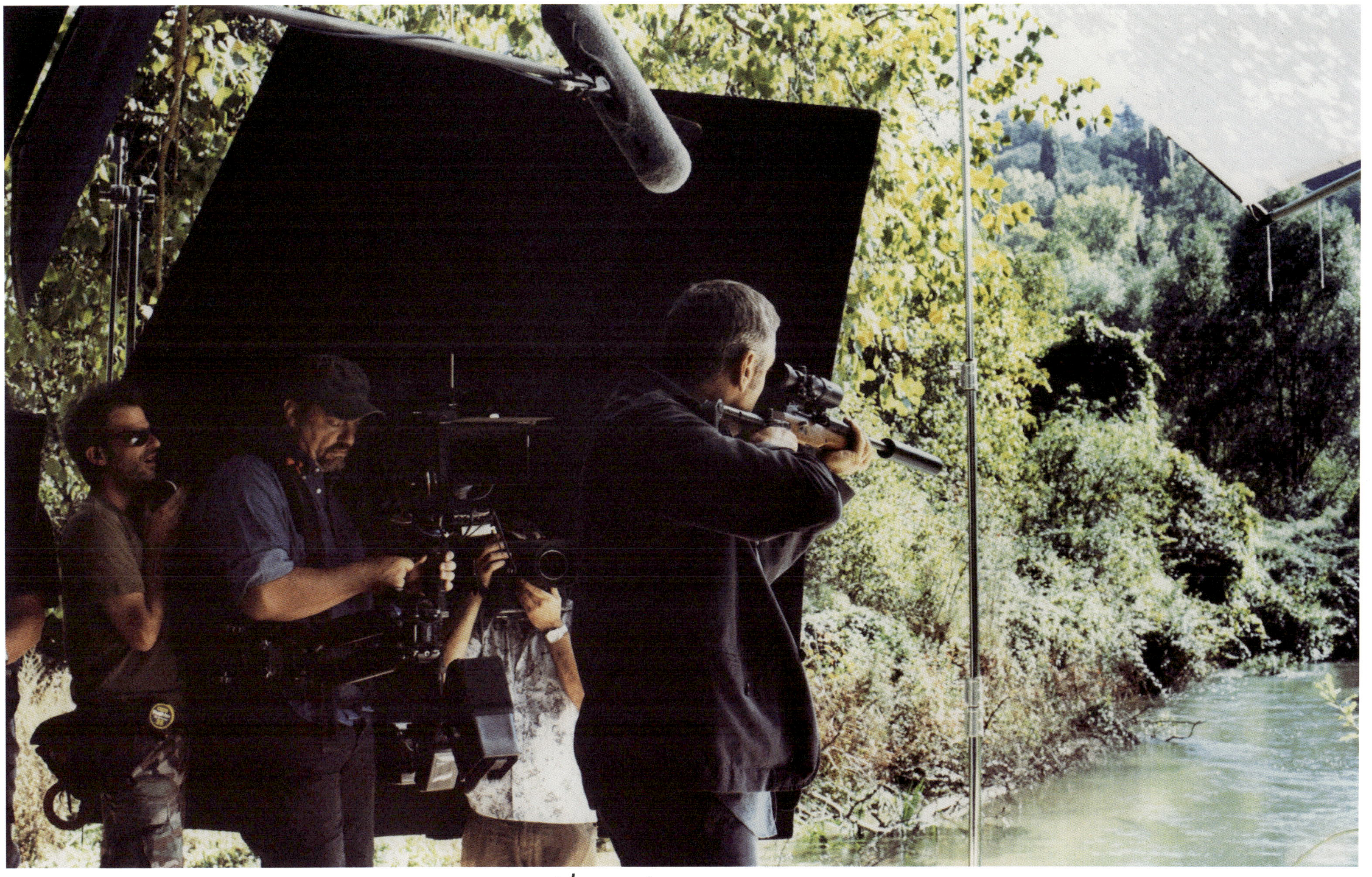

George practising the gun he assembled, shooting at reeds in the river.

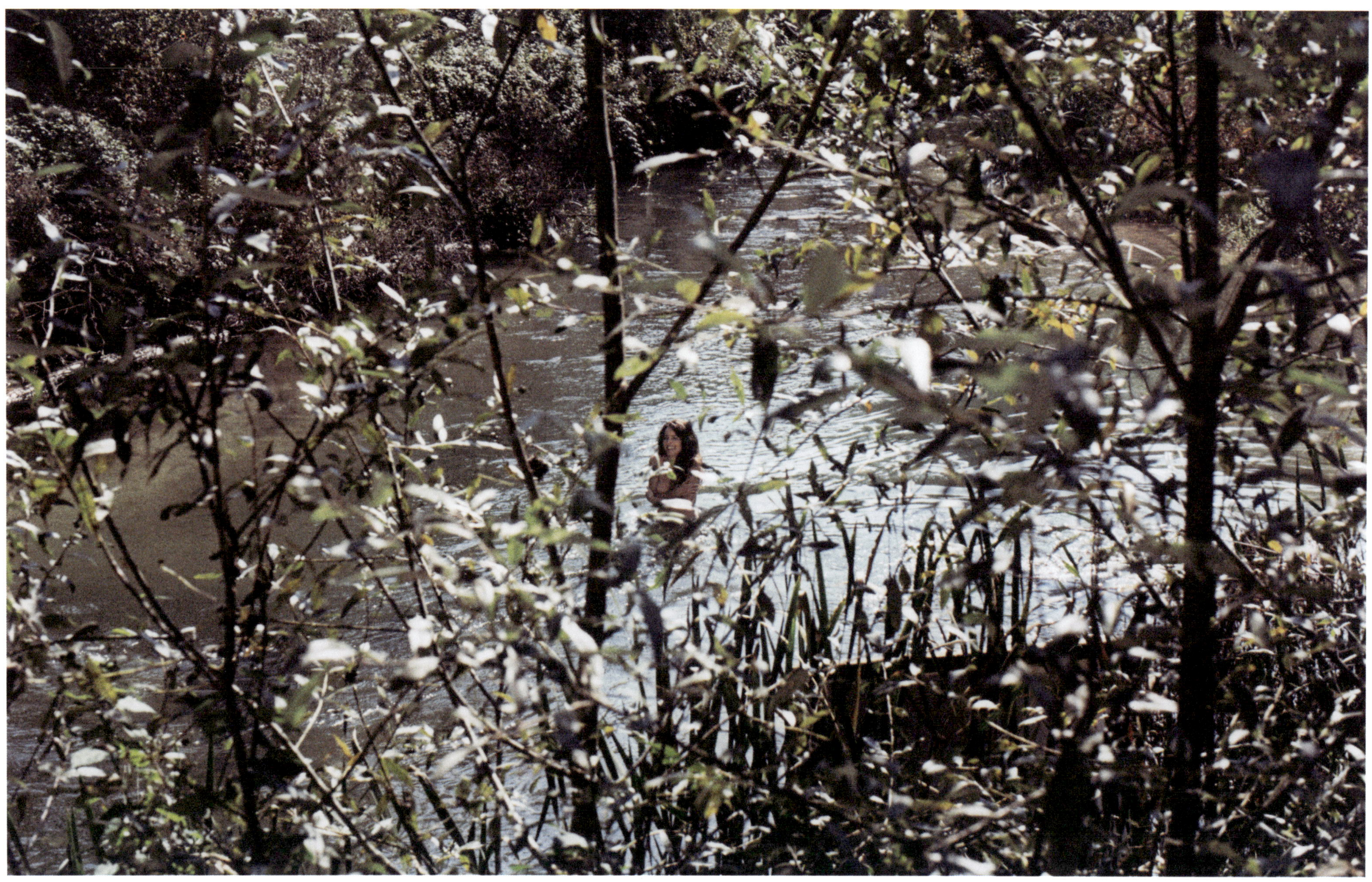

Violante during the river scene. We did takes from different angles which was very hard on her as the water was pretty cold but she made it look summery and easy.

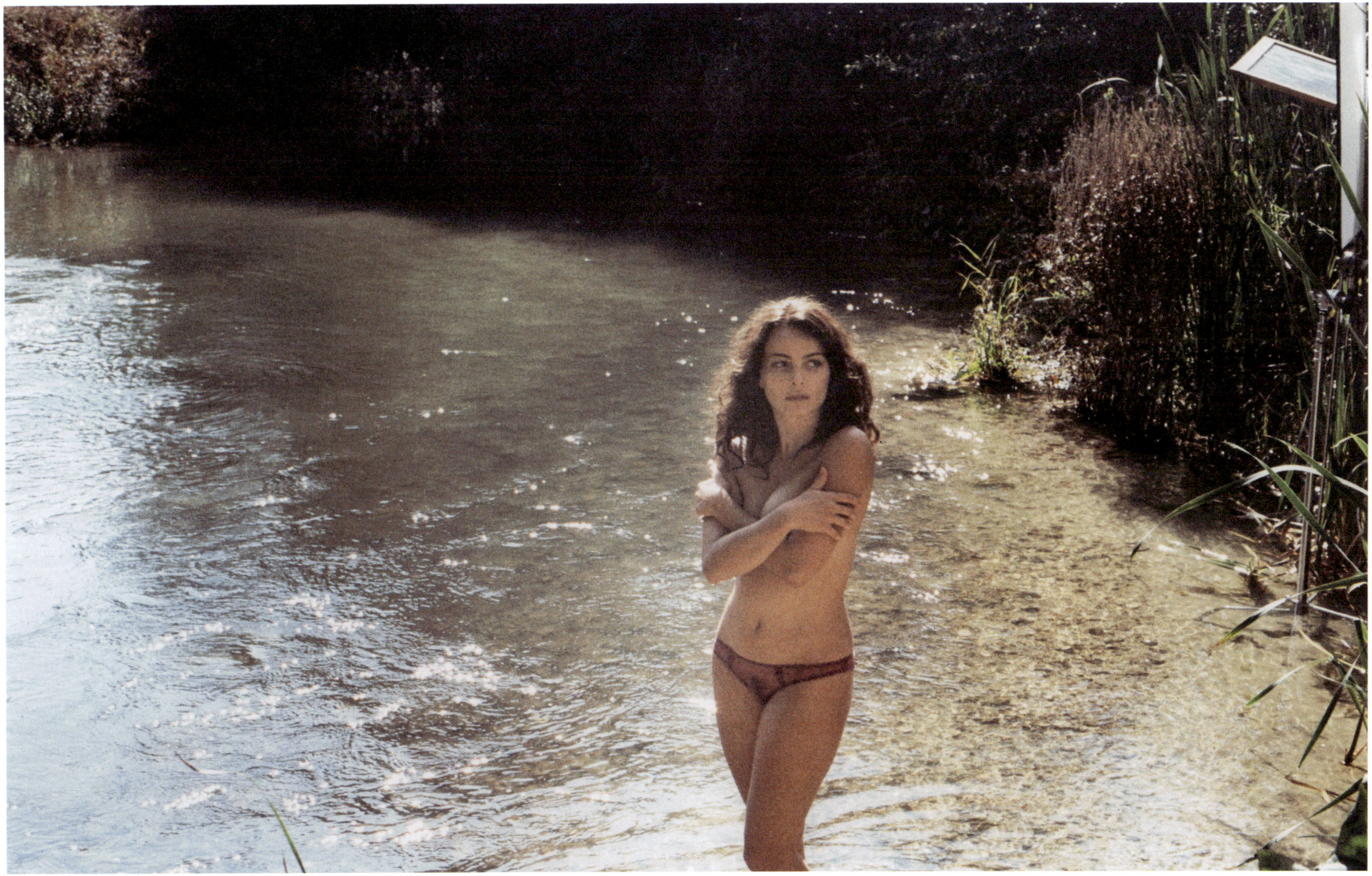

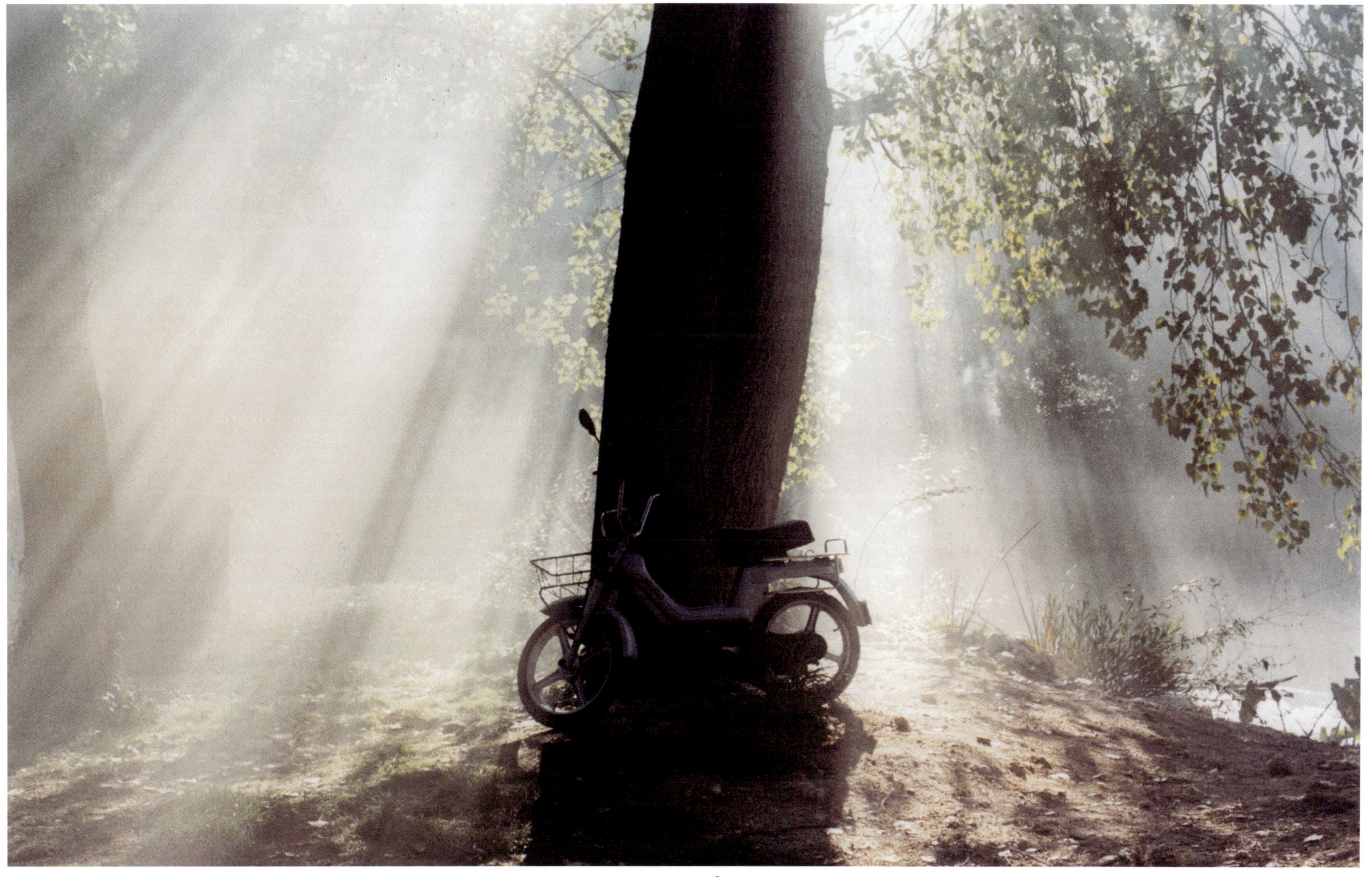

The endscene looks like paradise and the angel arrived on this moped.

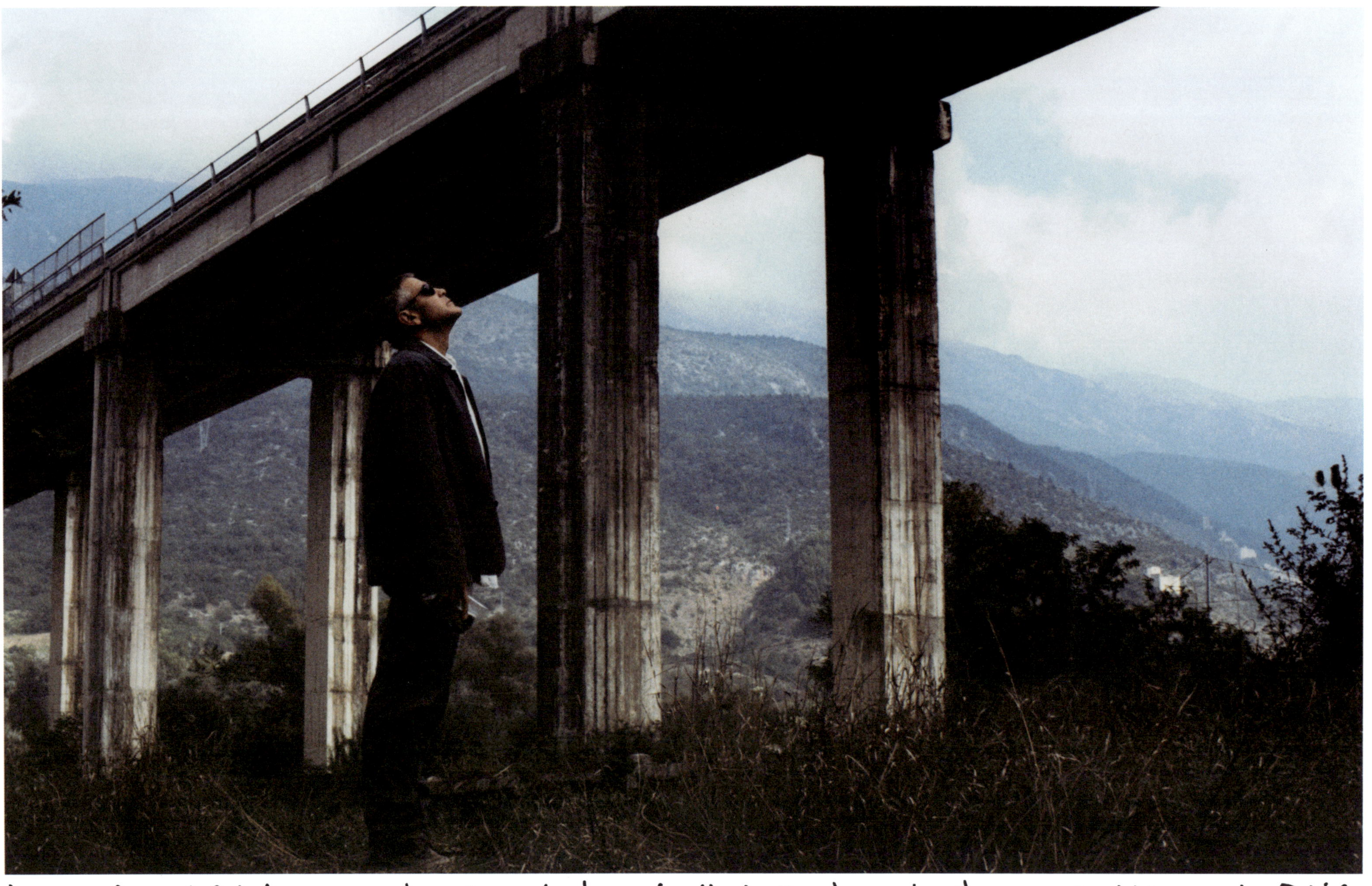

image of a deleted scene where George's character finds the phone he threw out of his car in Fabio's workplace and asks Fabio where did he get this, to which he replies "it was a gift from above".

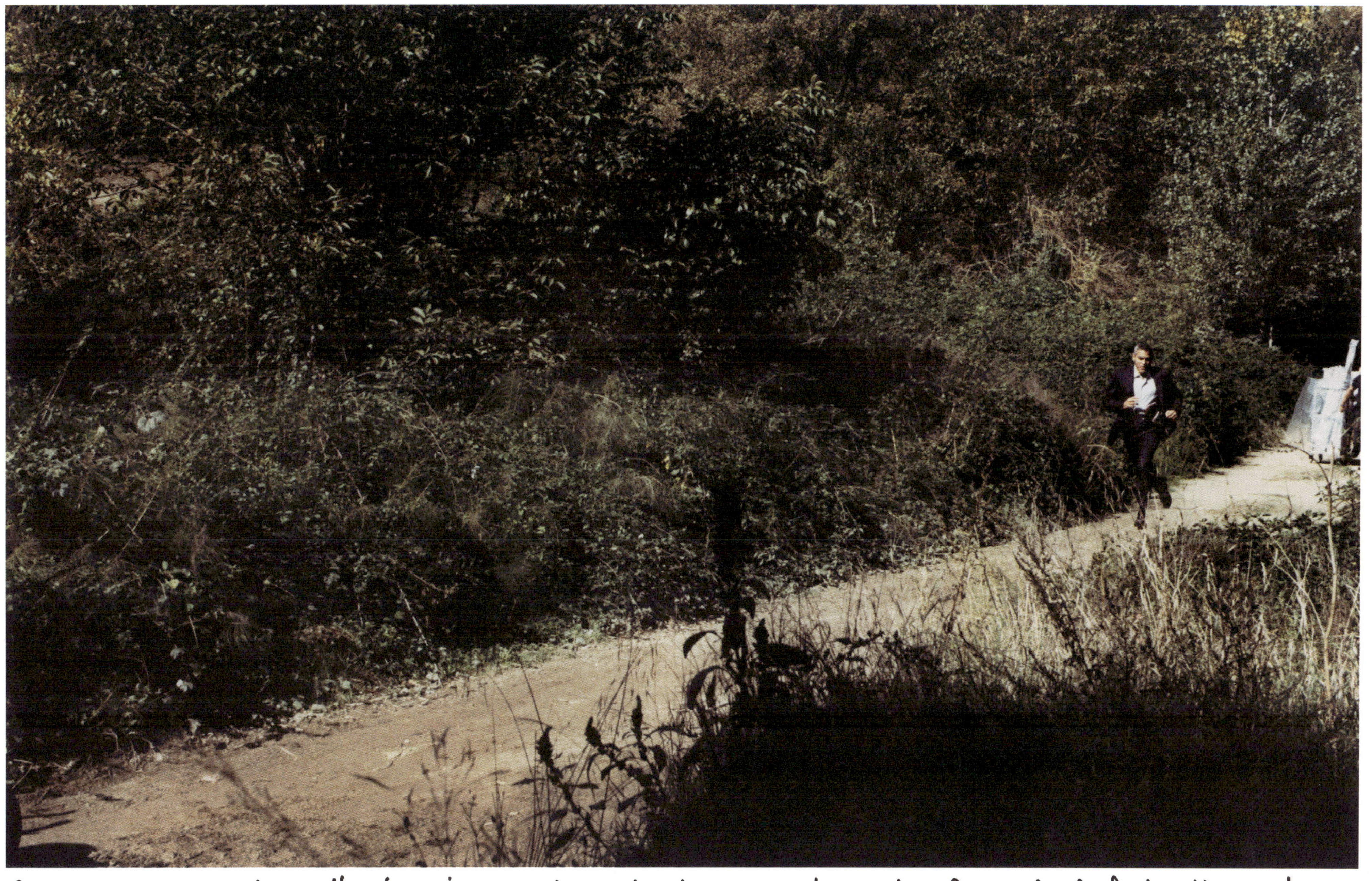

George is running in the burning sun in order to prepare for natural sweaty look for the endscene.

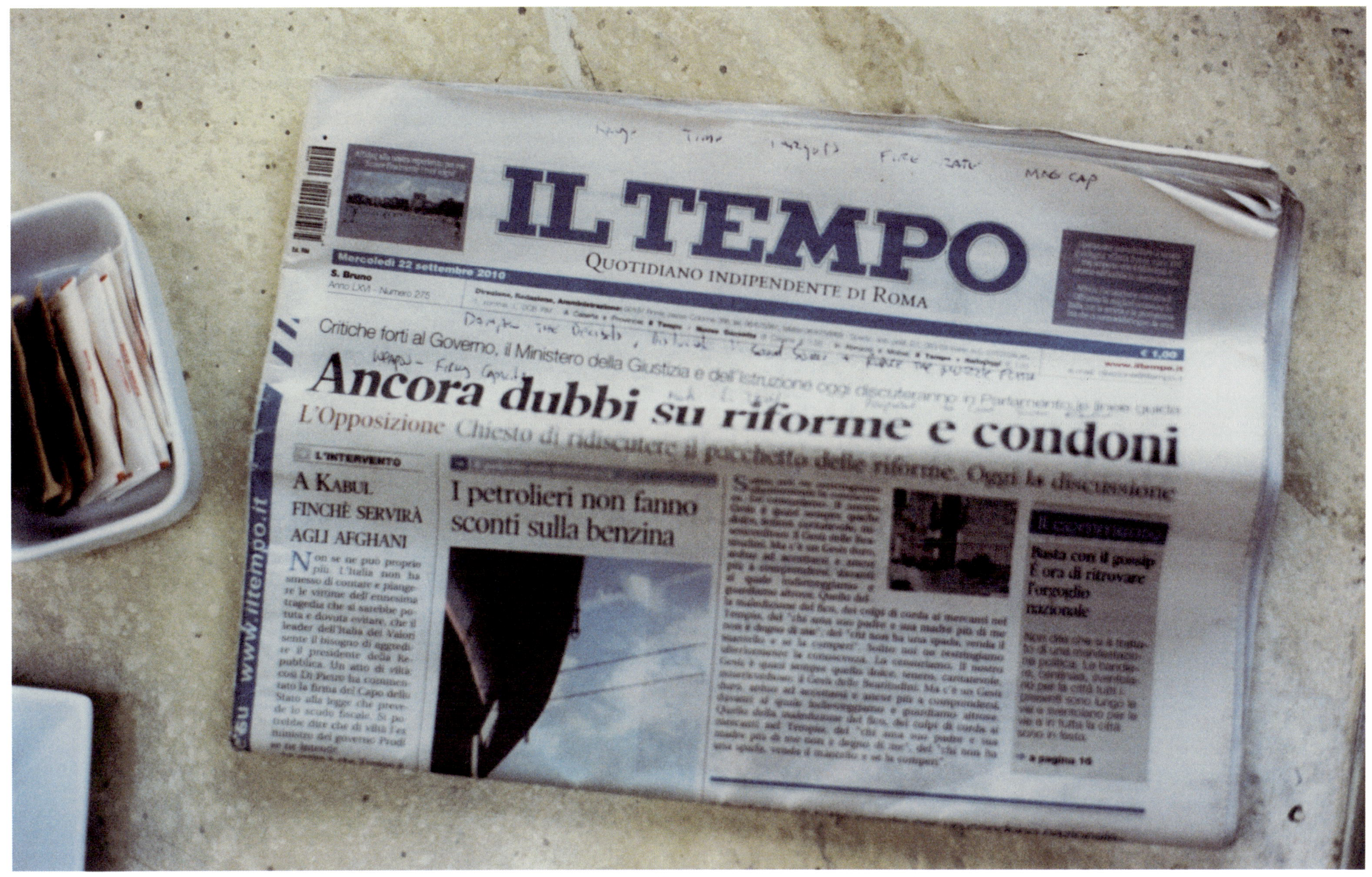

Scribbled notes on the newspaper during the market scene.

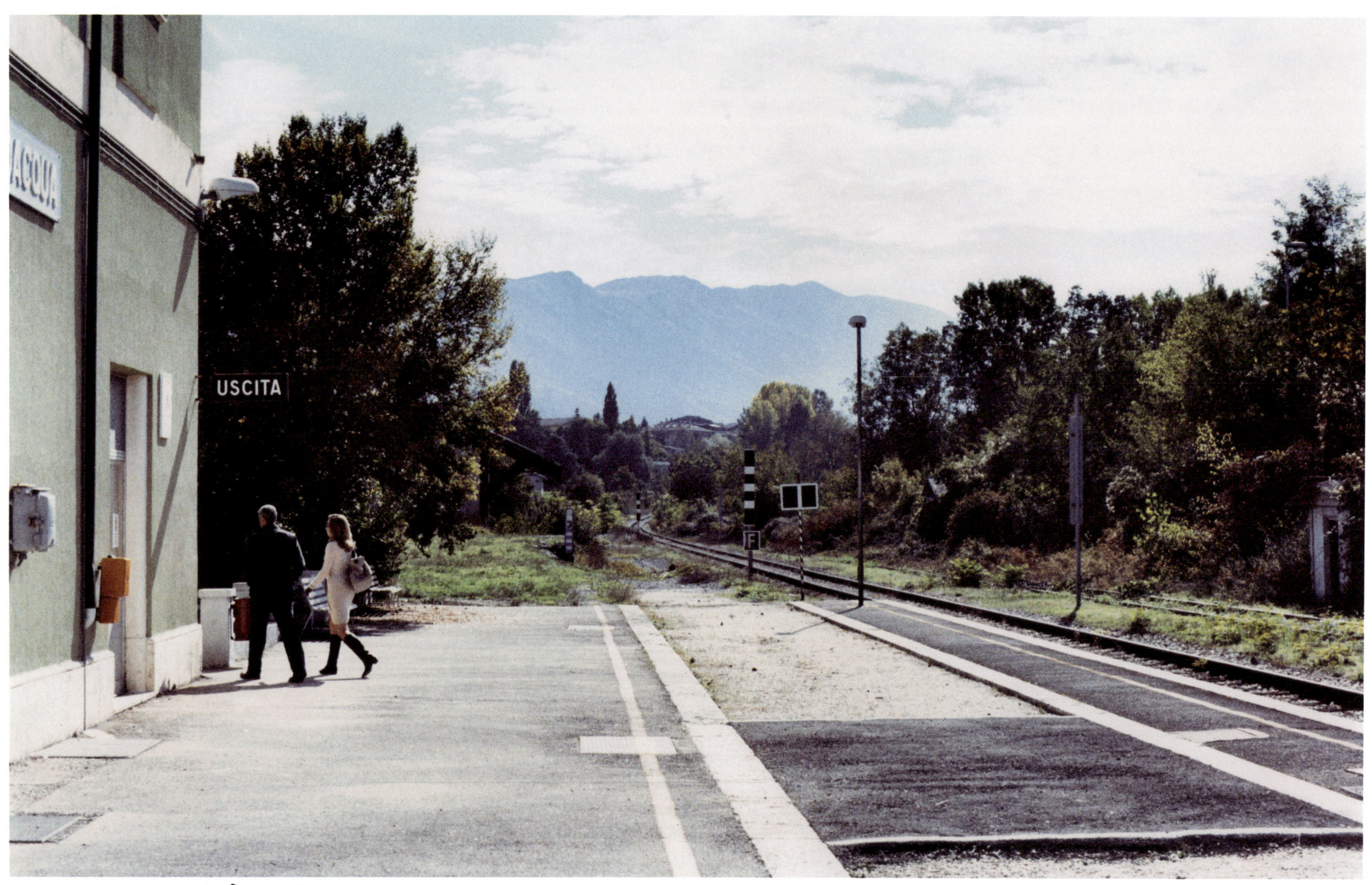

George and Thekla leaving the station in this very Western setting.

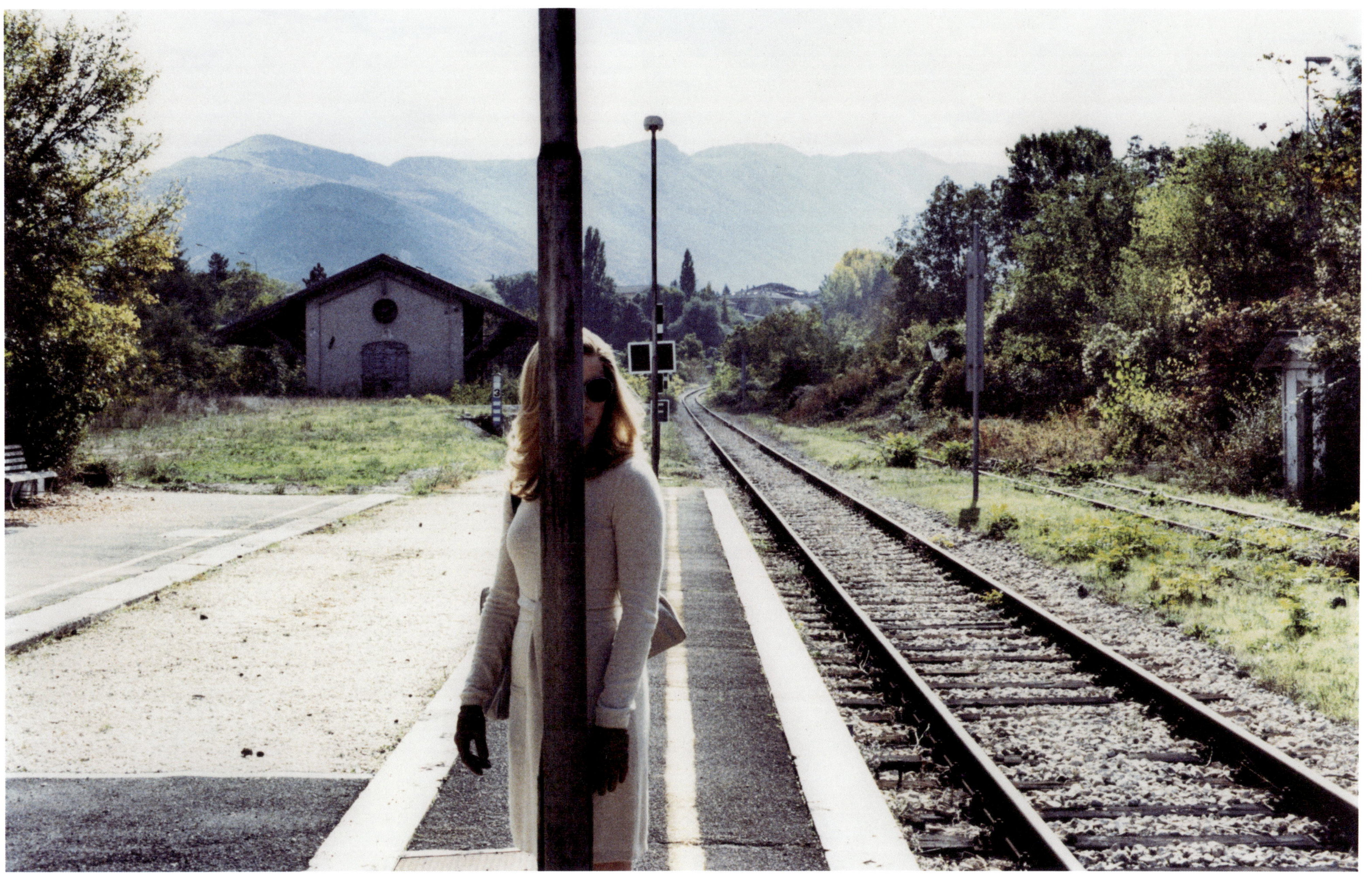

Thekla hiding at this small but GREAT station near Sulmona.

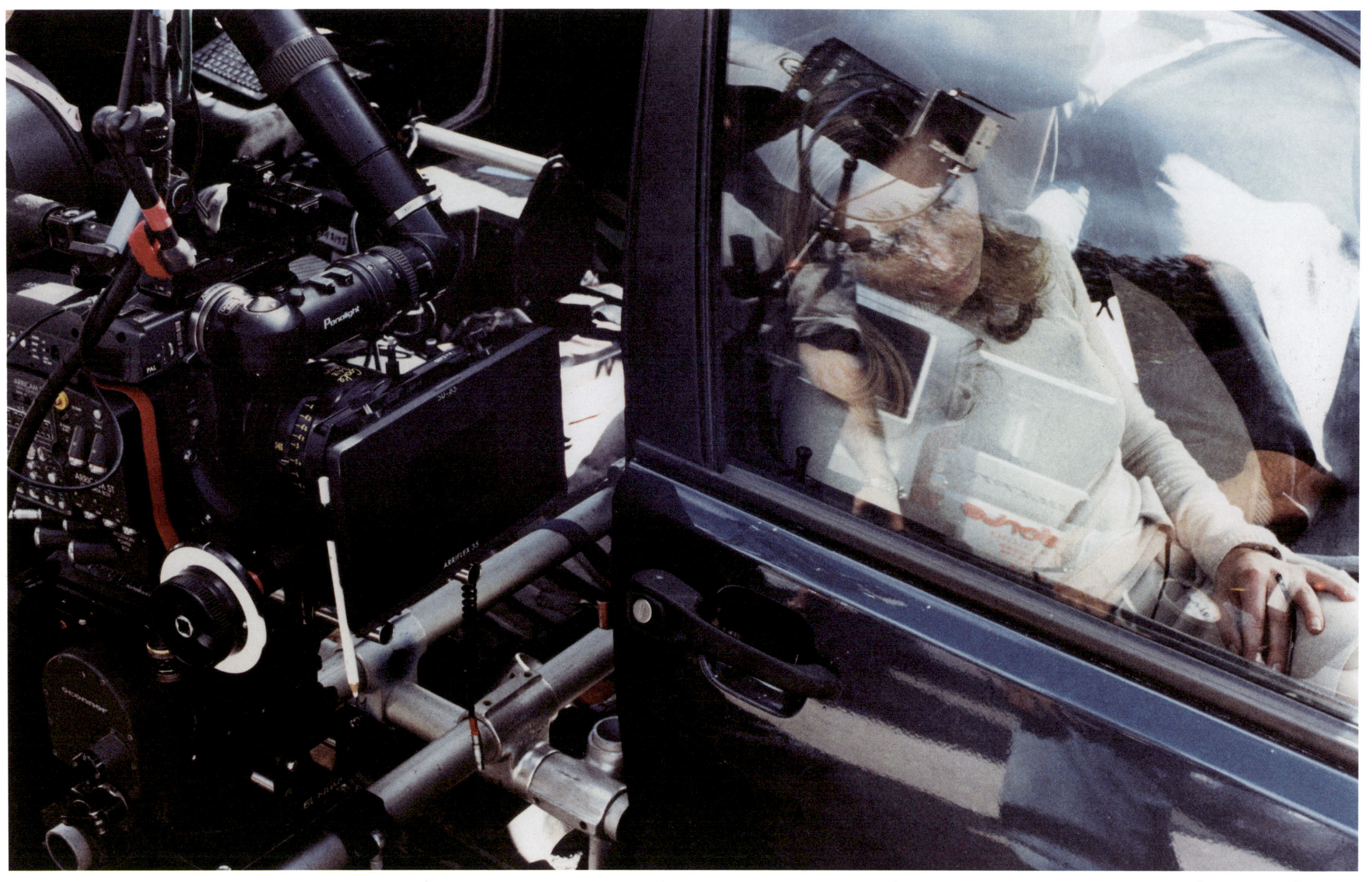

Setting up the shot of Mathilde's reflection in the car mirror at her way from the picnic to the station.

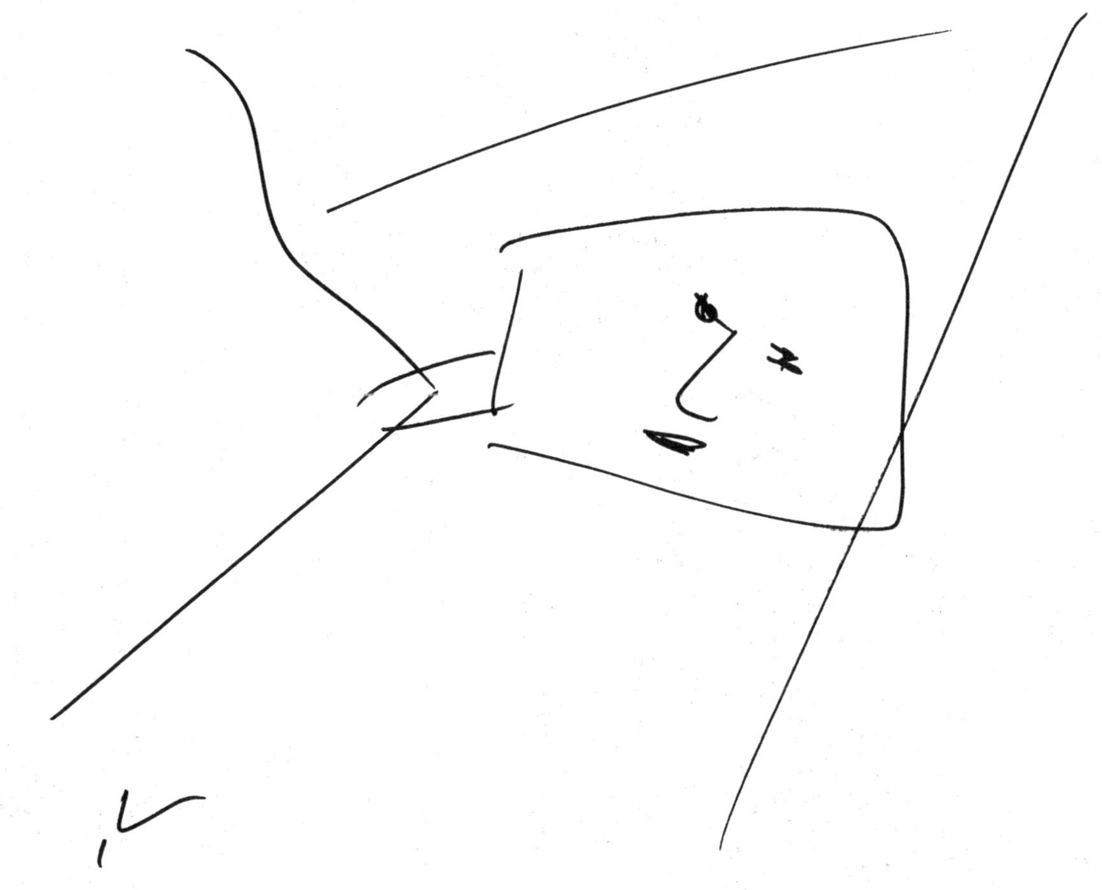

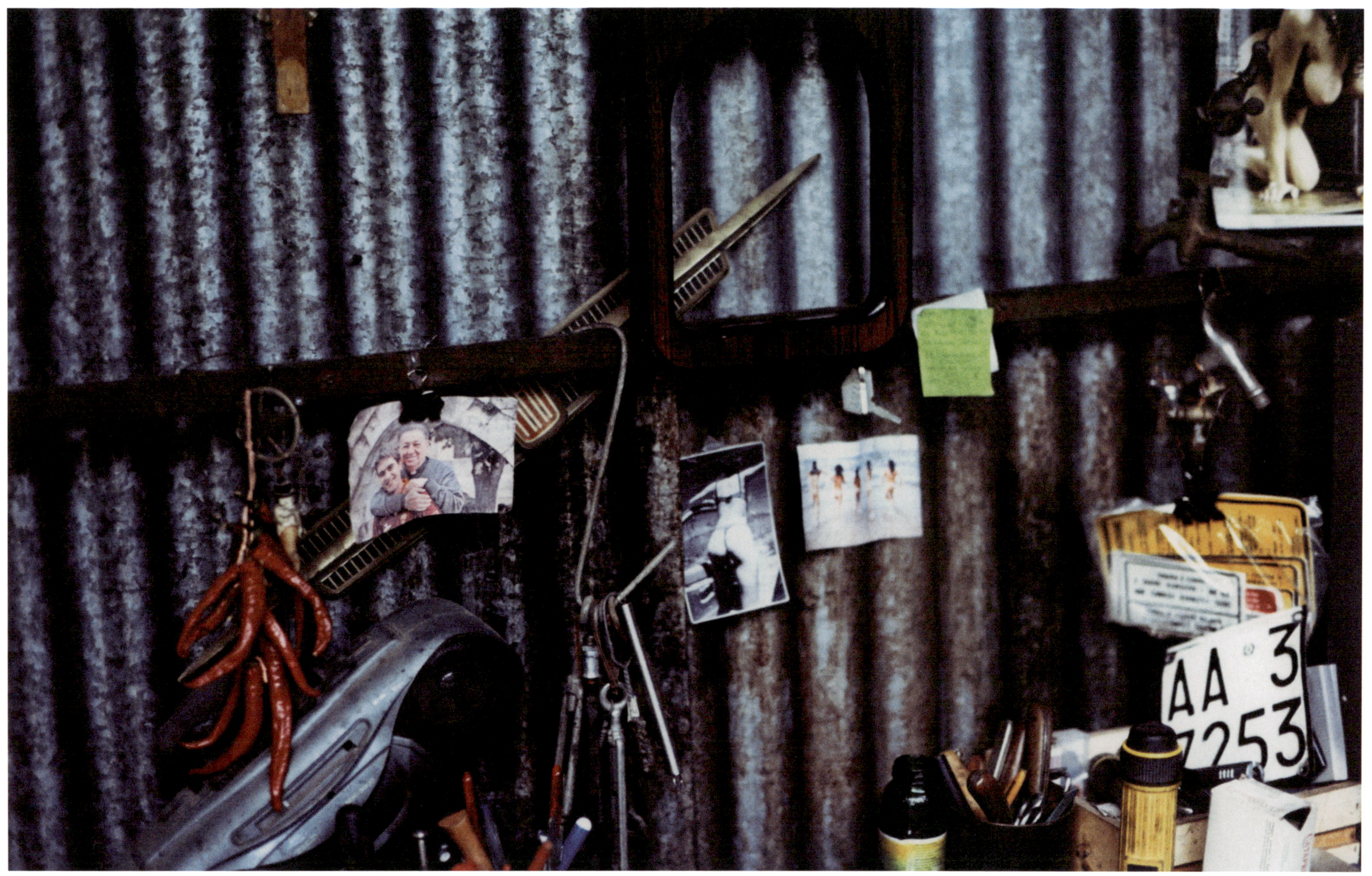

important detail in Fabio's workplace: the photograph of him as a young boy with the priest, his father.

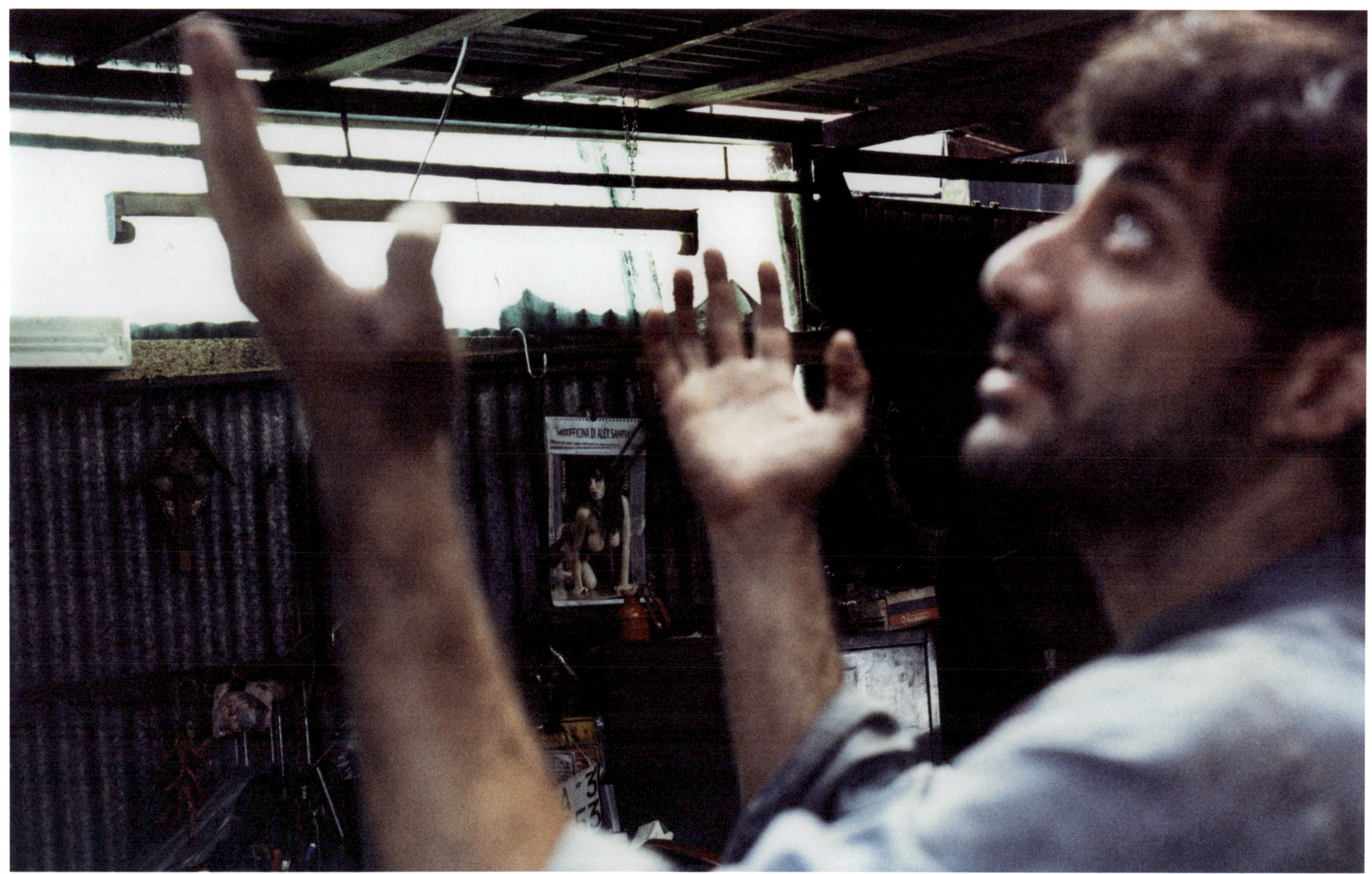

Filippo Timi's character (Fabio) explaining how he got hold of JACK's phone ("a gift from above")

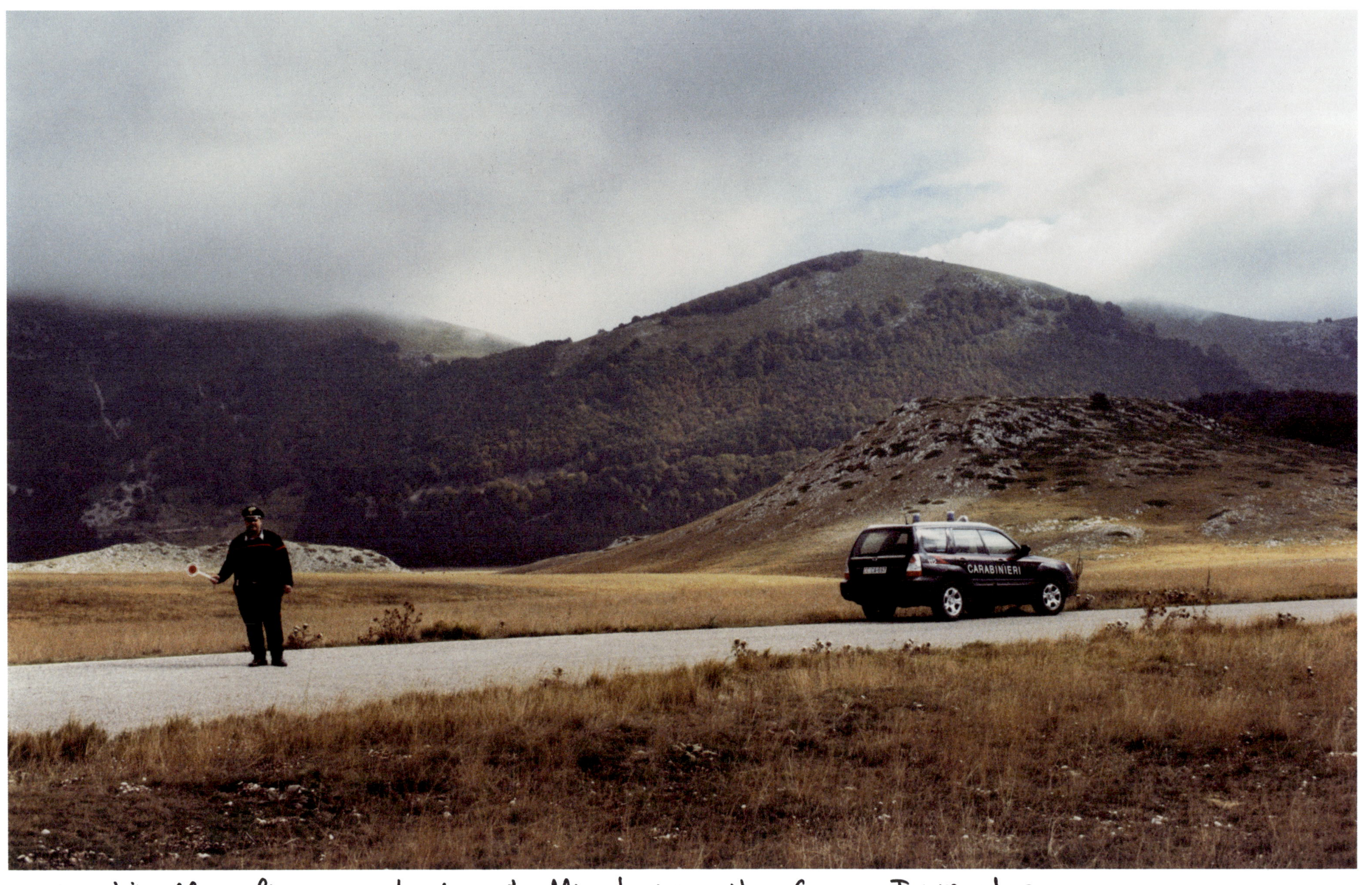

a very friendly policeman stopping traffic for us on the Campo Imperatore.

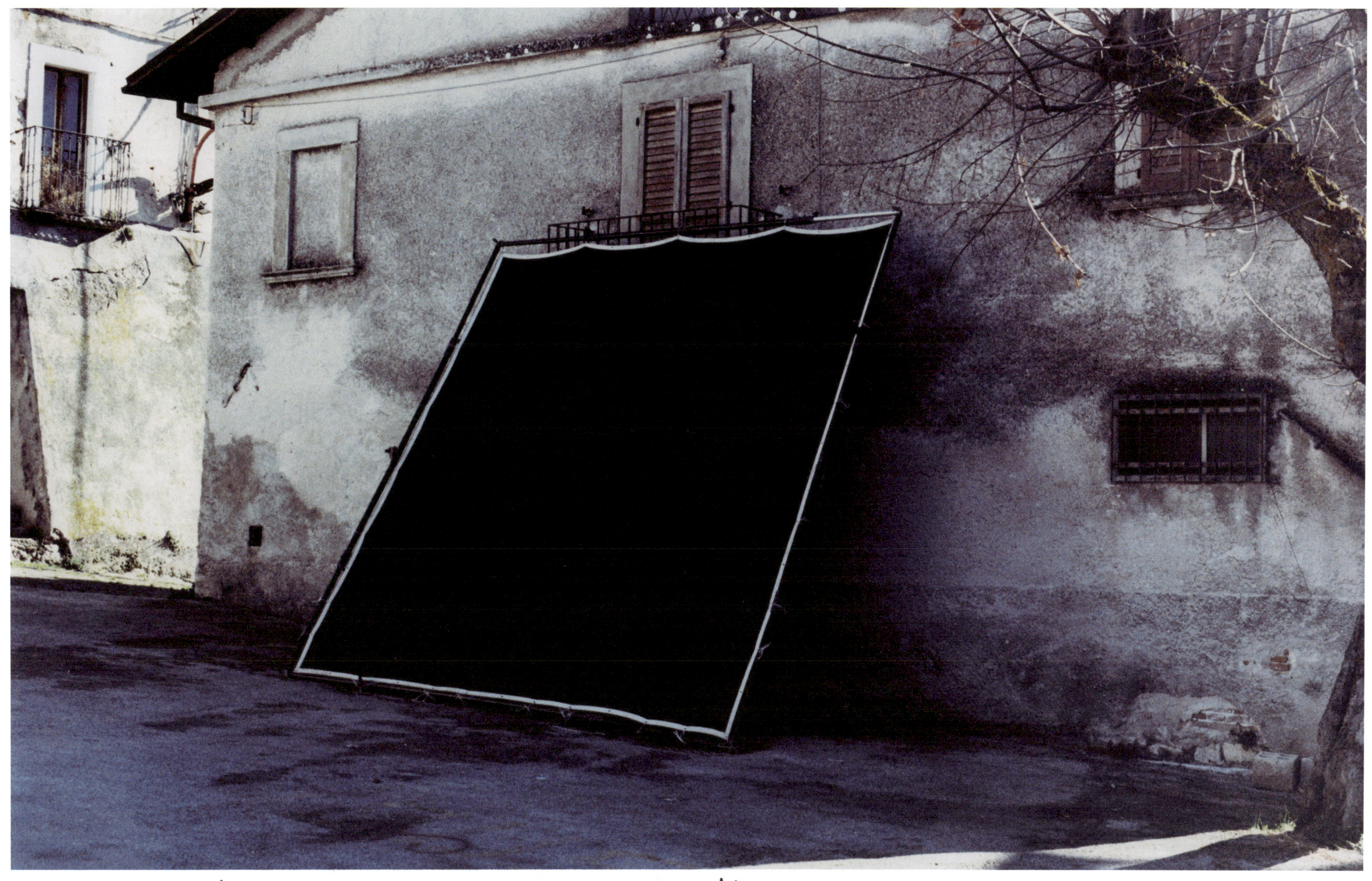

a negative fill leaning against a house in Castelvecchio.

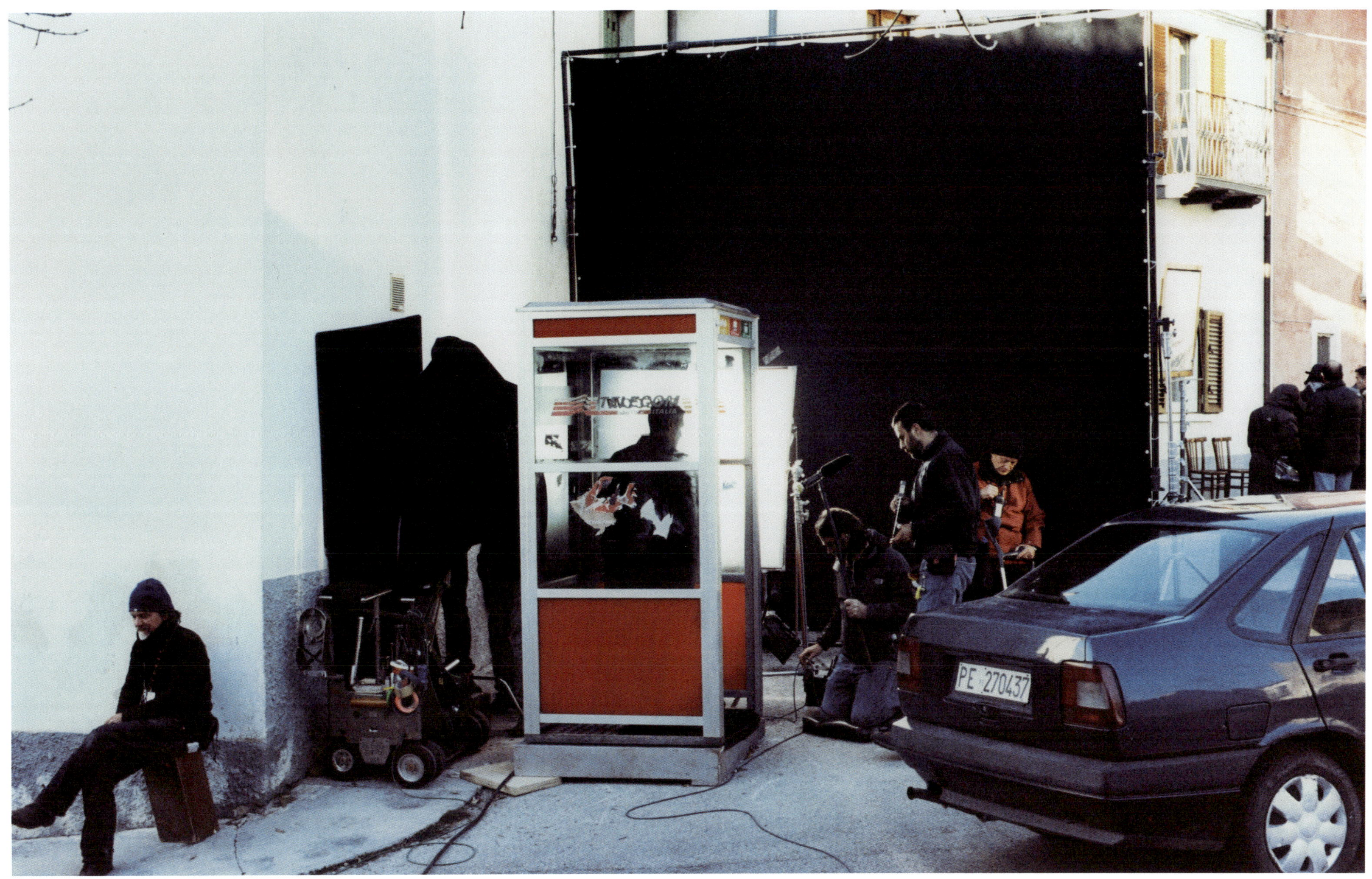

the fill in use for one of the telephone recordings.

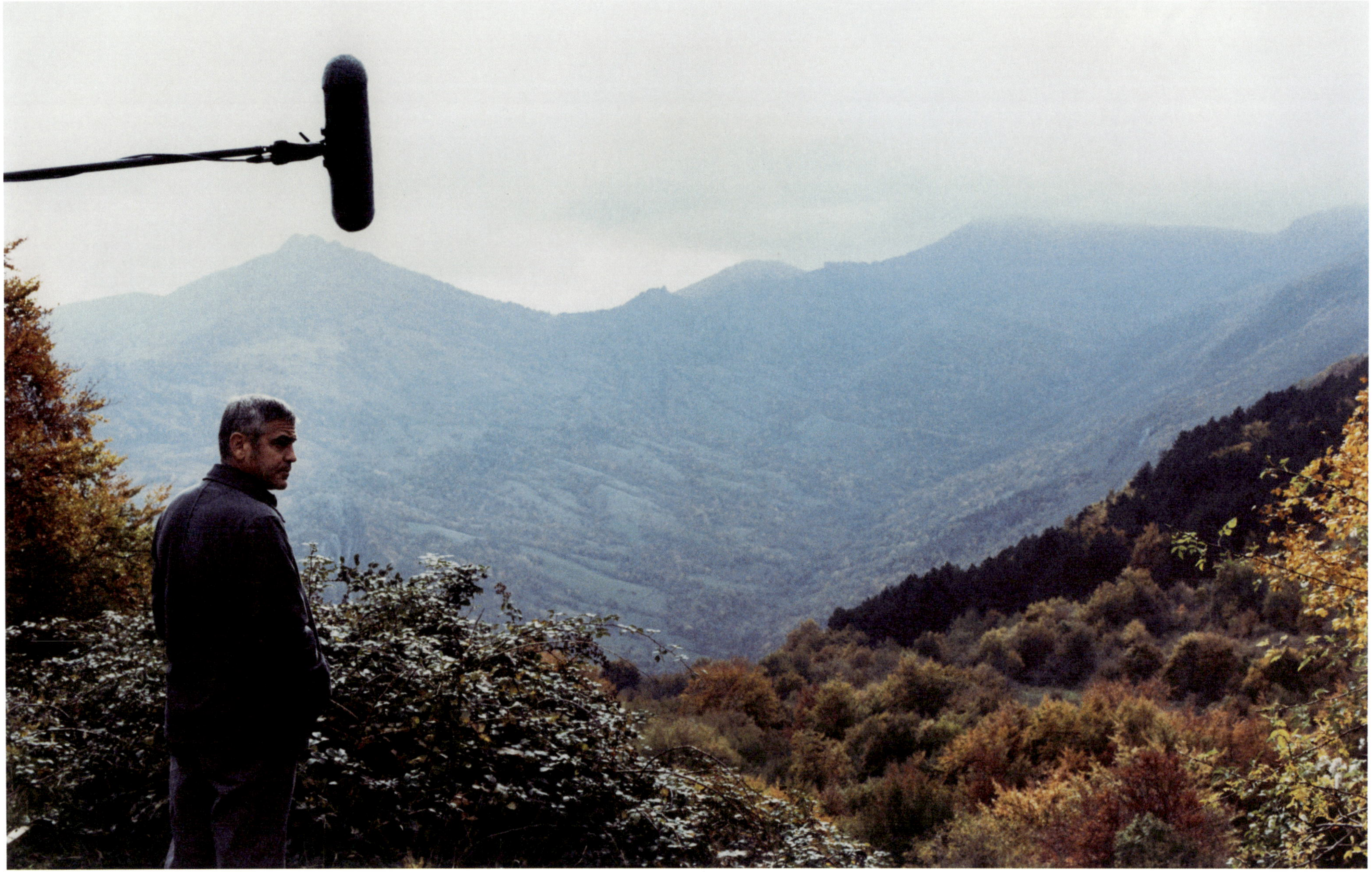

In a scene that's no longer in the film, George gets out of the car to check on a car following him.

57

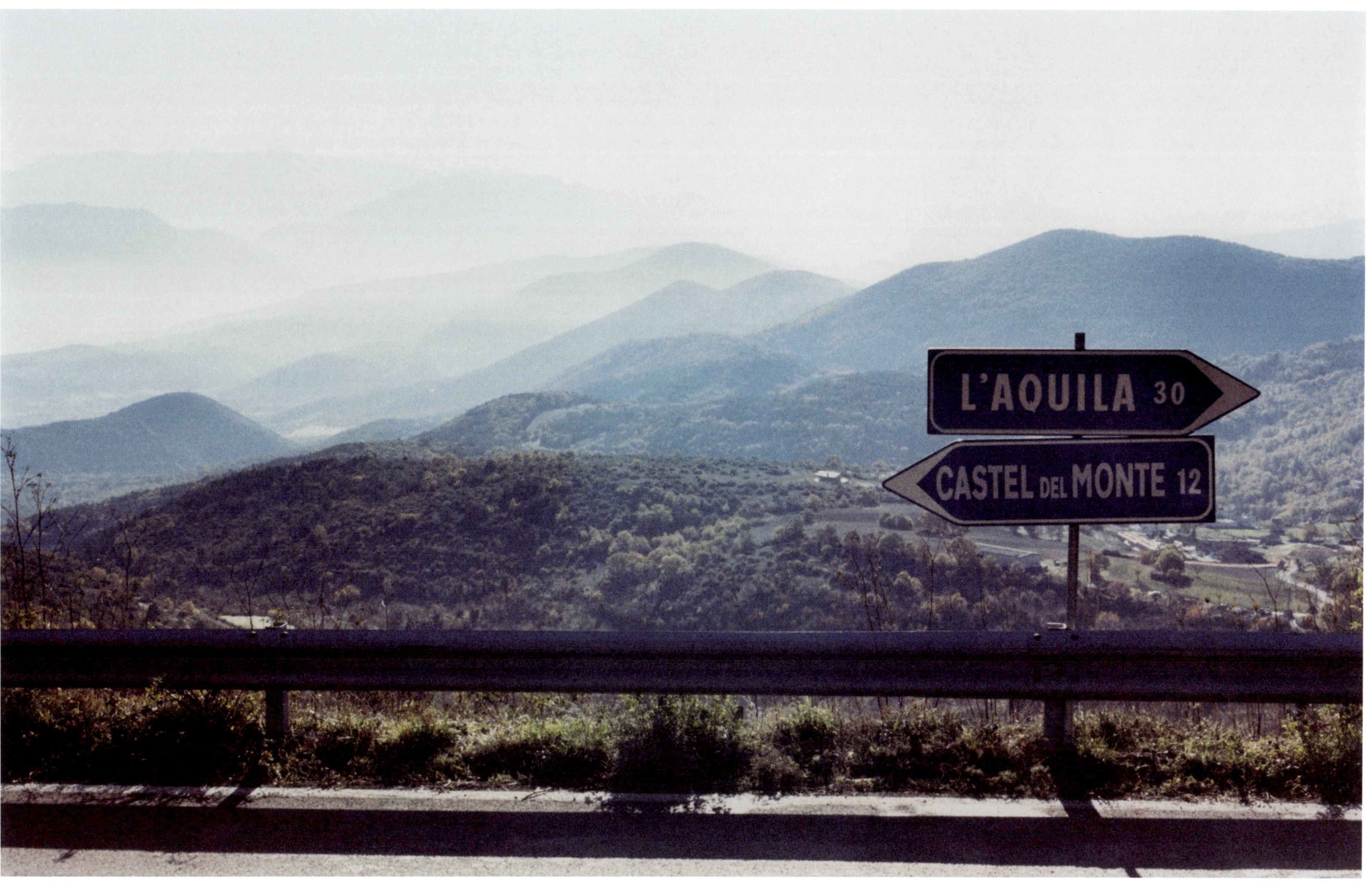

When Jack leaves Castelvecchio he takes a left turn to Castel del Monte.

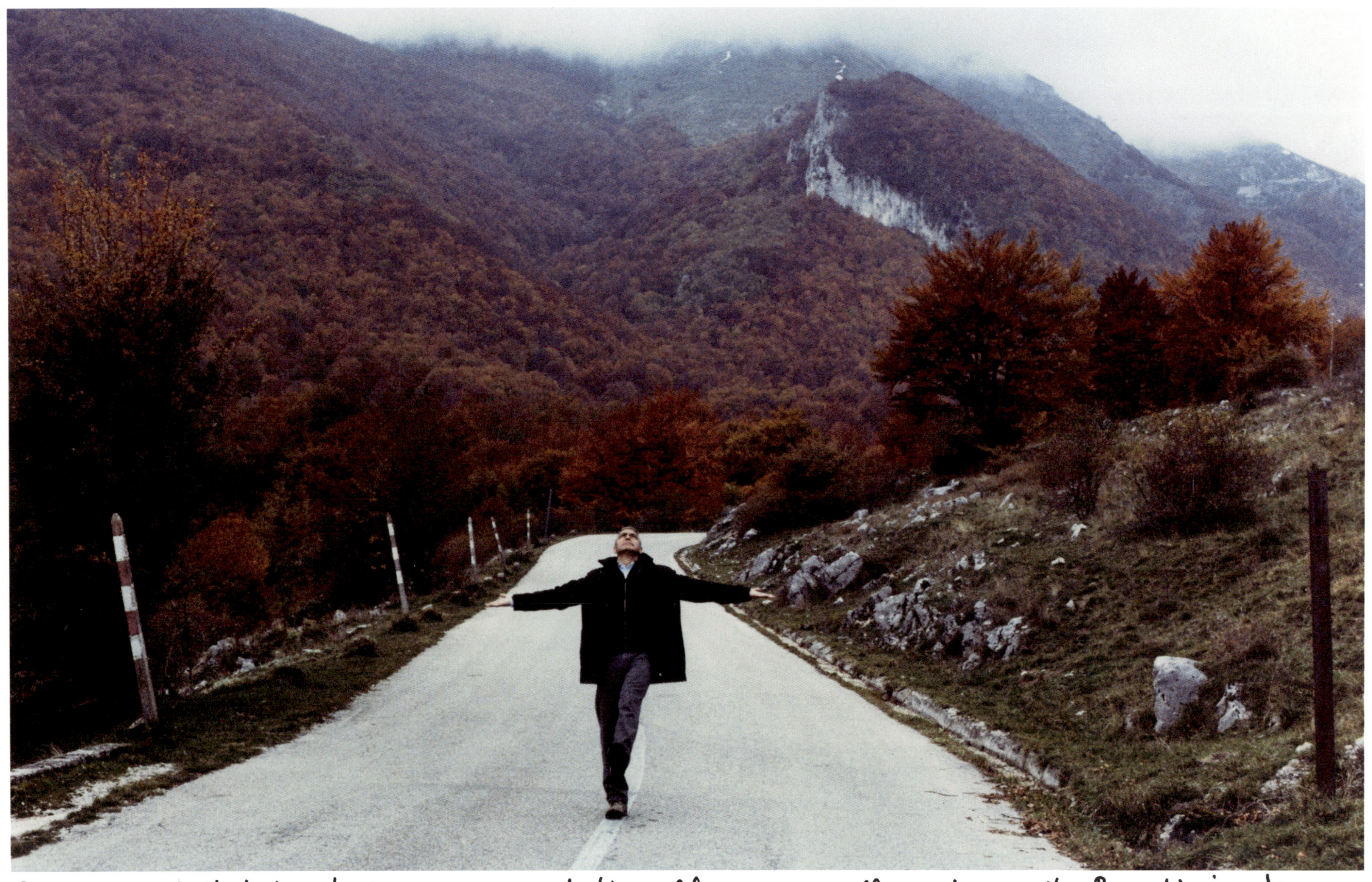

George entertaining the troops, me and himself on a small road near the Parco Nazionale del Gran Sasso

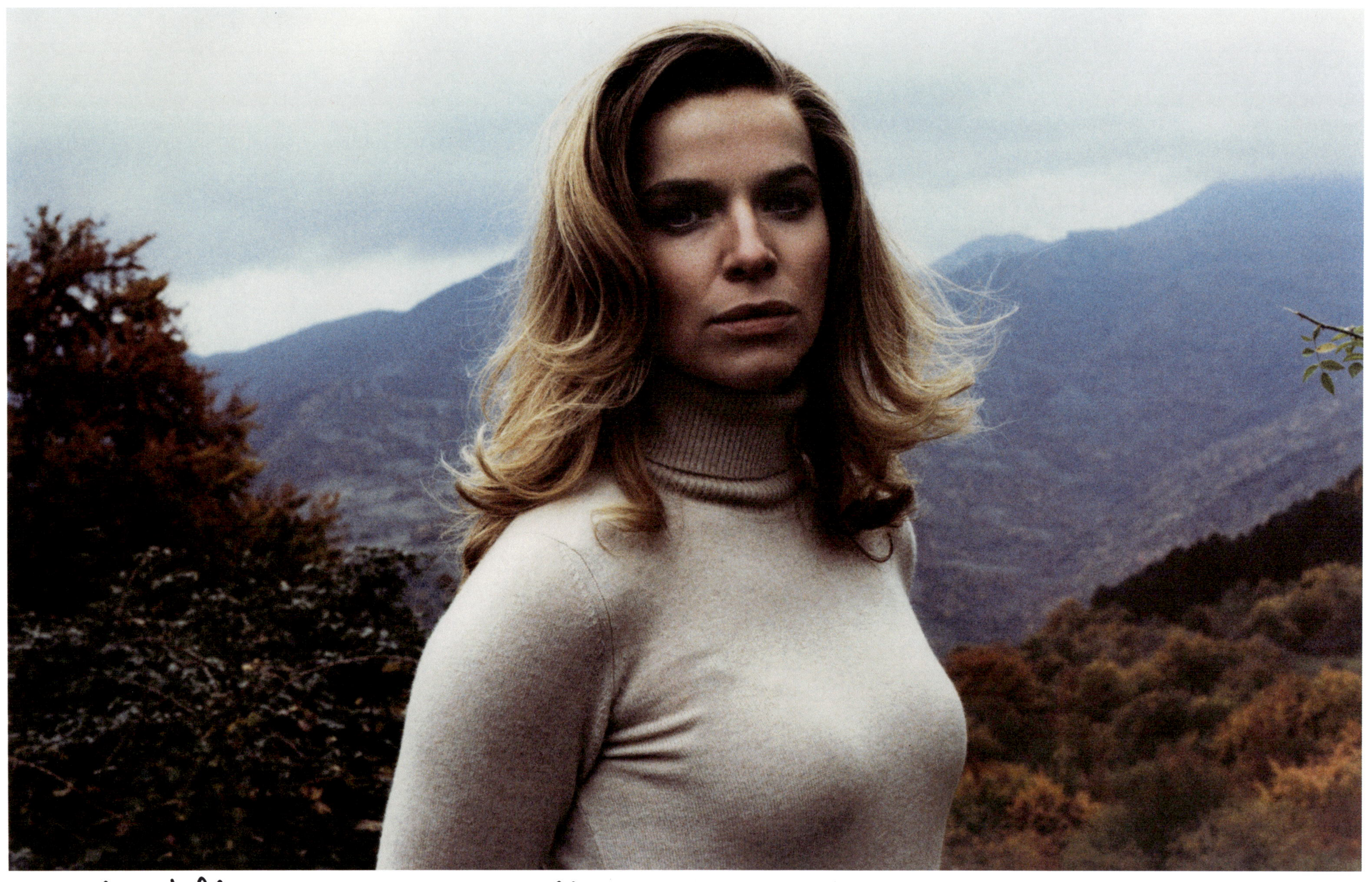

Beautiful Thekla in the autumnal hills resembling 70's Catherine Deneuve unintentionally.

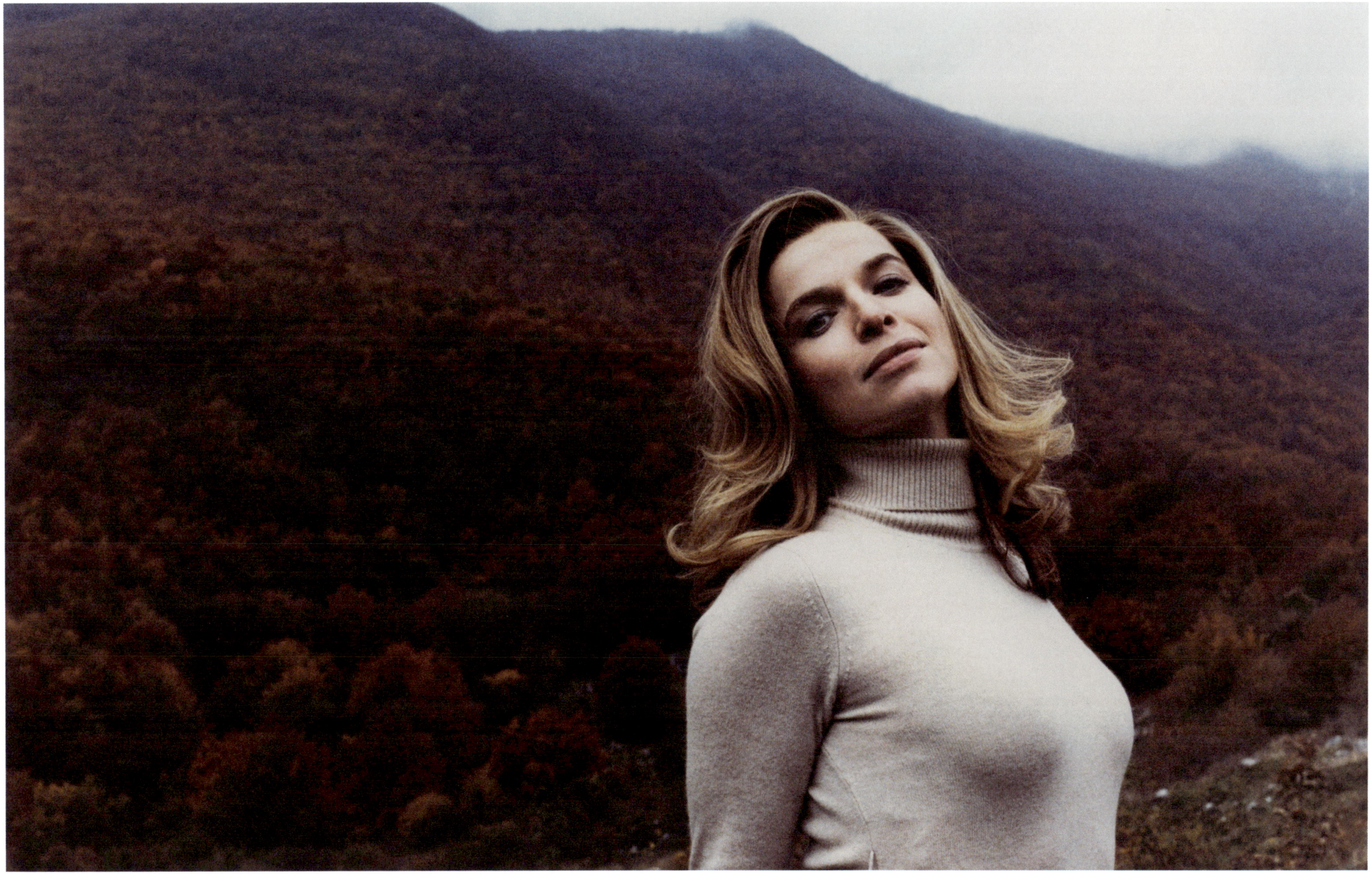

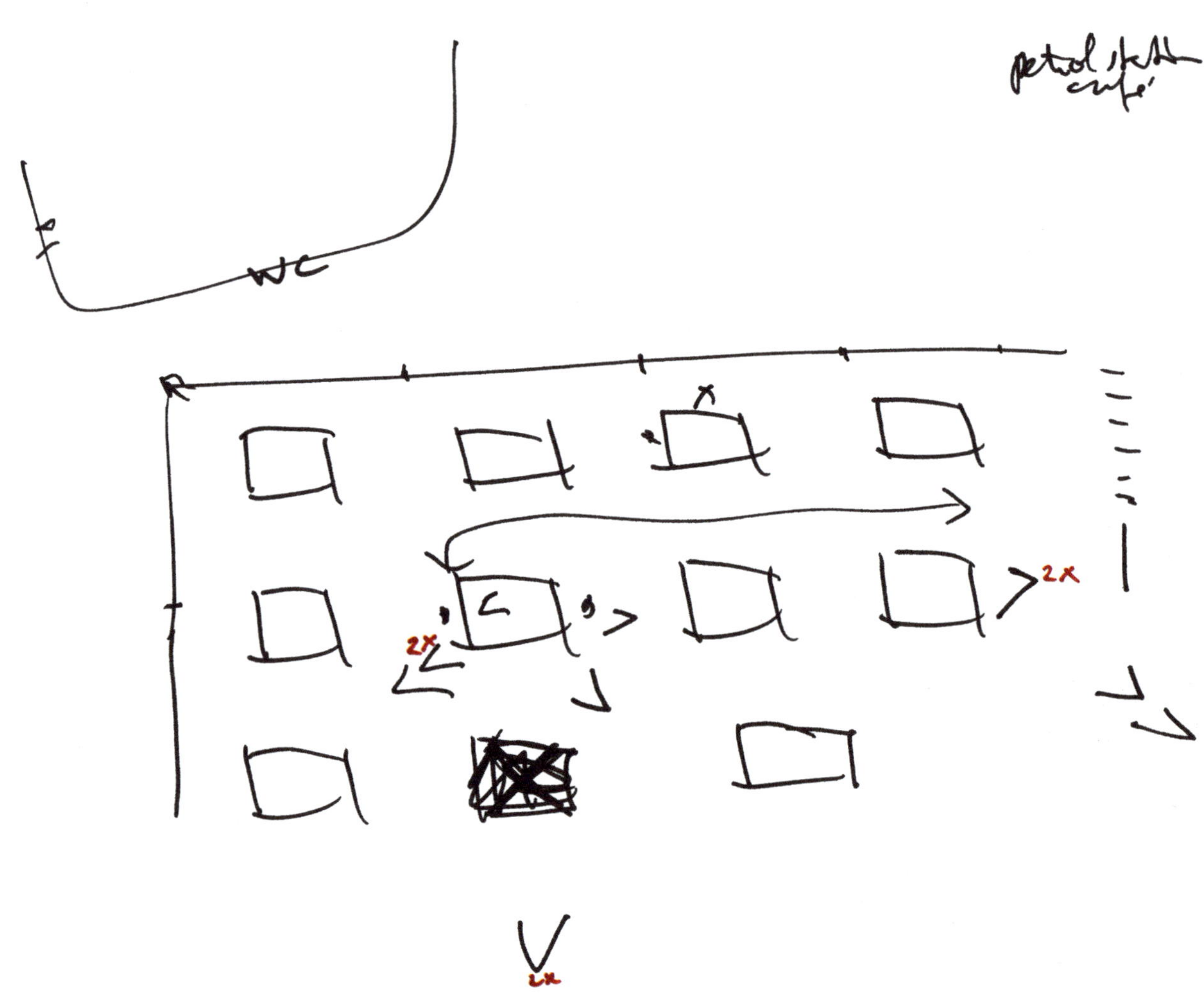
WC
2X
2X
2X

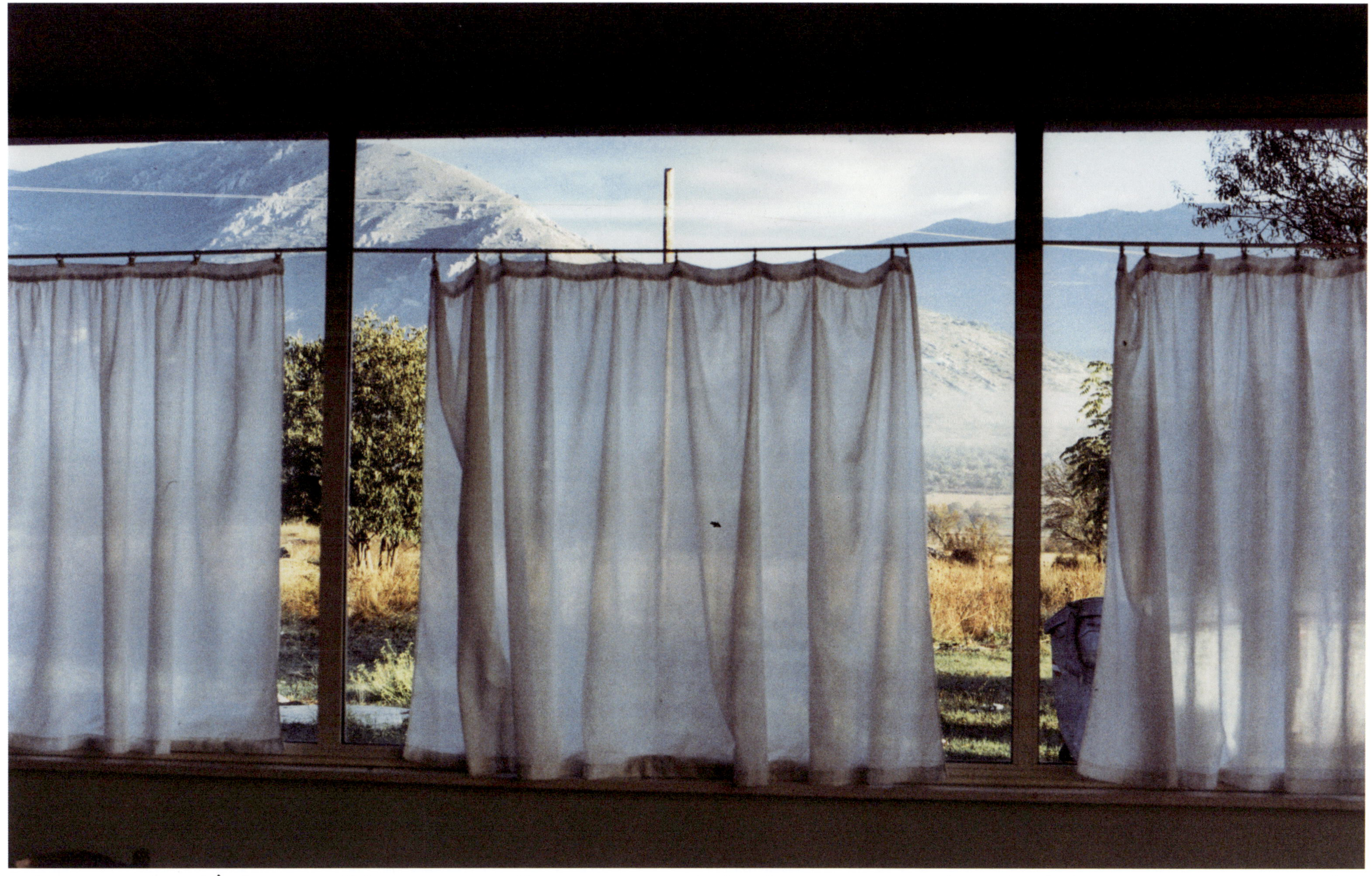

when we stumbled upon this petrolstation restaurant building i realised we had just found my favorite location of the film. part Hopper, part Wenders, part Americana, and used for a great scene.

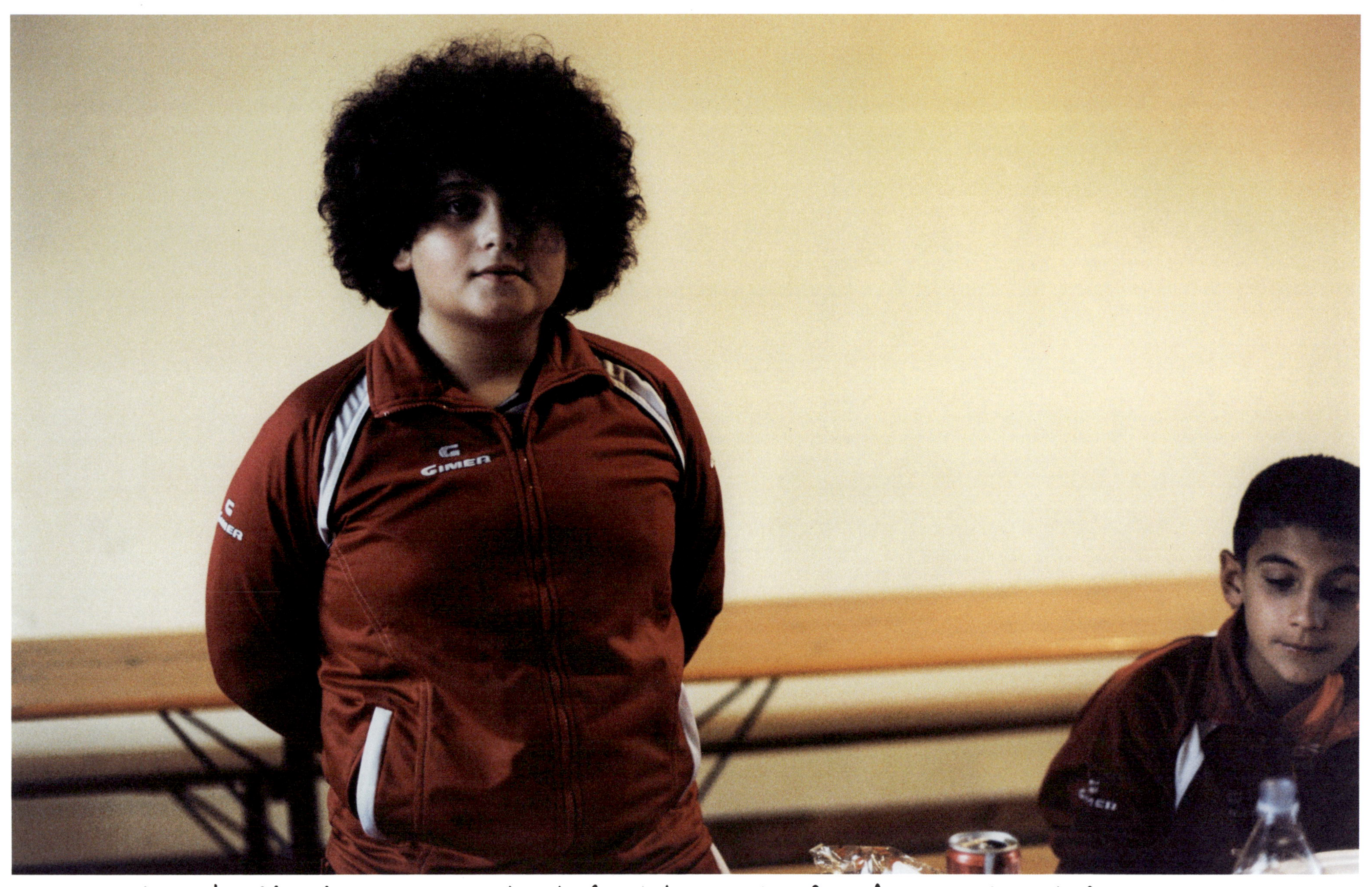

two of the schoolbus kids in their footbal clothes during lunch near the petrol station.

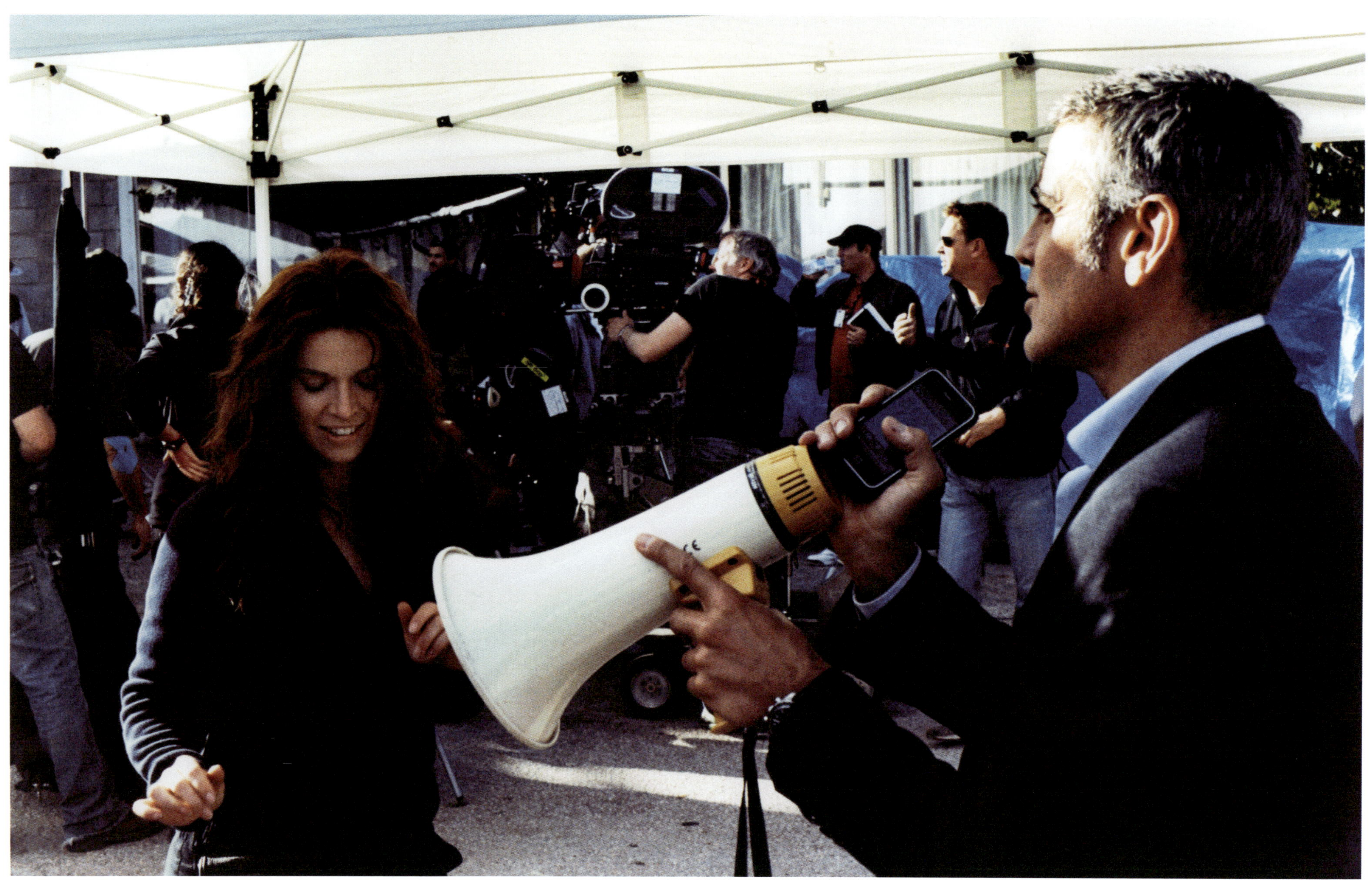

thekla dances to the tunes George is playing from his iphone outside the petrolstation cafe'.

67

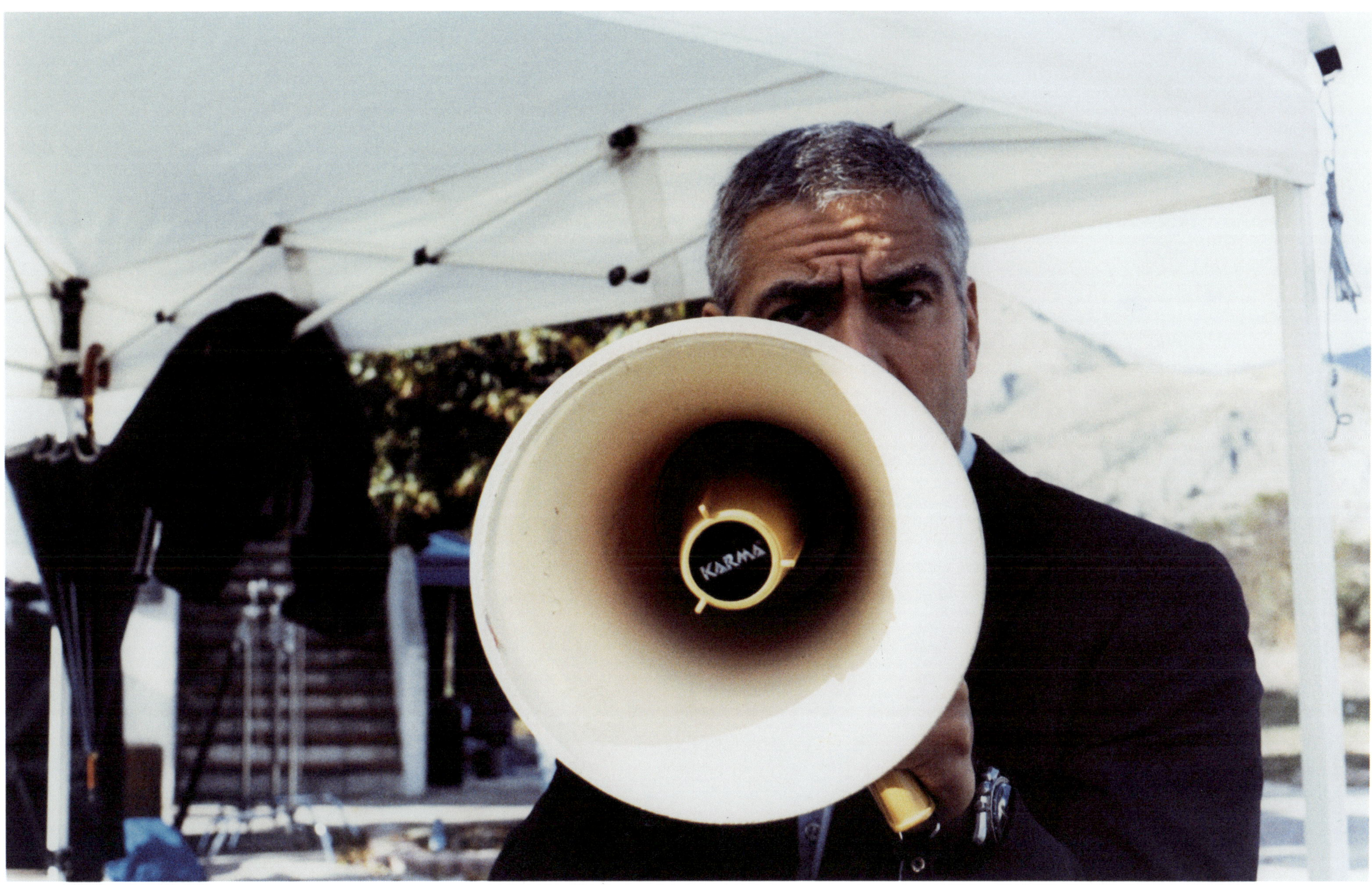

instant!

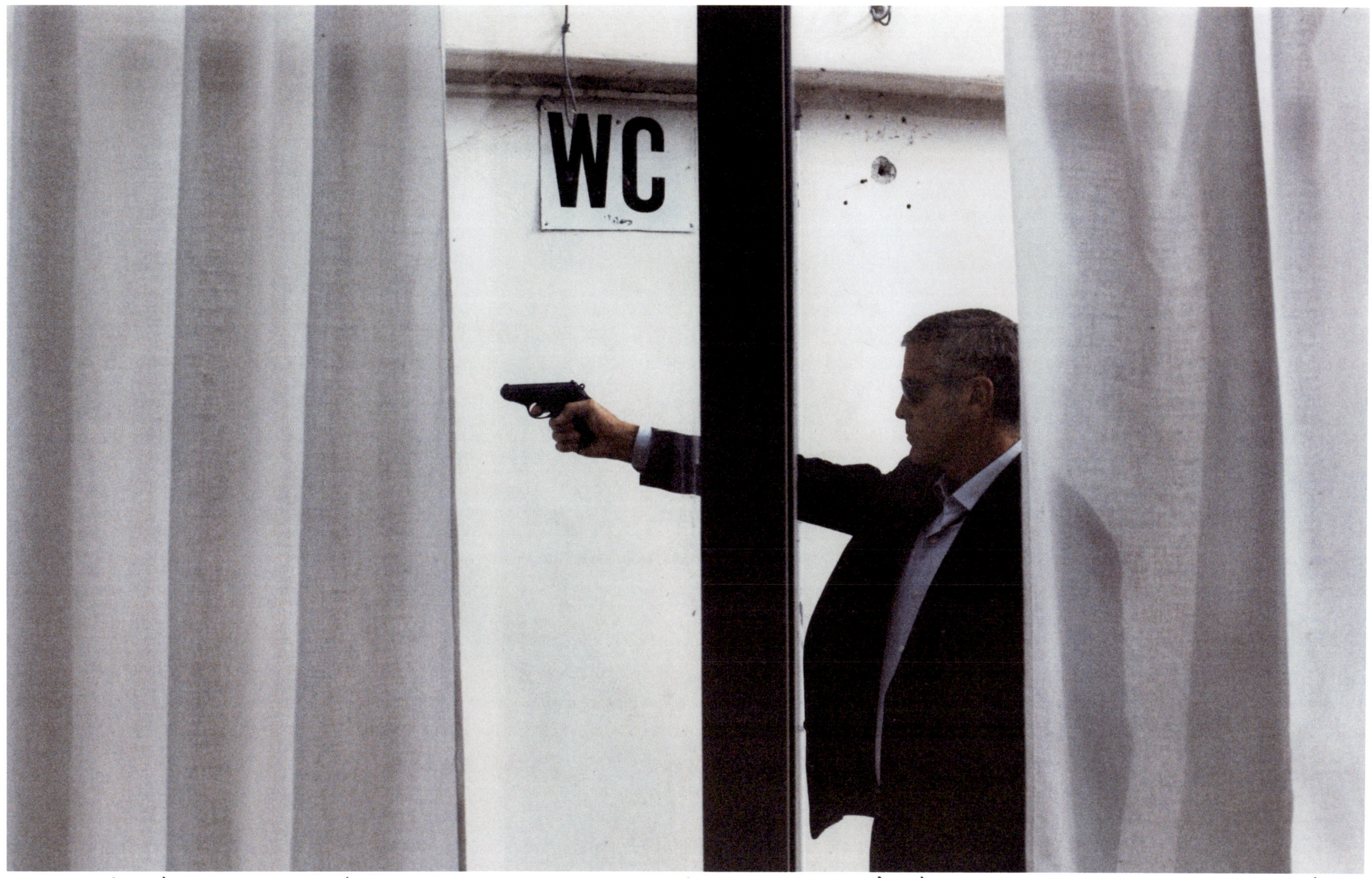

i enjoy shooting photographs through windows and that's what this photo is all about, as i so loved this location (roadside café) with its outdoor toilet.

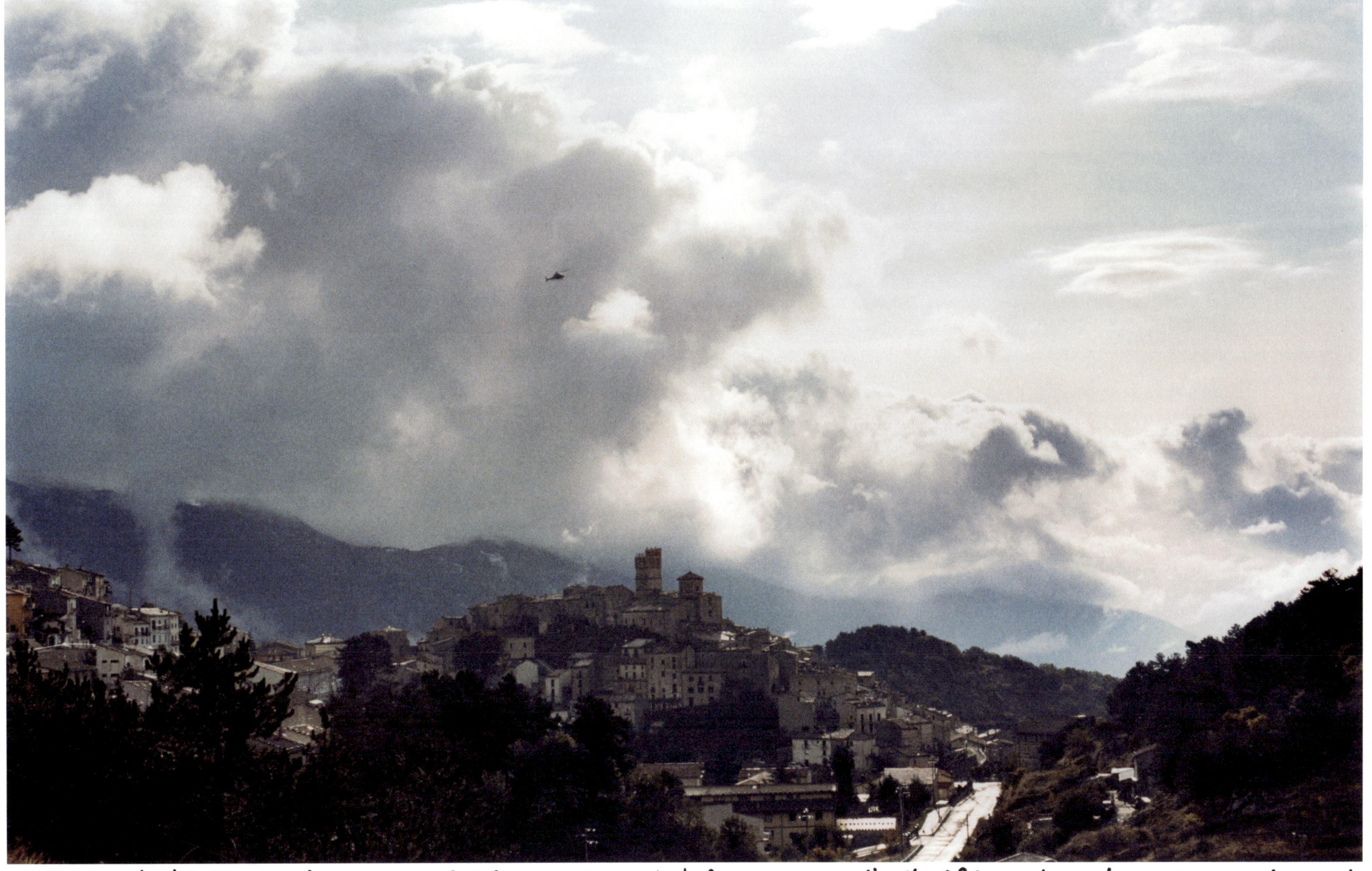

shooting the bird's eye view of Castel del Monte from the helicopter. Martin the DP is onboard, i went on the next trip 20 minutes later, just before it suddenly started to snow and the heli was grounded for 24 hours.

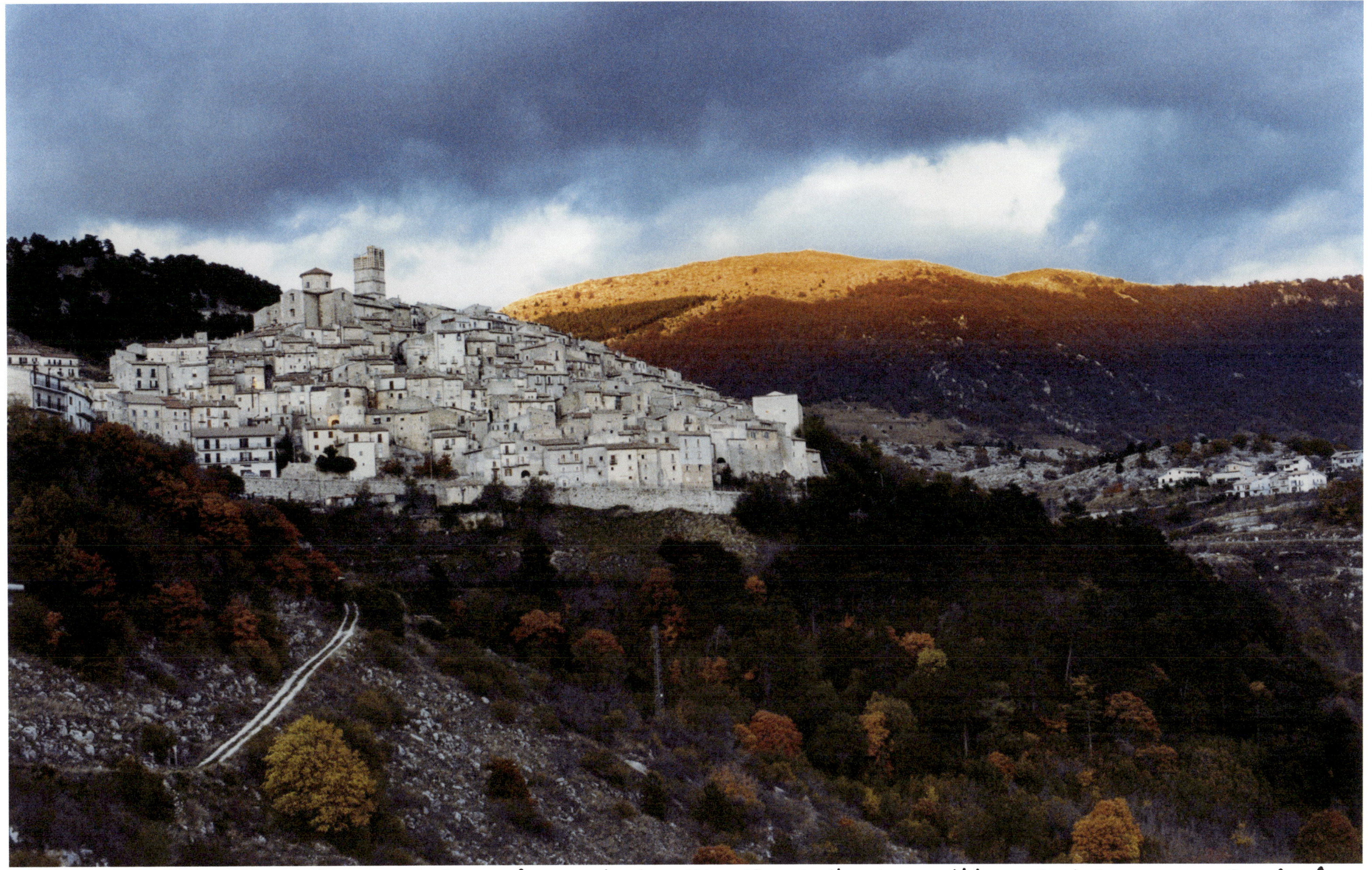

Every day the light in the mountains make you look differently at the same thing. Driving up to Castel del Monte late afternoon during the nightshoot, i had to stop the car to shoot this before it disappeared a minute later.

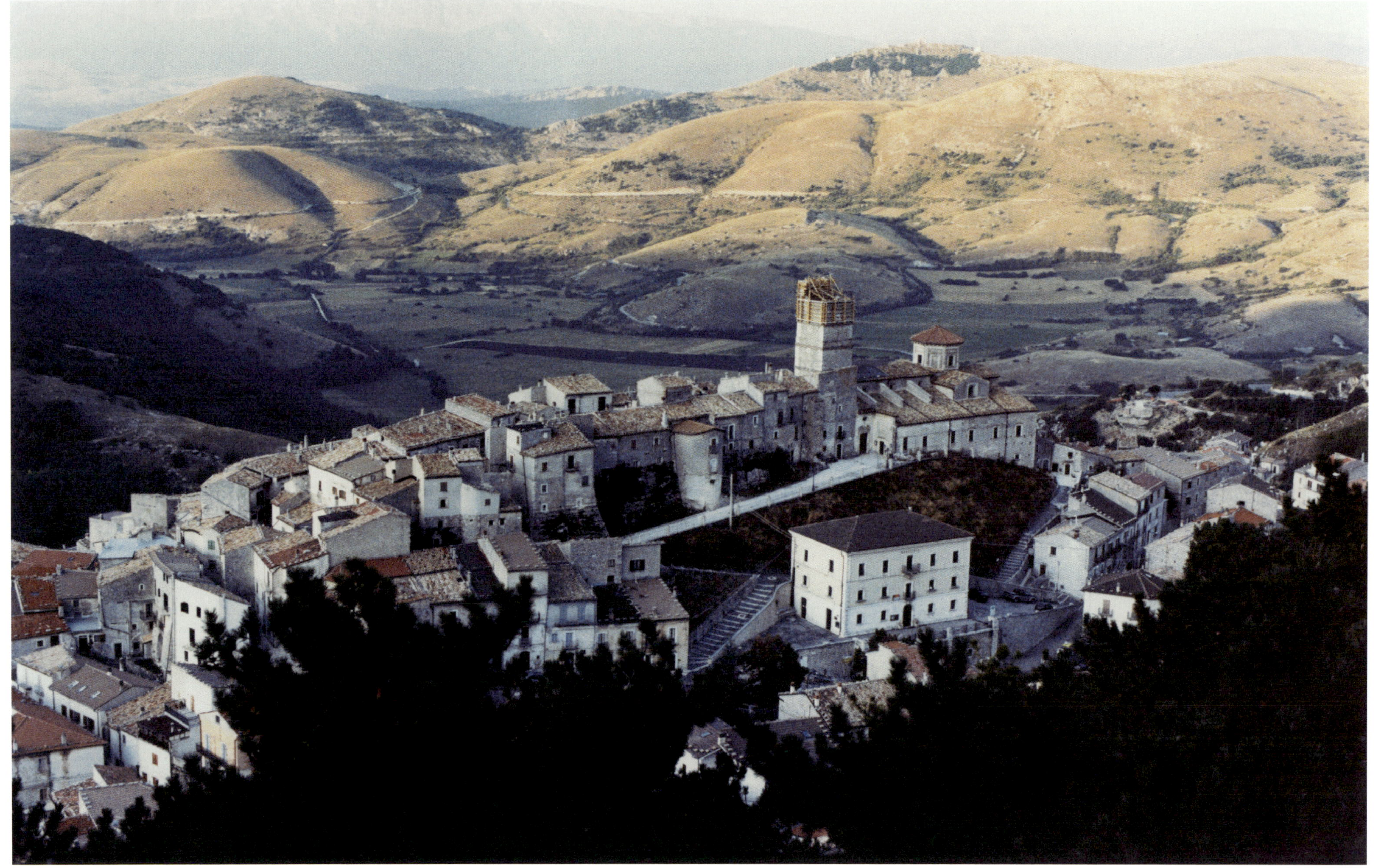

this view of CdM shows very well the damaged tower caused by the earthquake. We fixed it in the film though.

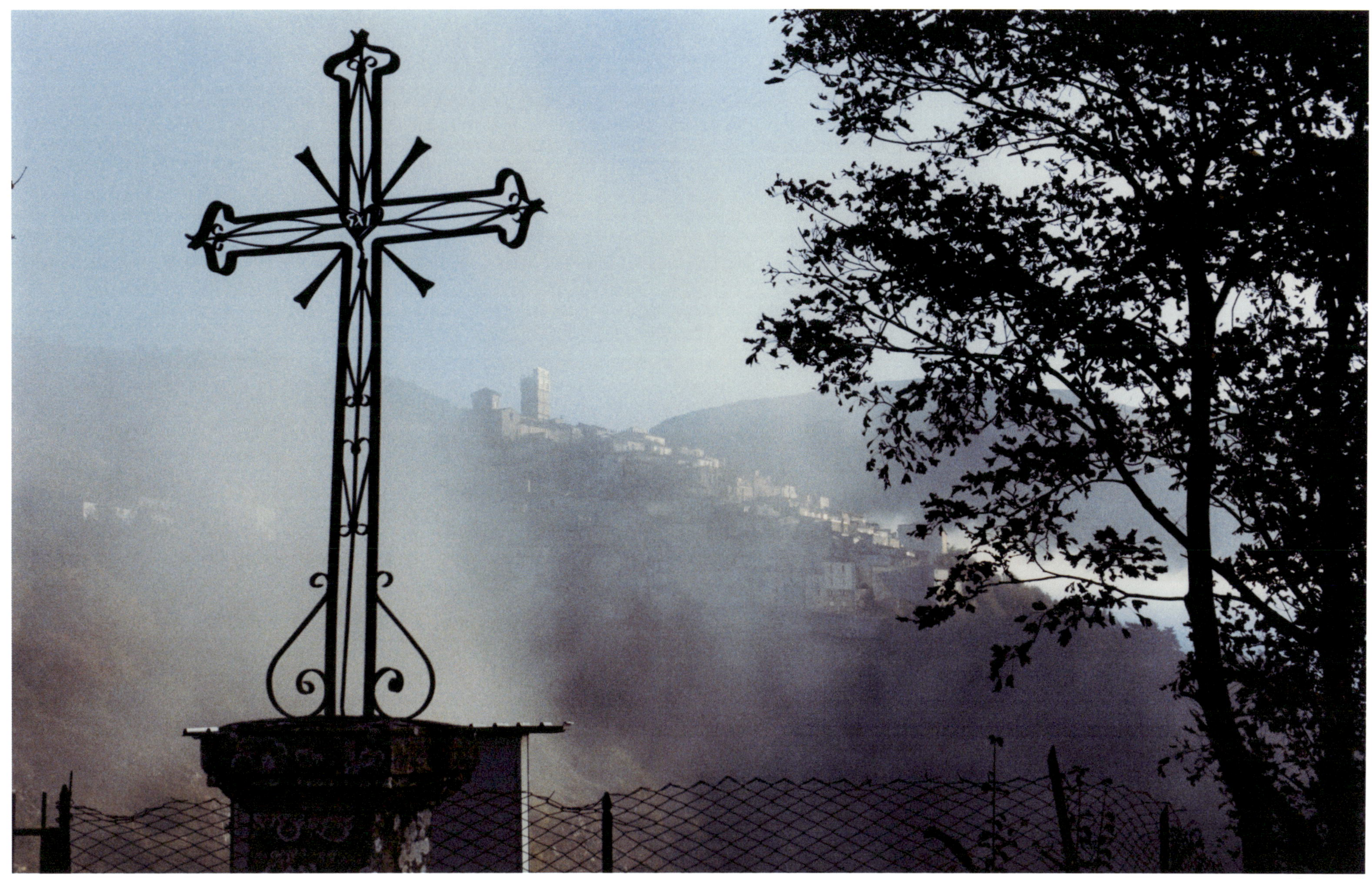

it was unclear to me why this cross stood on this corner but it worked well against the foggy background

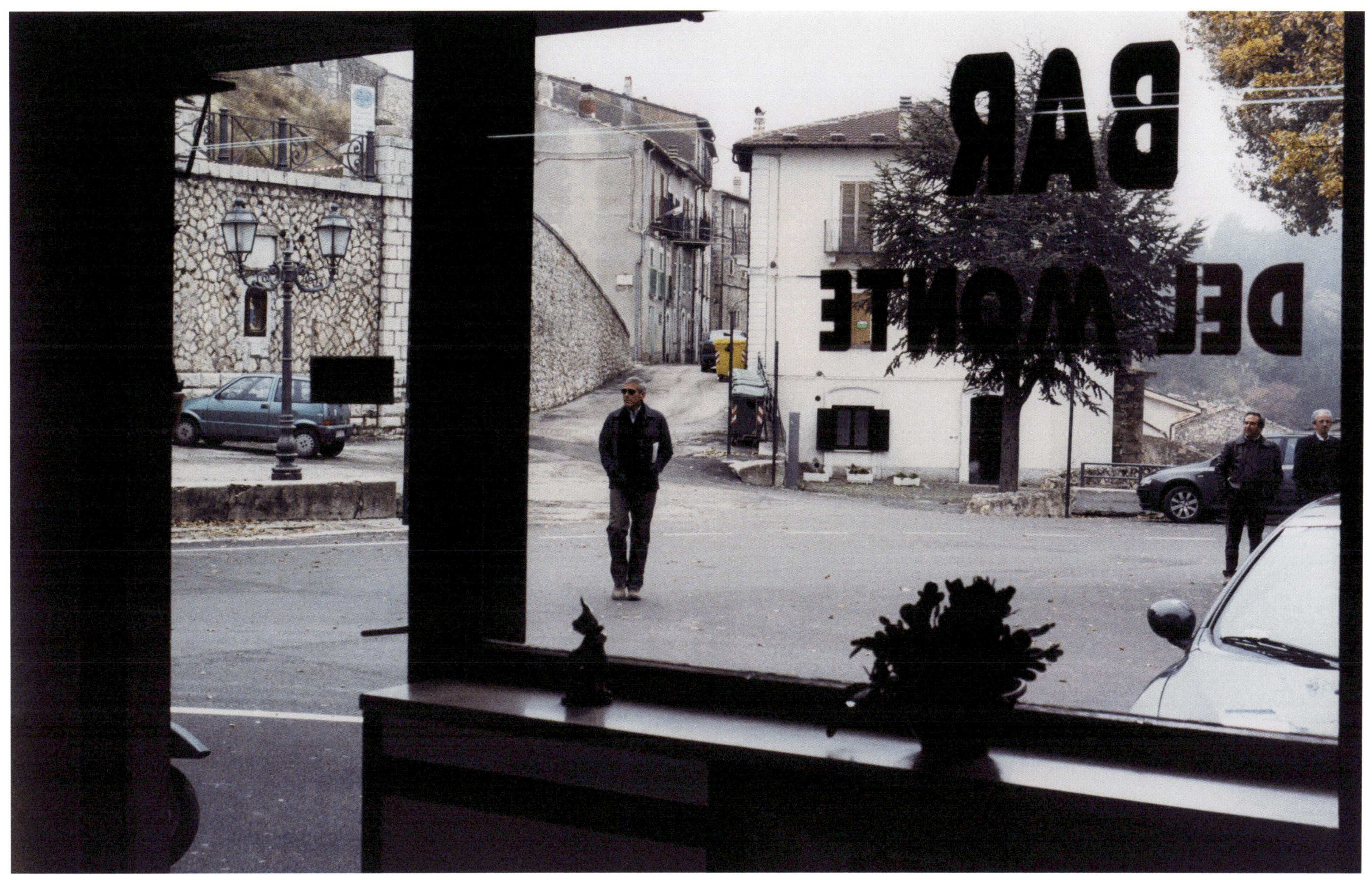

George walking back to the bar in Castel del Monte – you can spot his car behind the yellow bin.

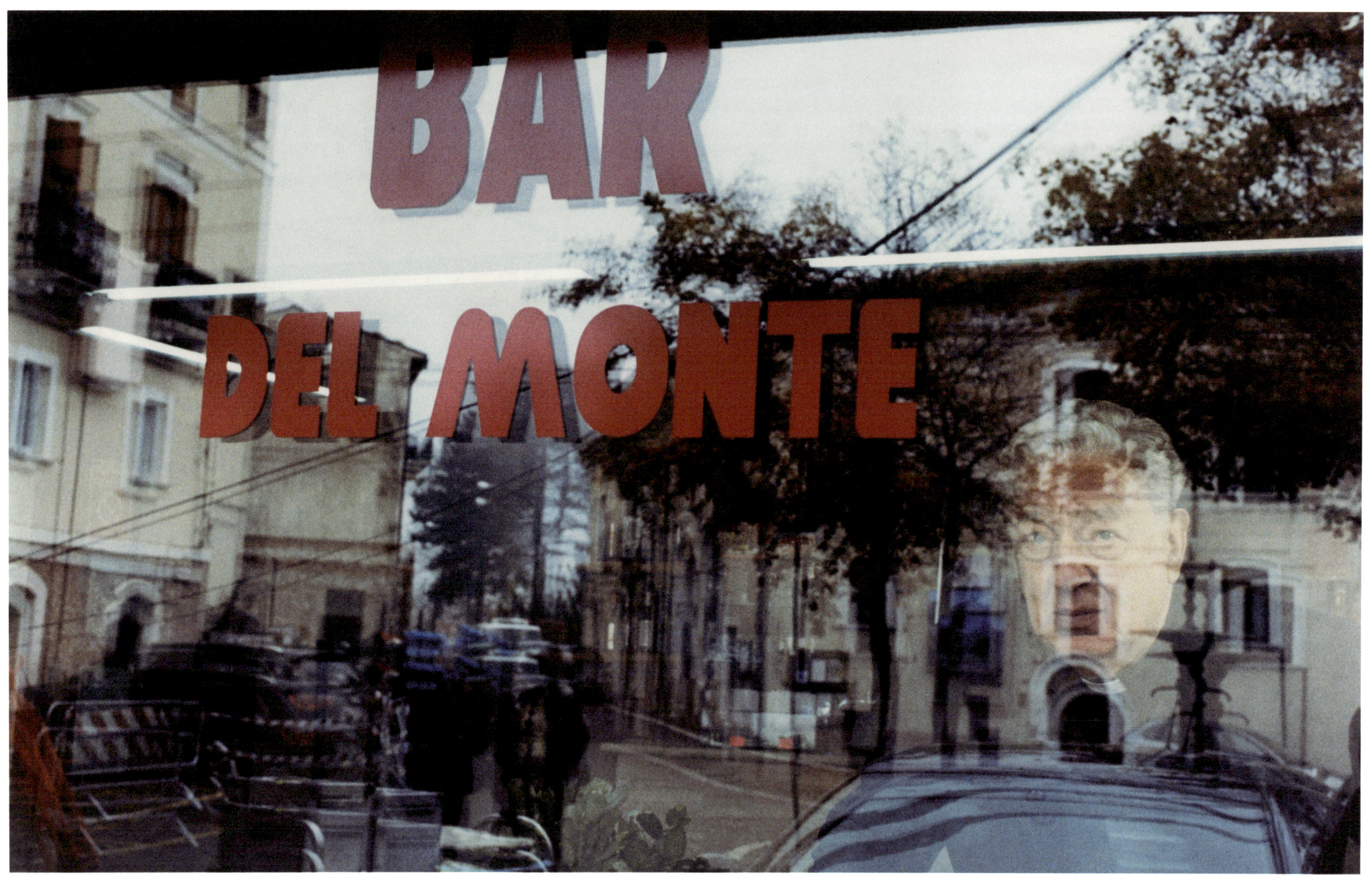

Father Benedetto, Paolo Bonacelli, looks out into the world.

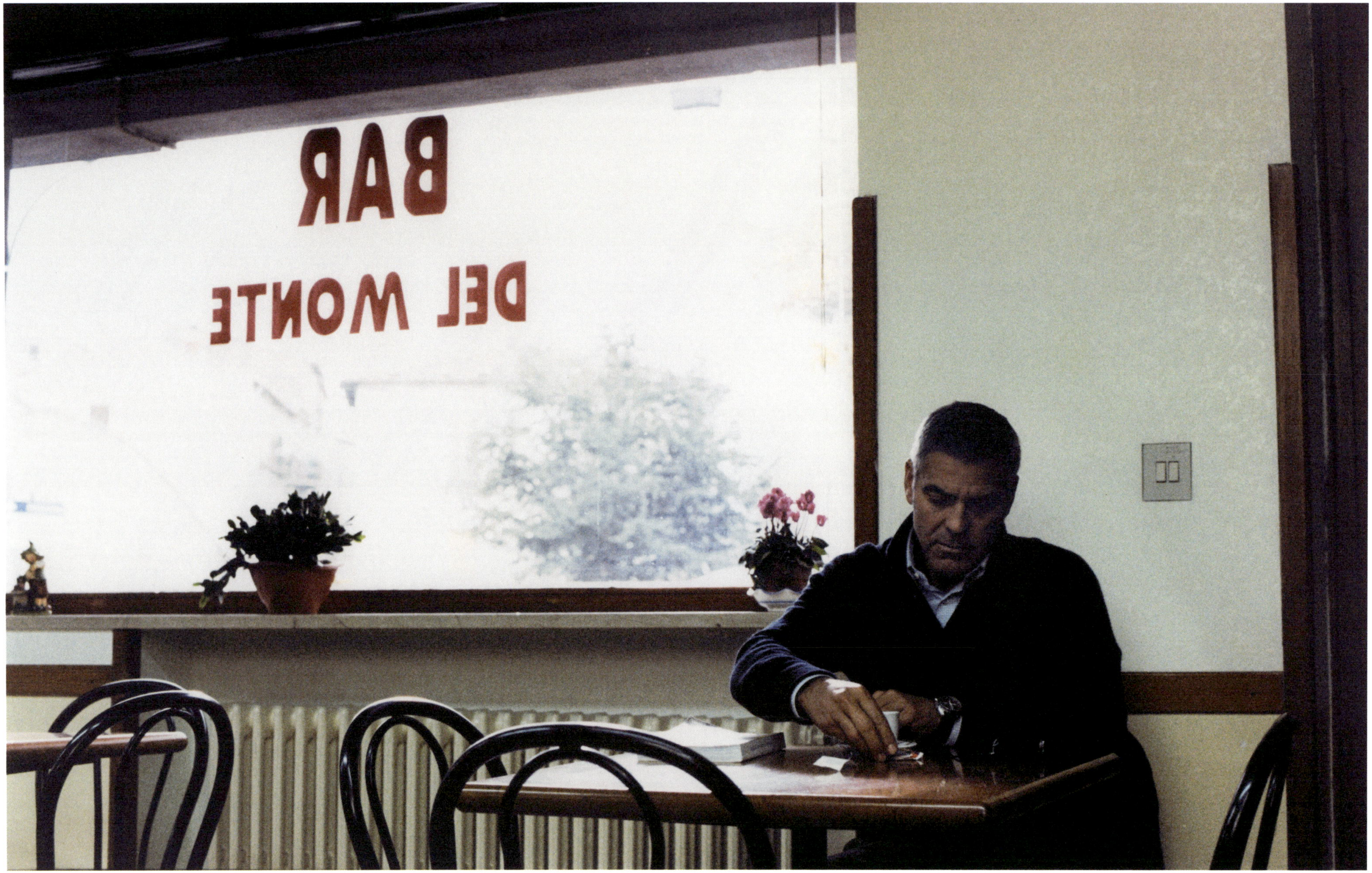

Inside the Bar del Monte, George is buying his first coffee while reading up on the region, Abruzzo.

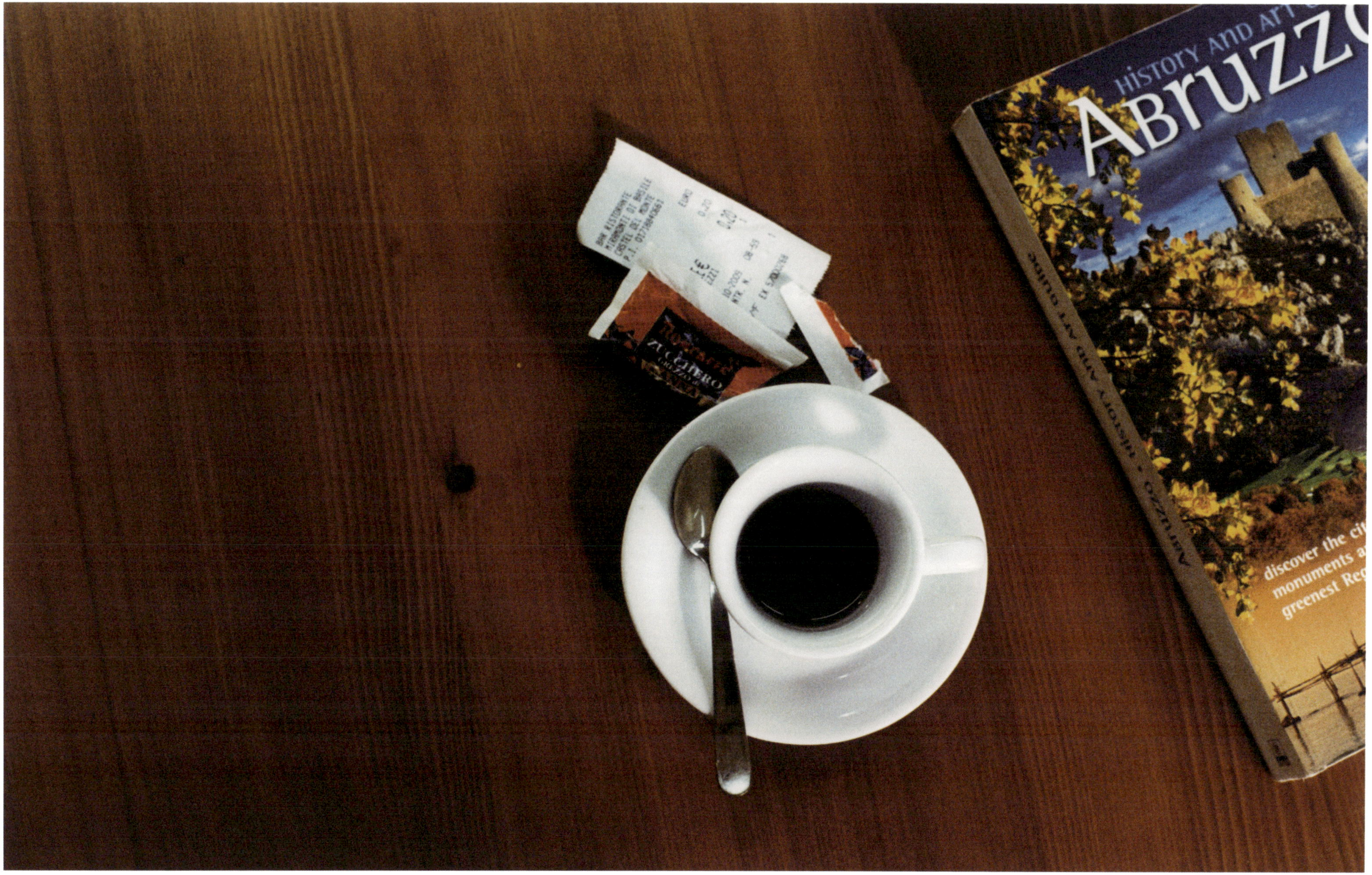

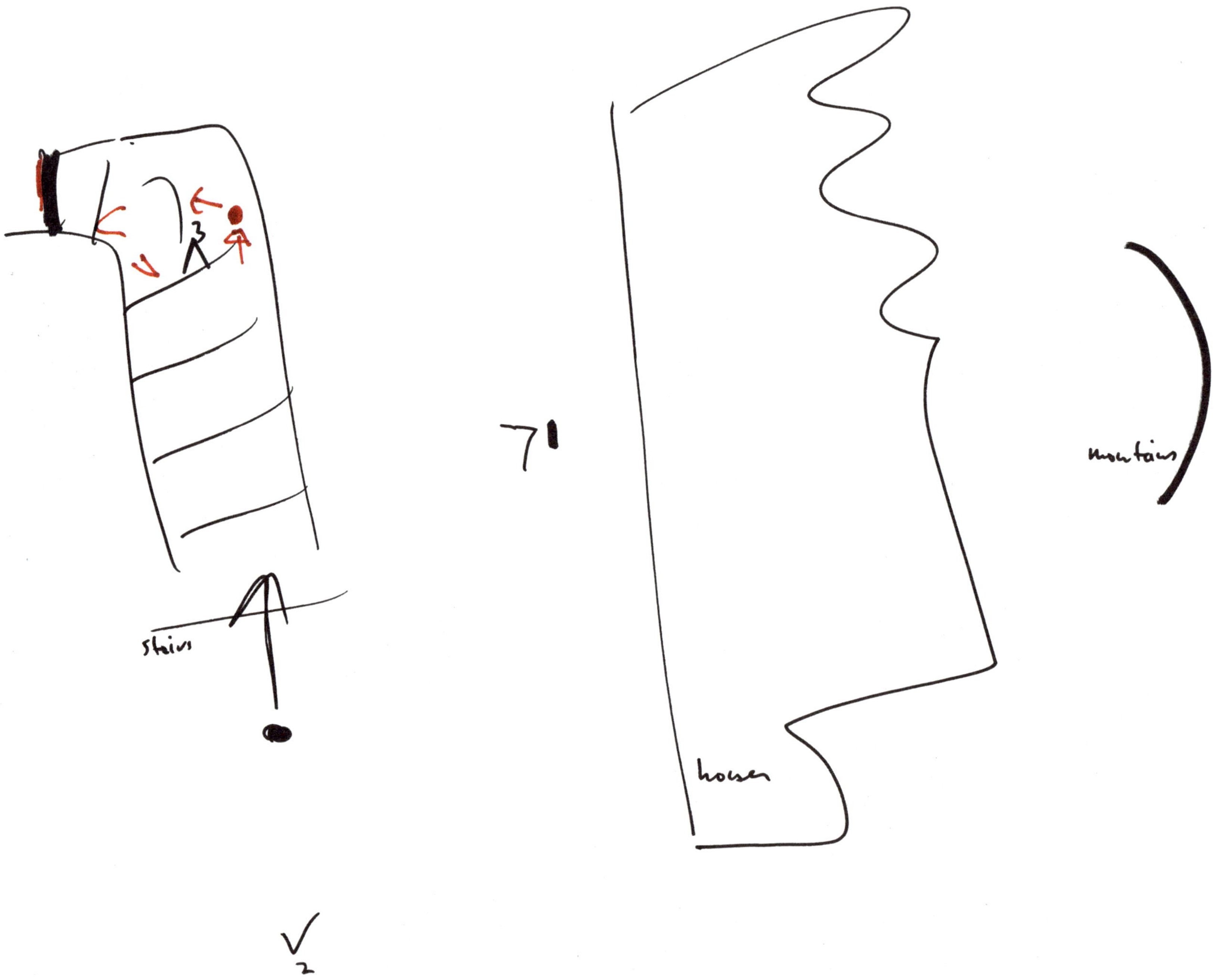

stairs

houses

mountains

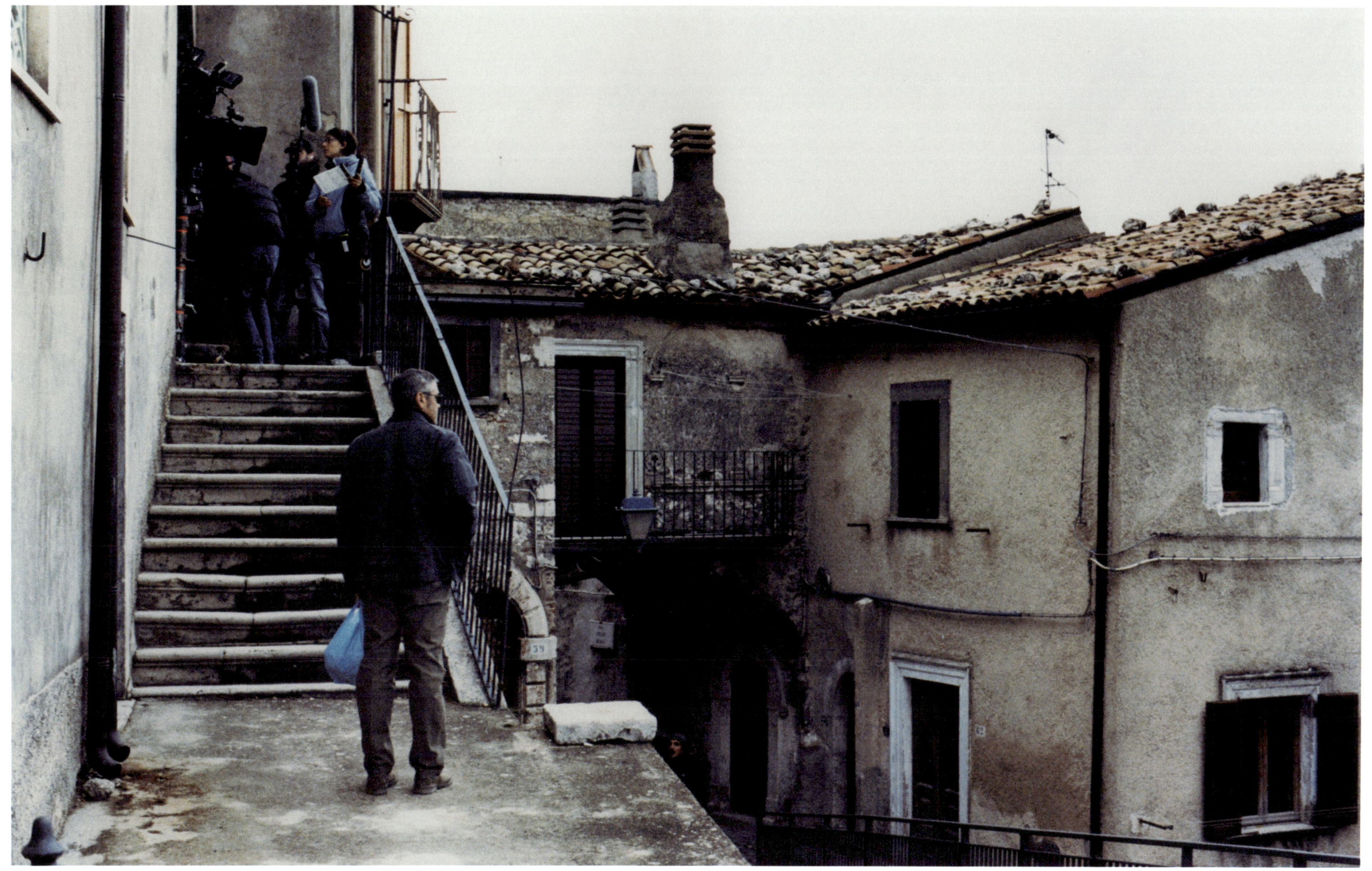

George about to go to 'his' apartment in CdM, it is to the left at the top of the stairs. I love the grey color of the houses in the village.

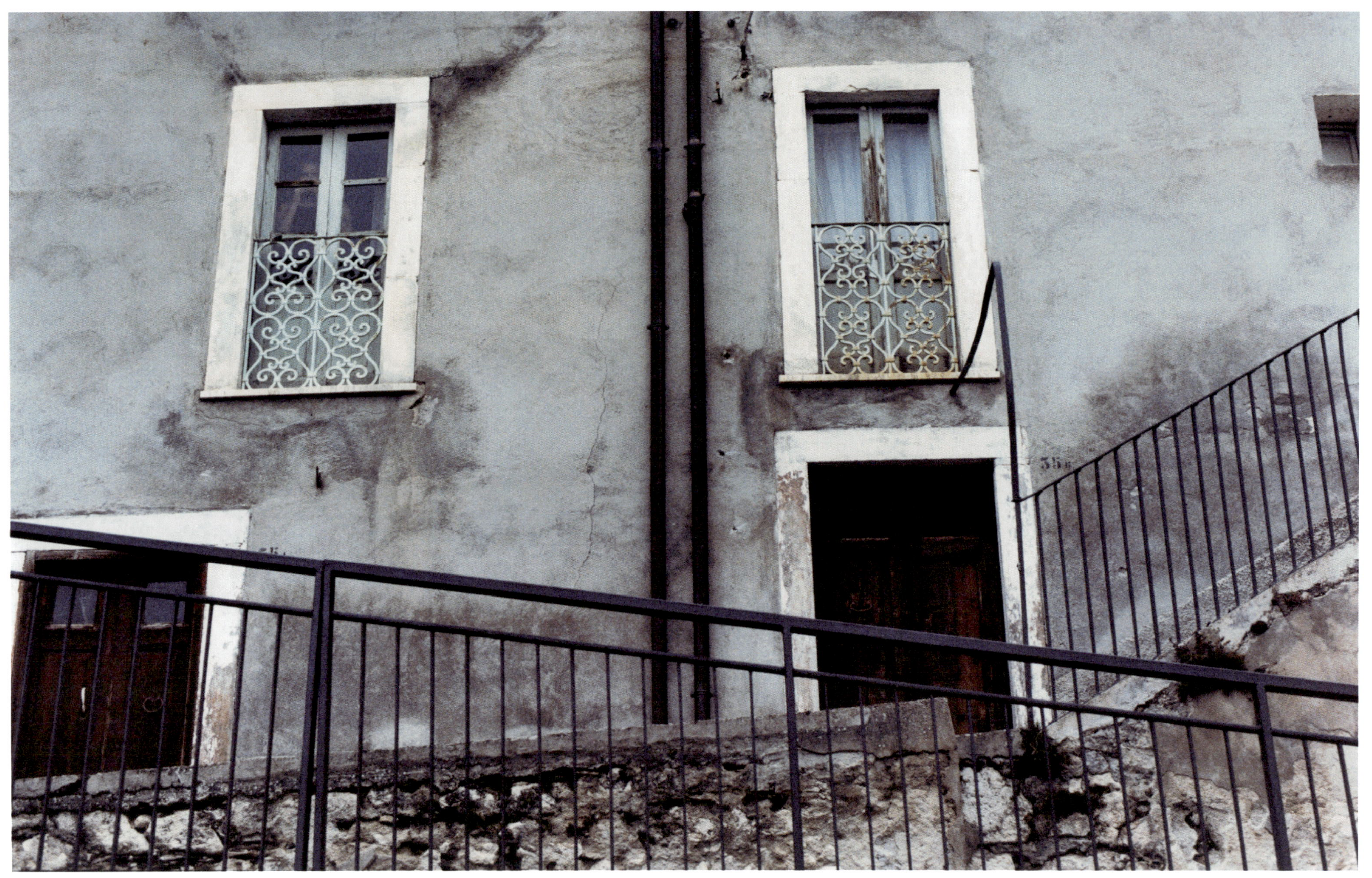

G is looking out of his window towards Castelvecchio prior to going there to make a phonecall.

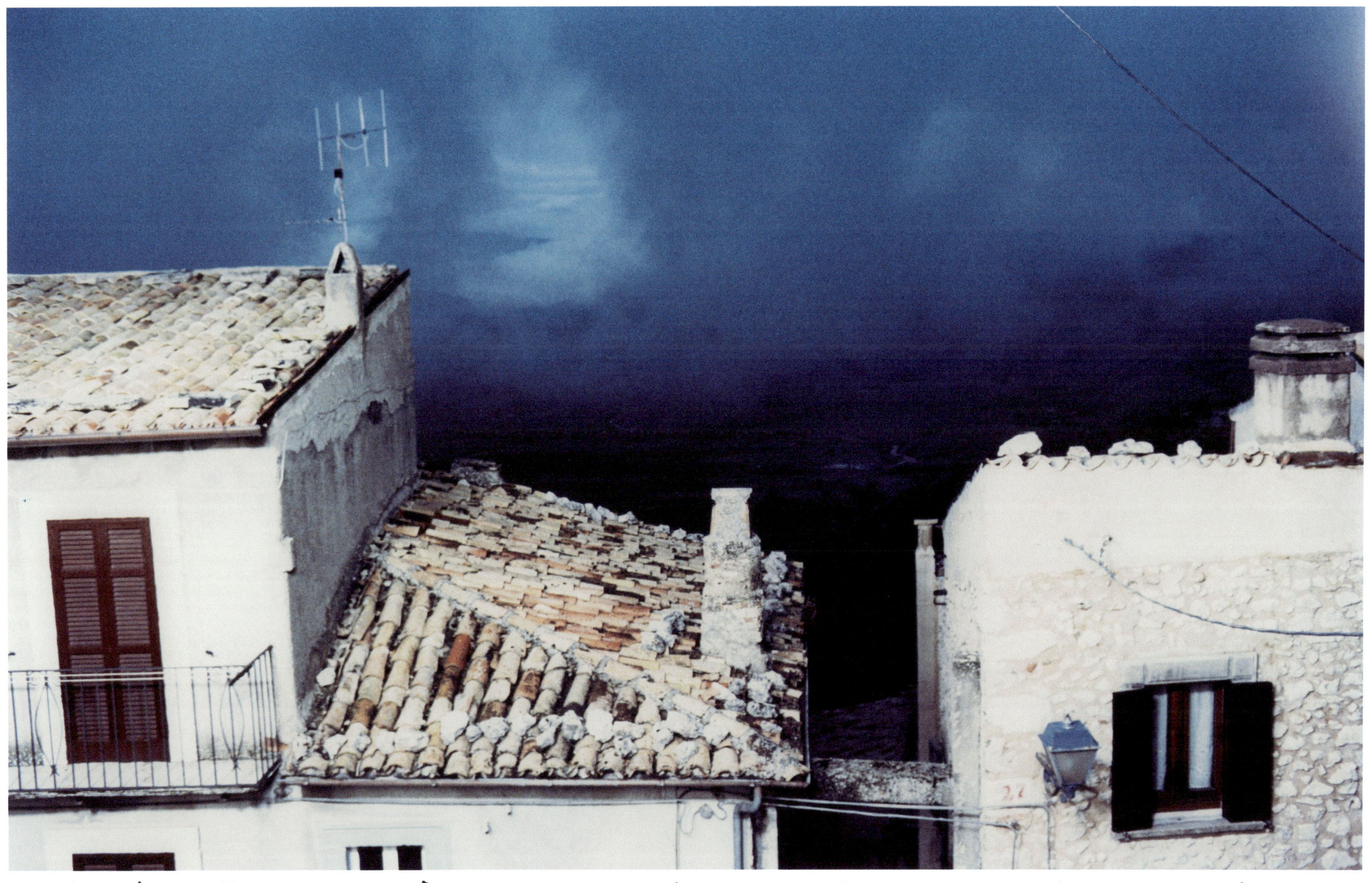

'on' lights reflecting on the houses opposite Jack's apartment and look very white instead of grey.

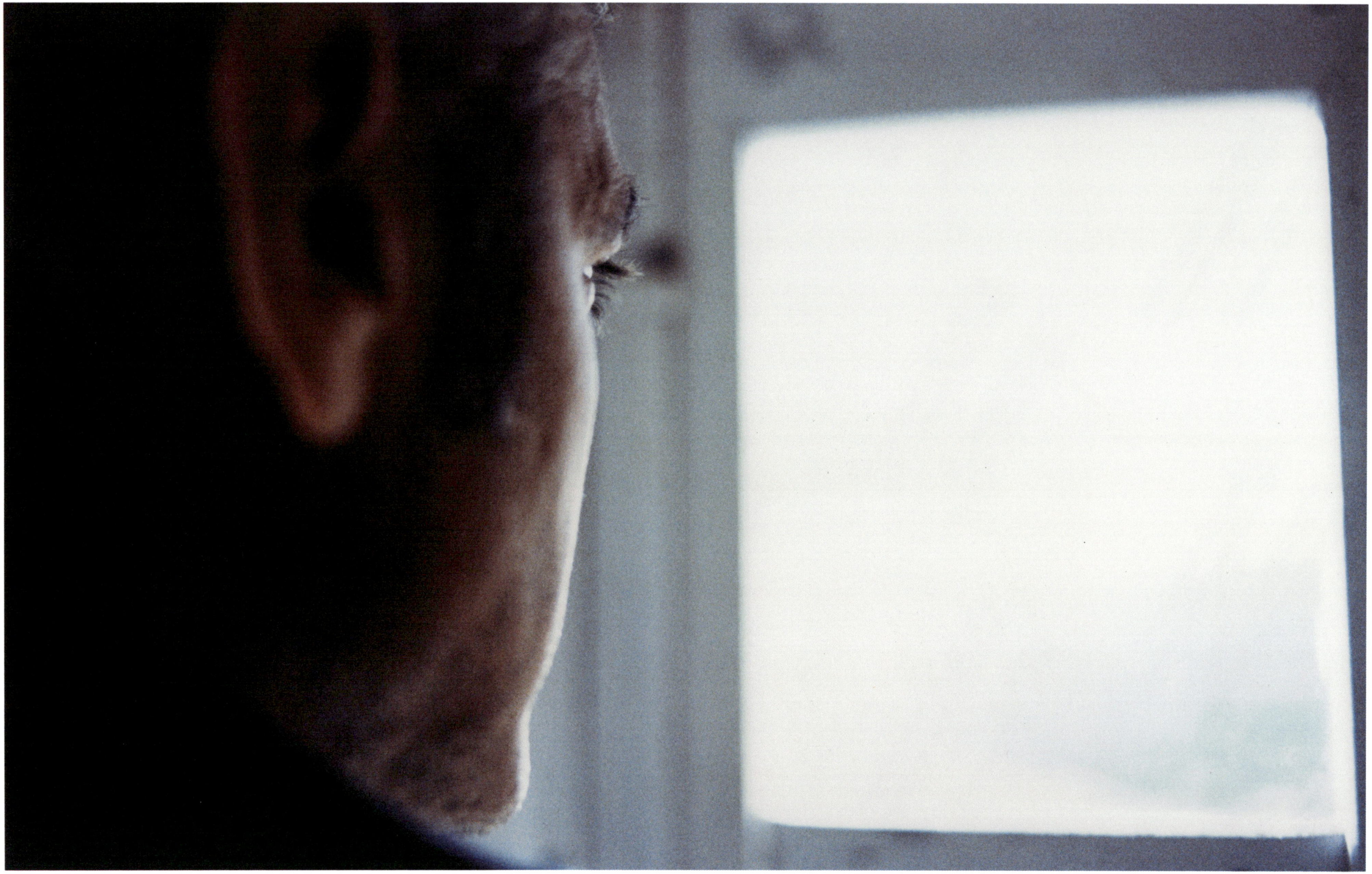

George looking out from the inside.

'Casa Abruzzo'

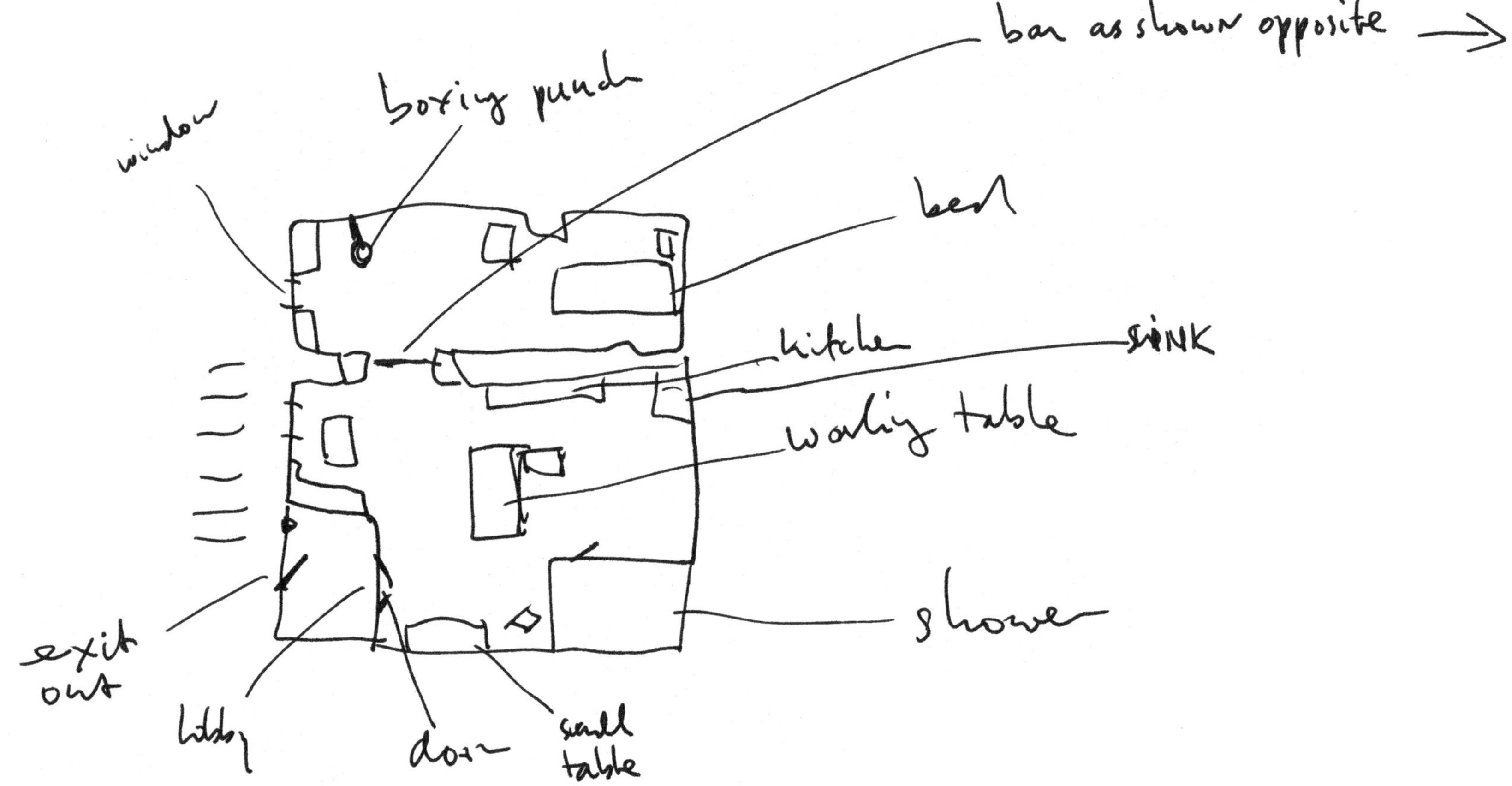

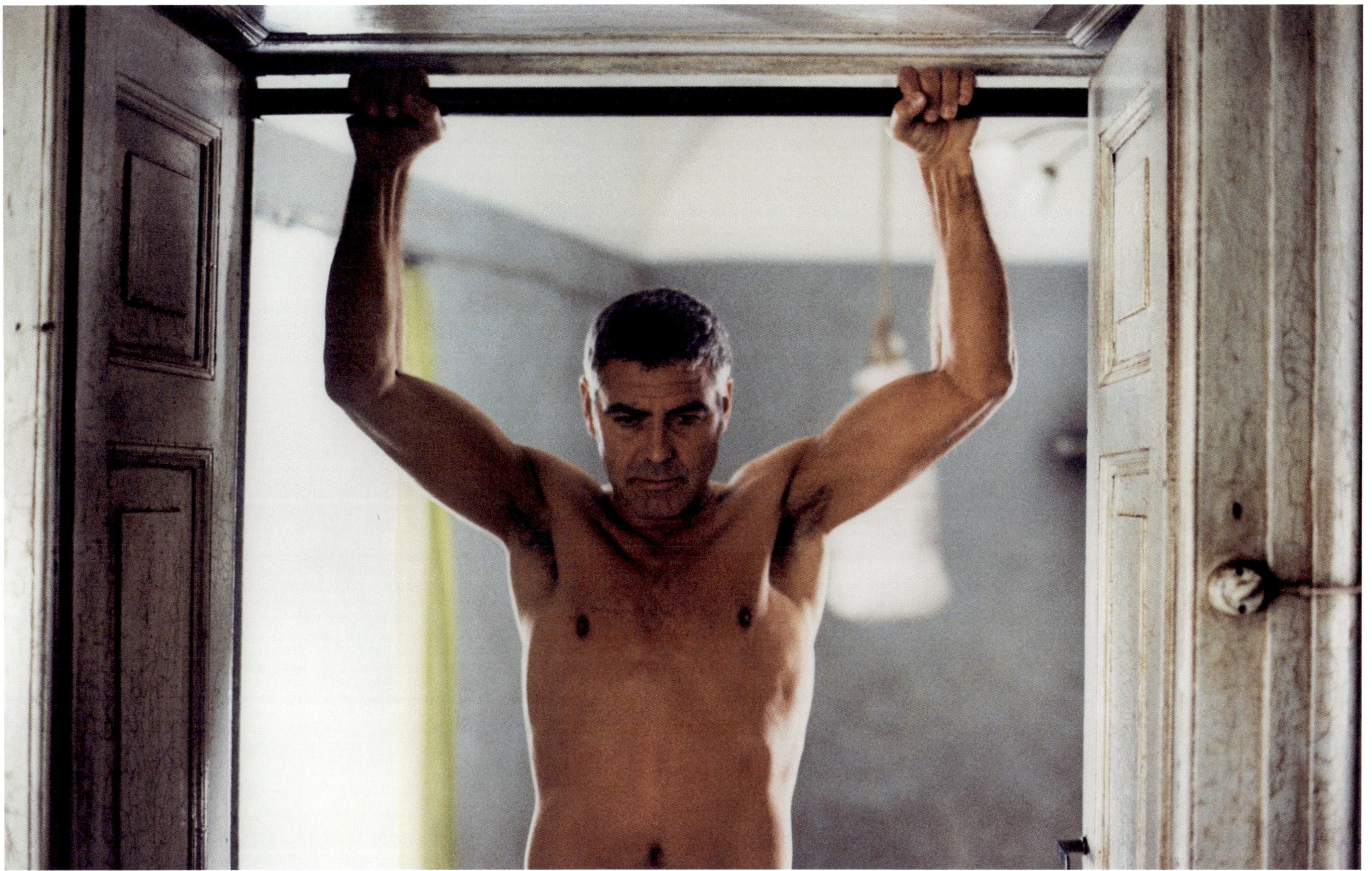

The apartment we used in CdM was perfect in size and we made it look amazing. it had what estate agents call 'lots of character'! The metal bar George is holding is the one he uses for workouts, stuck in the doorway between rooms

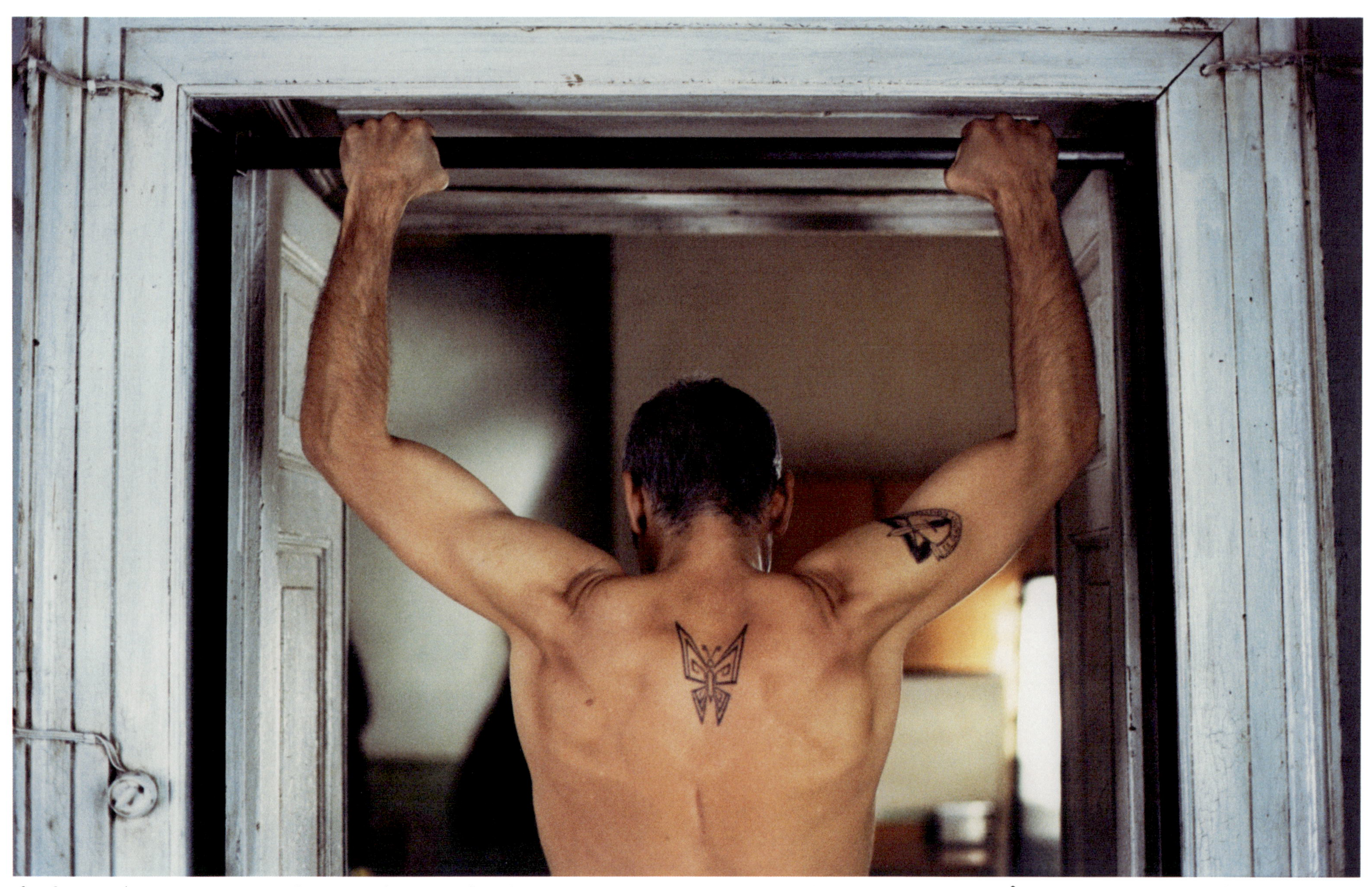

i love the angular shaped butterfly tattoo on George's back. Suits the character very well.

90

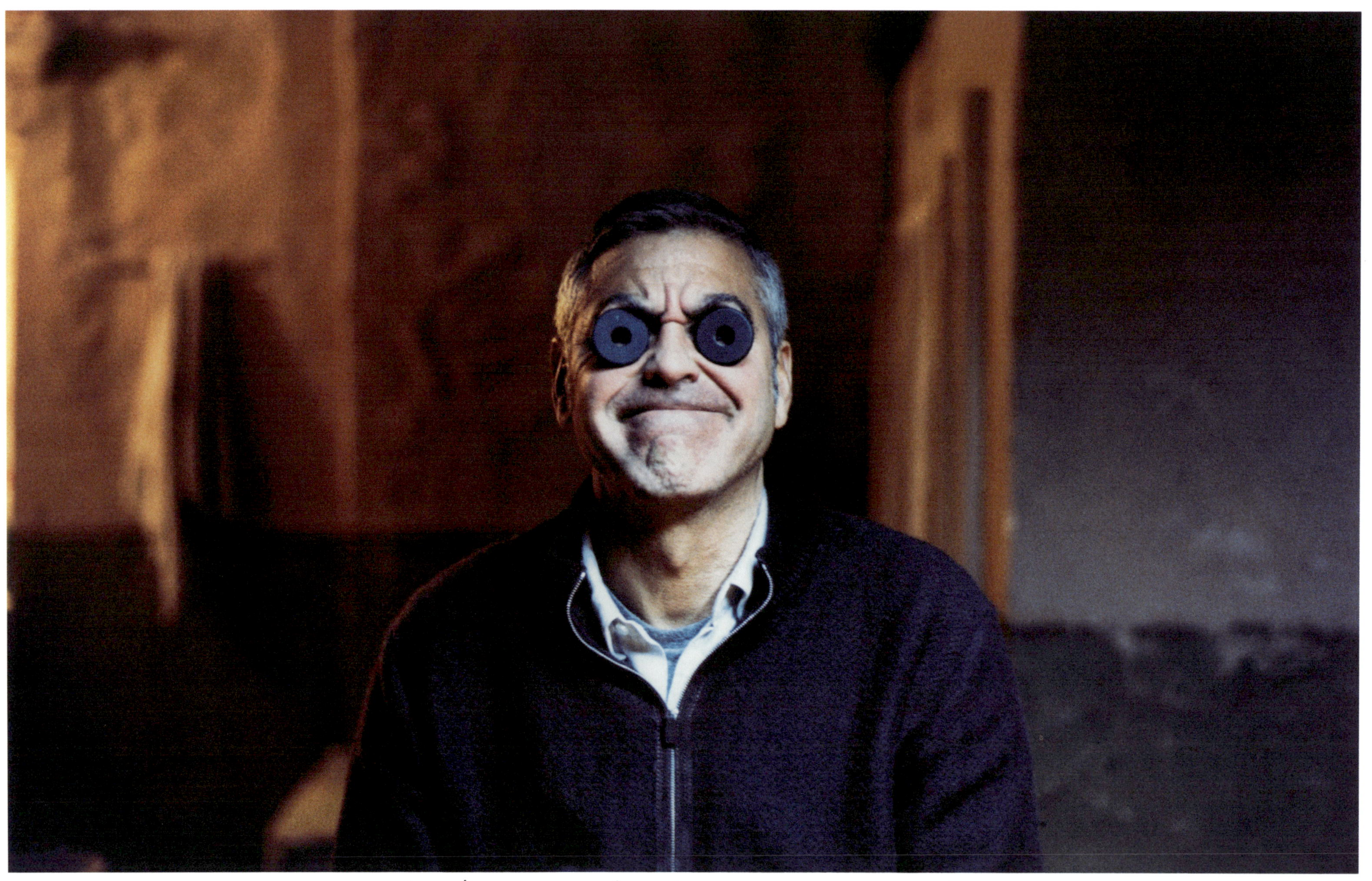

in between takes there are many moments.

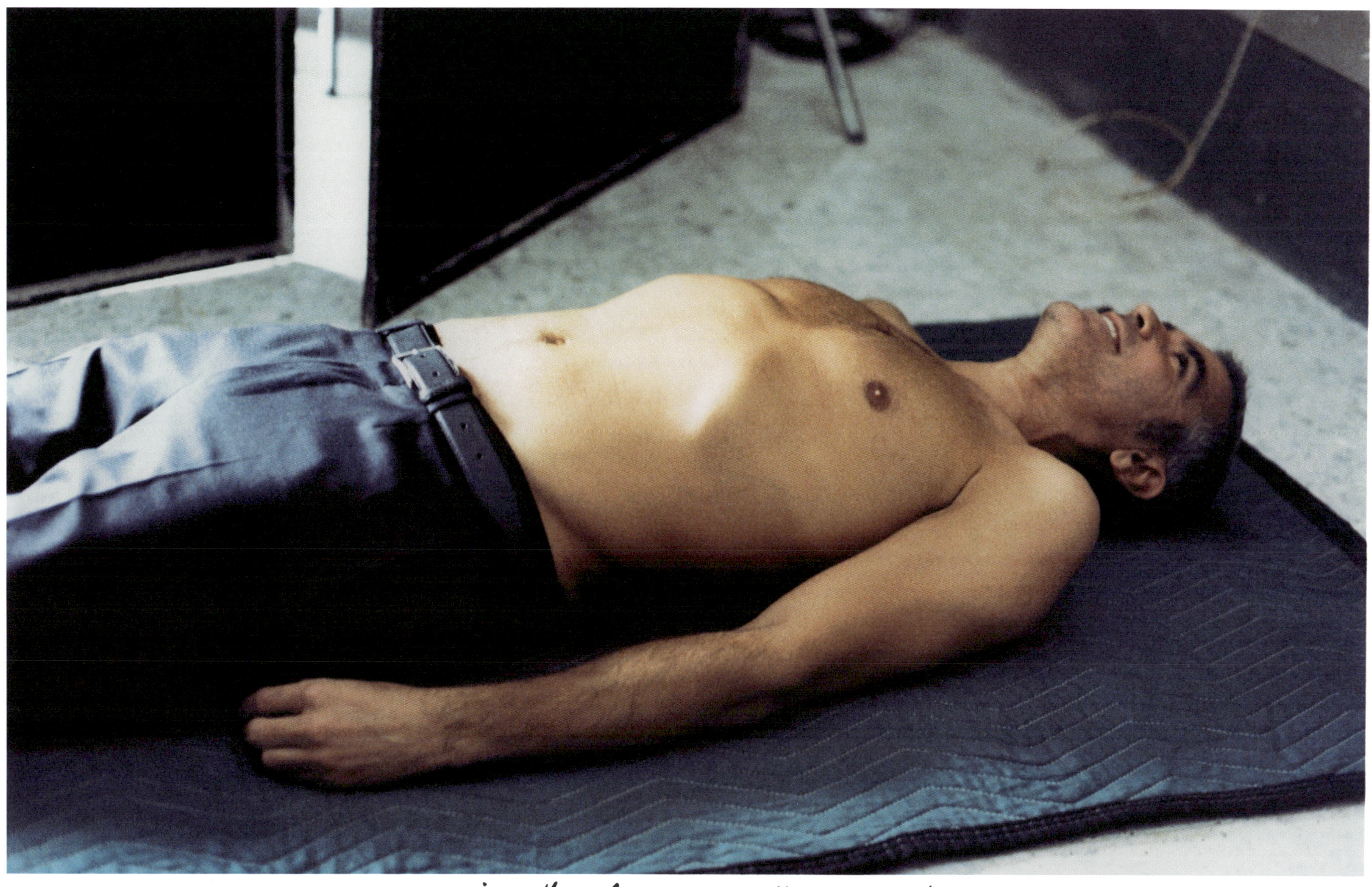

preparing the close-up for the yoga-shot.

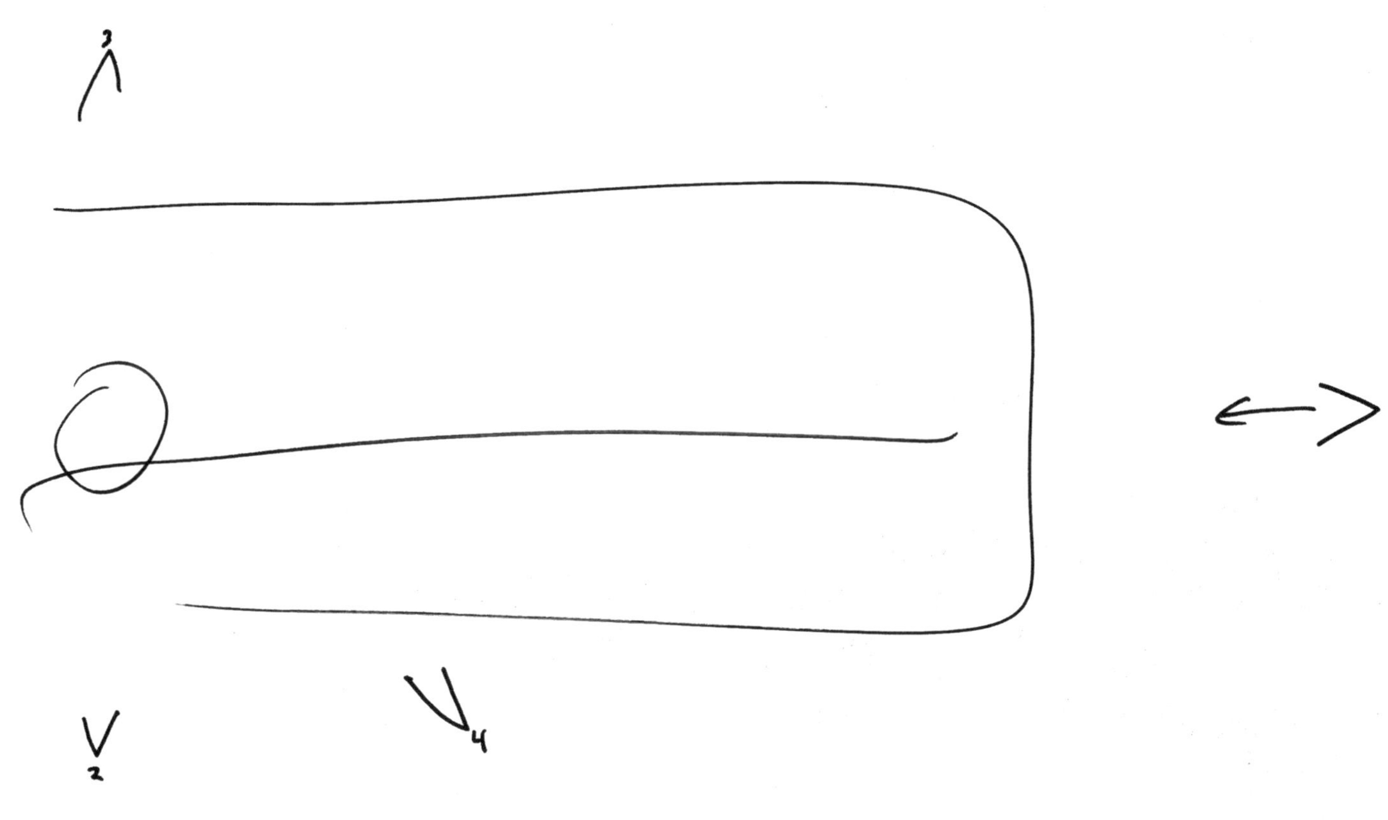

95

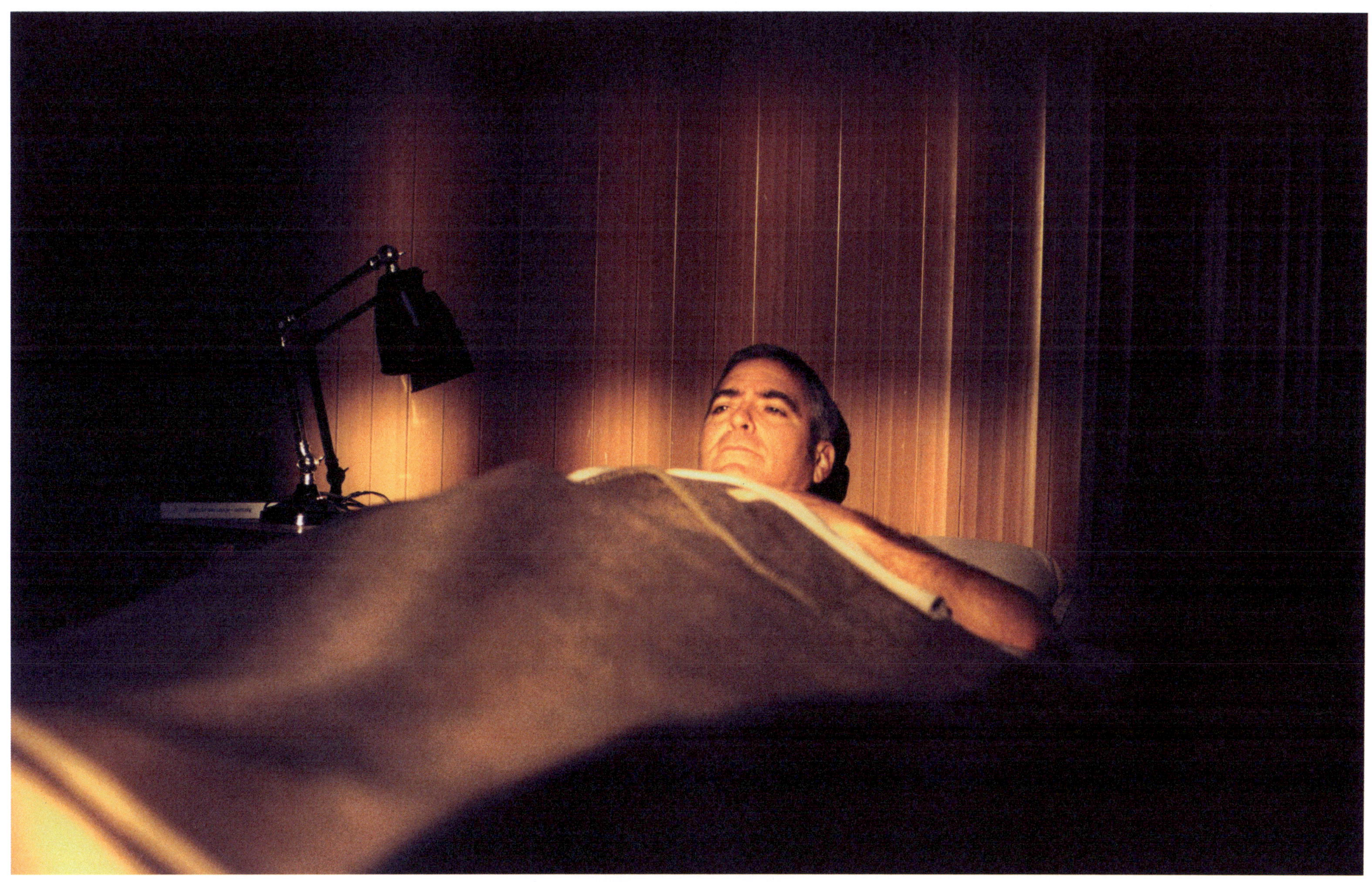

the nightmare scene

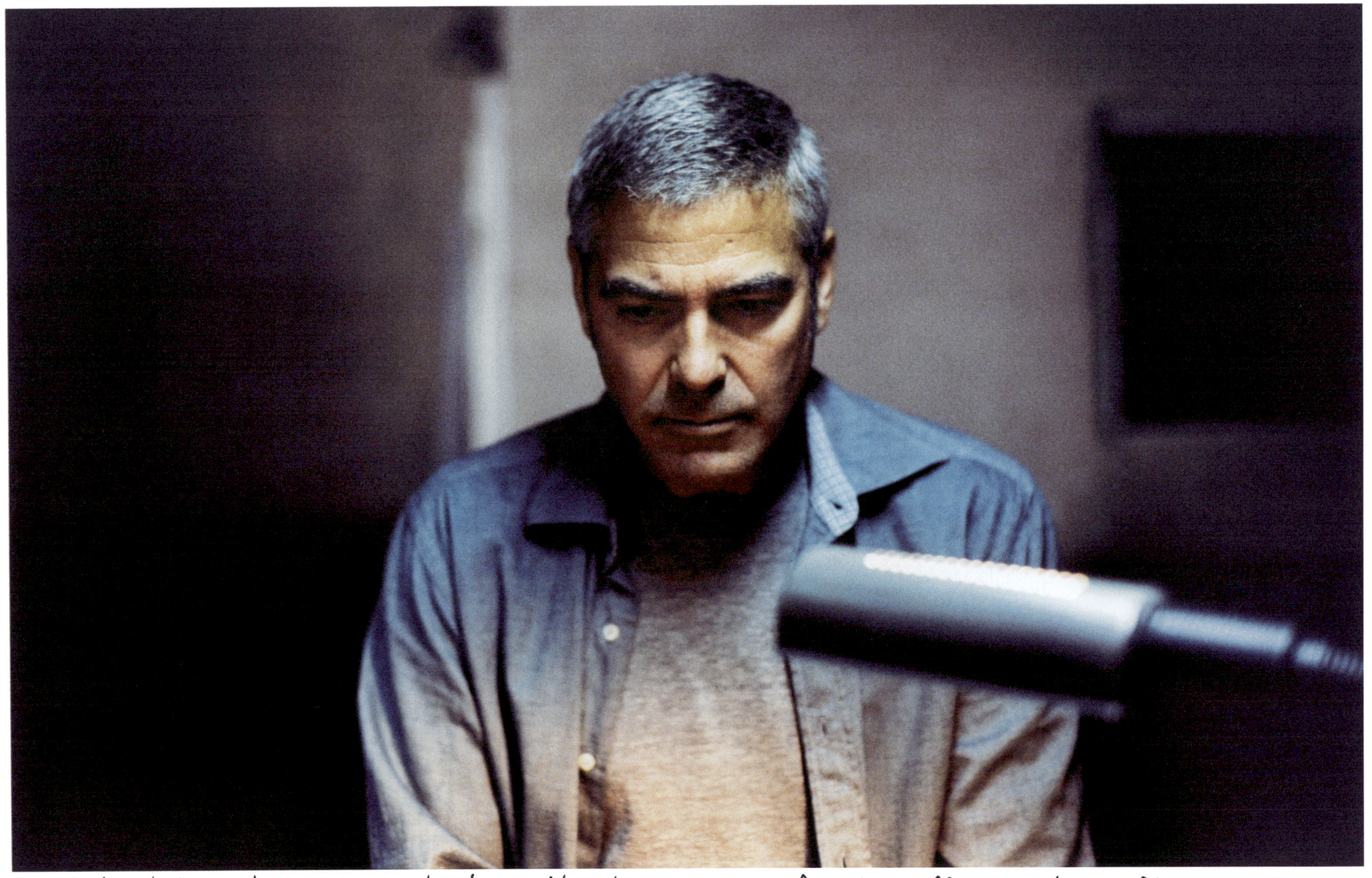

we did a lot of shots at the kitchen table which was a worktable really. I like working in confined spaces as it forces you to become creative with what you got instead of with what you can get.

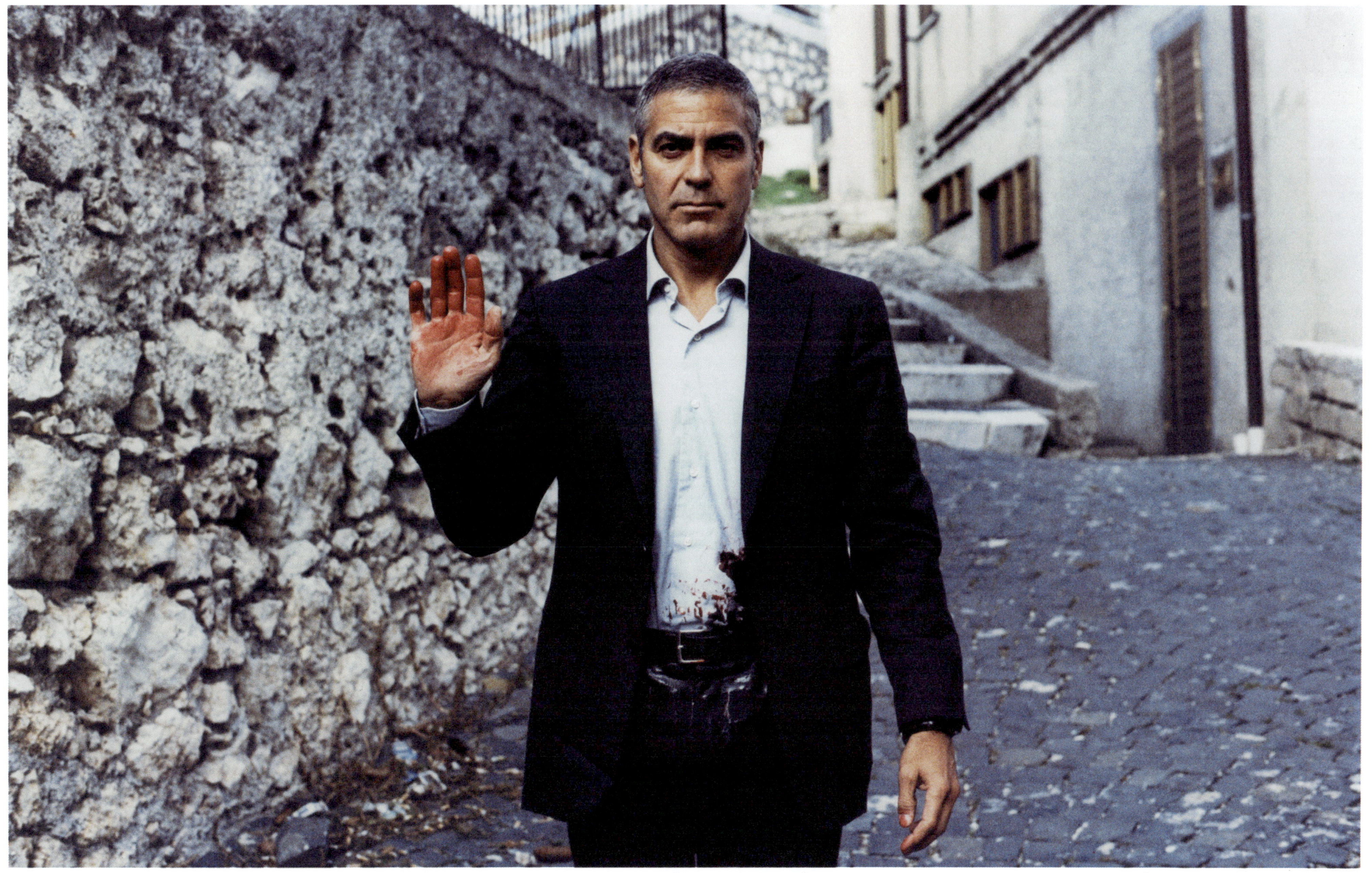

A bloody hello! we did 2 great scenes that day: Jack's final drive from the village to the river and the walk in the park with the priest. this photo is taken just after the driving scene.

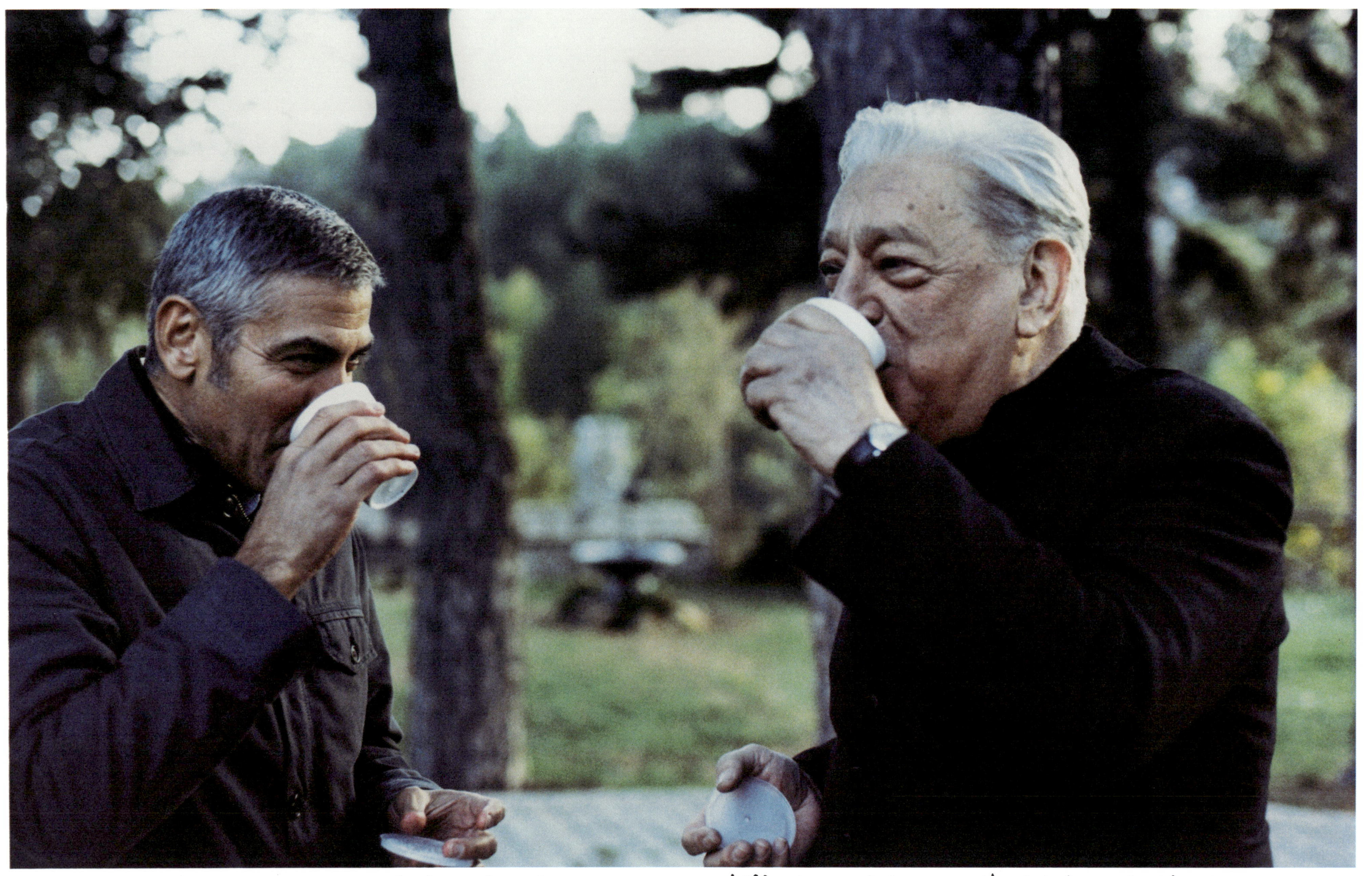

warming up for the cold end of day shoot, it gets very chilly in october on the higher altitudes. The scene plays as an early morning scene which we shot over 2 days.

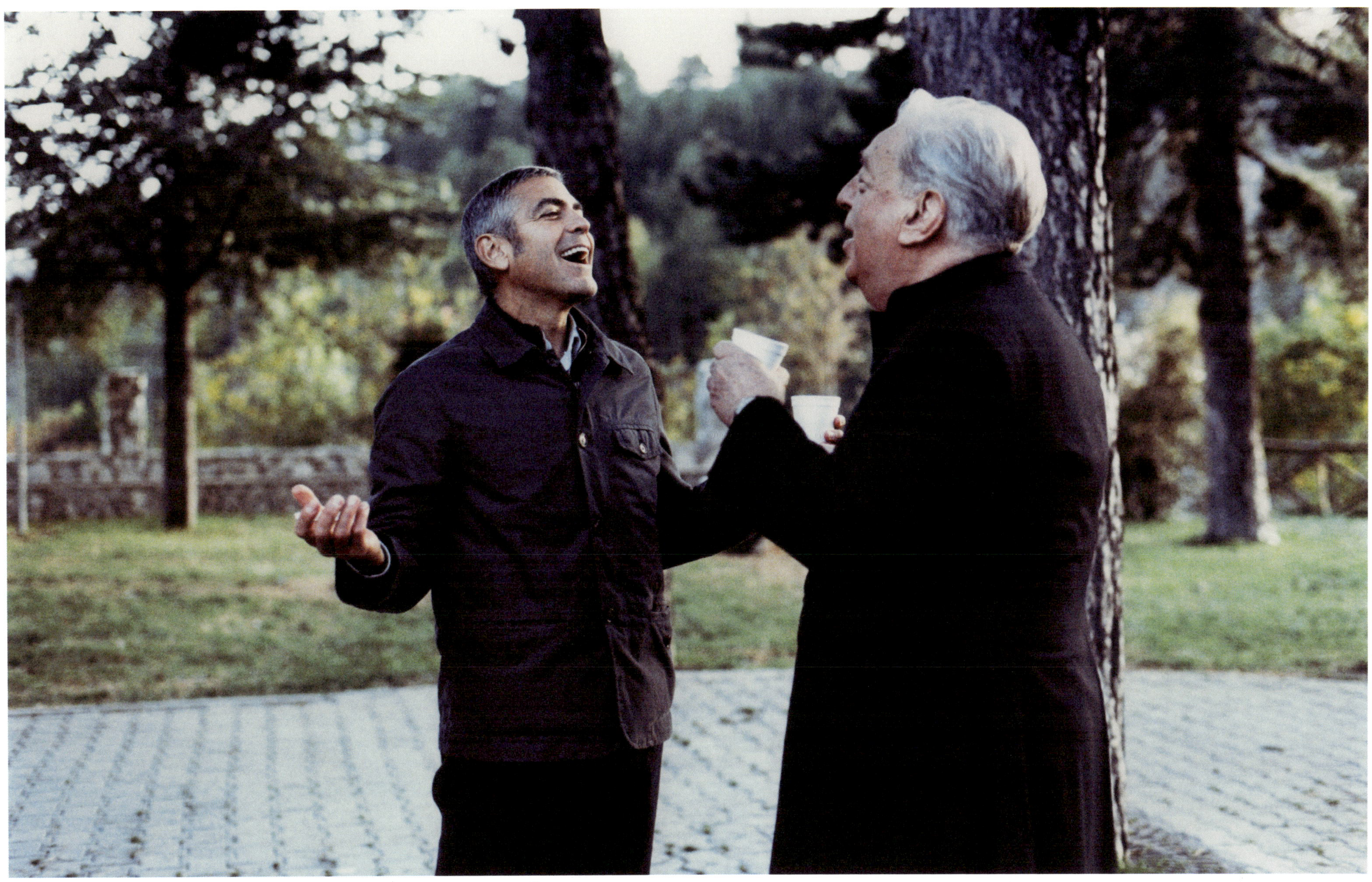

George and Paolo are discussing my directions.

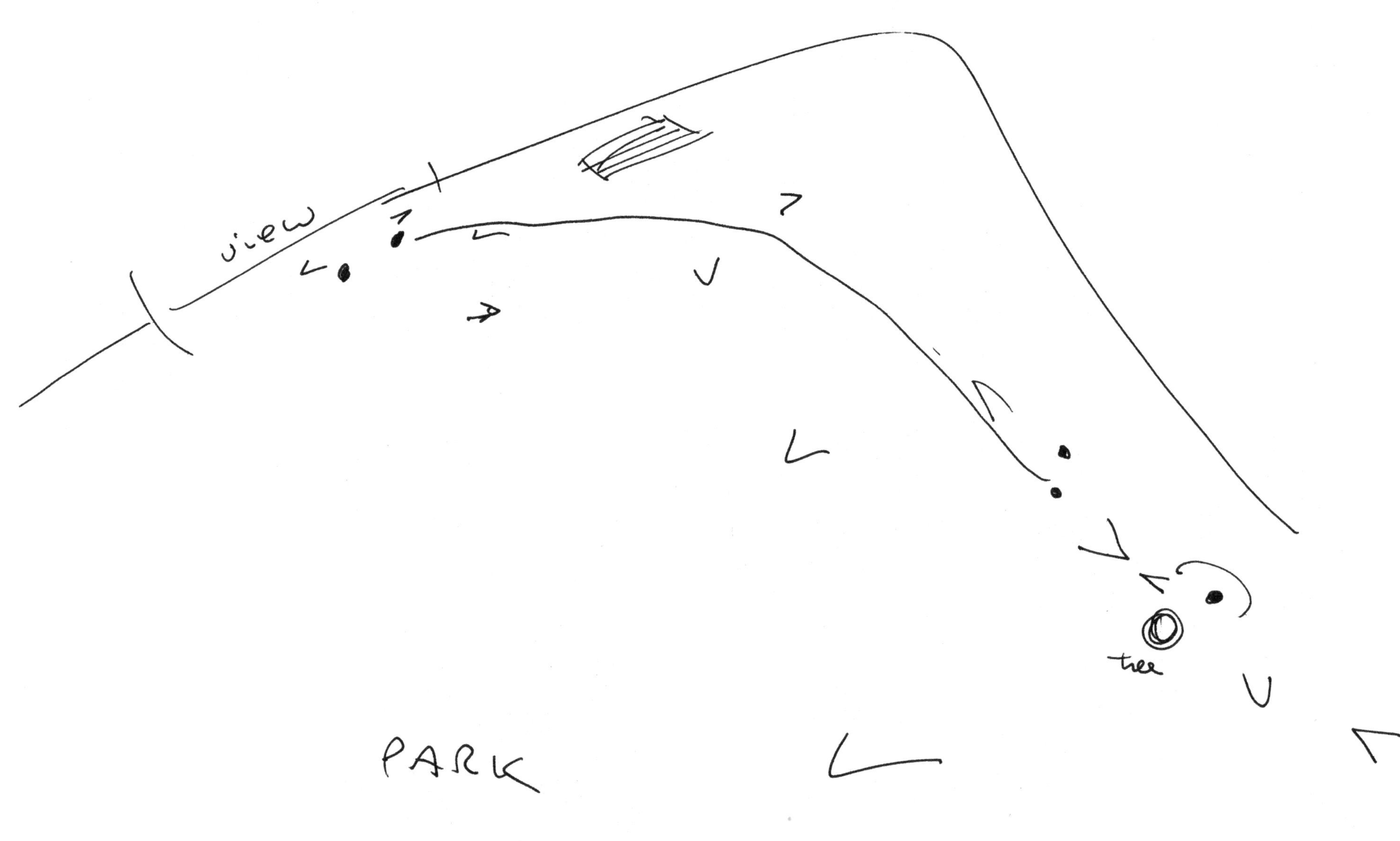
view
tree
PARK

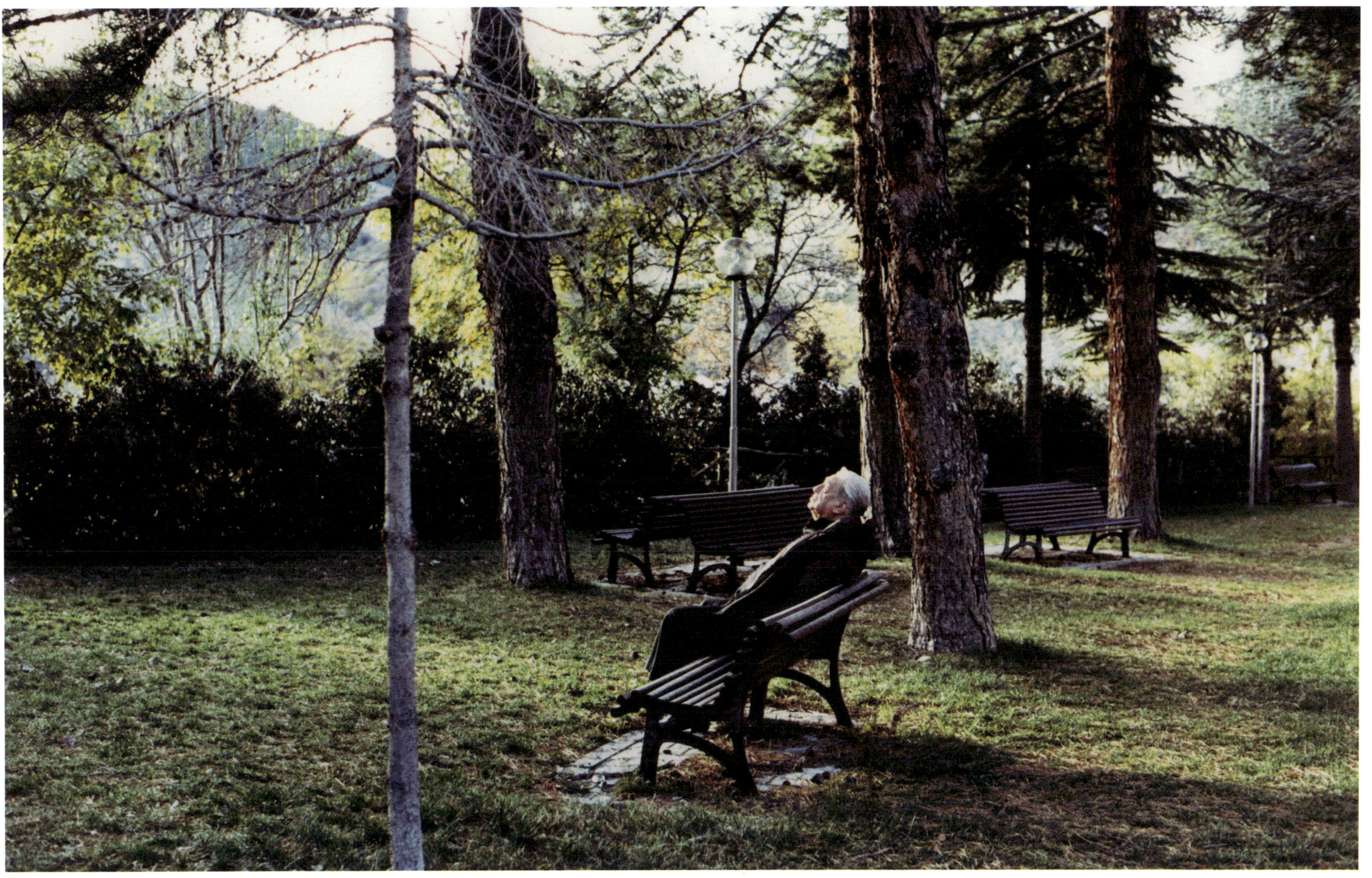

Paolo was the priest for me from the moment i saw him. i'm a minister's son so no-one could argue with me.

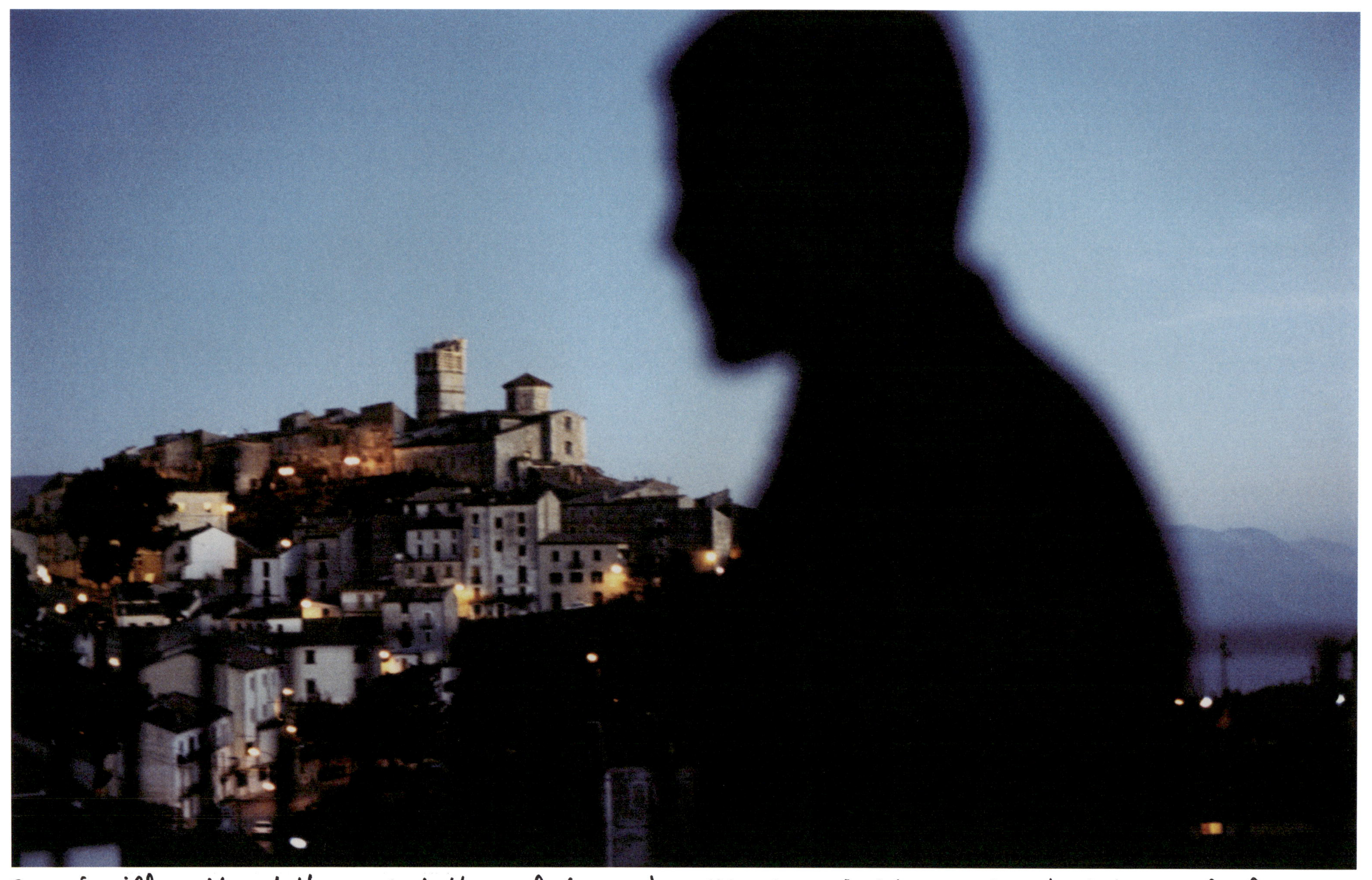

George's silhouette at the end of the park from where this view of CdM exists. that town looks great any time of the day, and in any light. often nothing short of amazing.

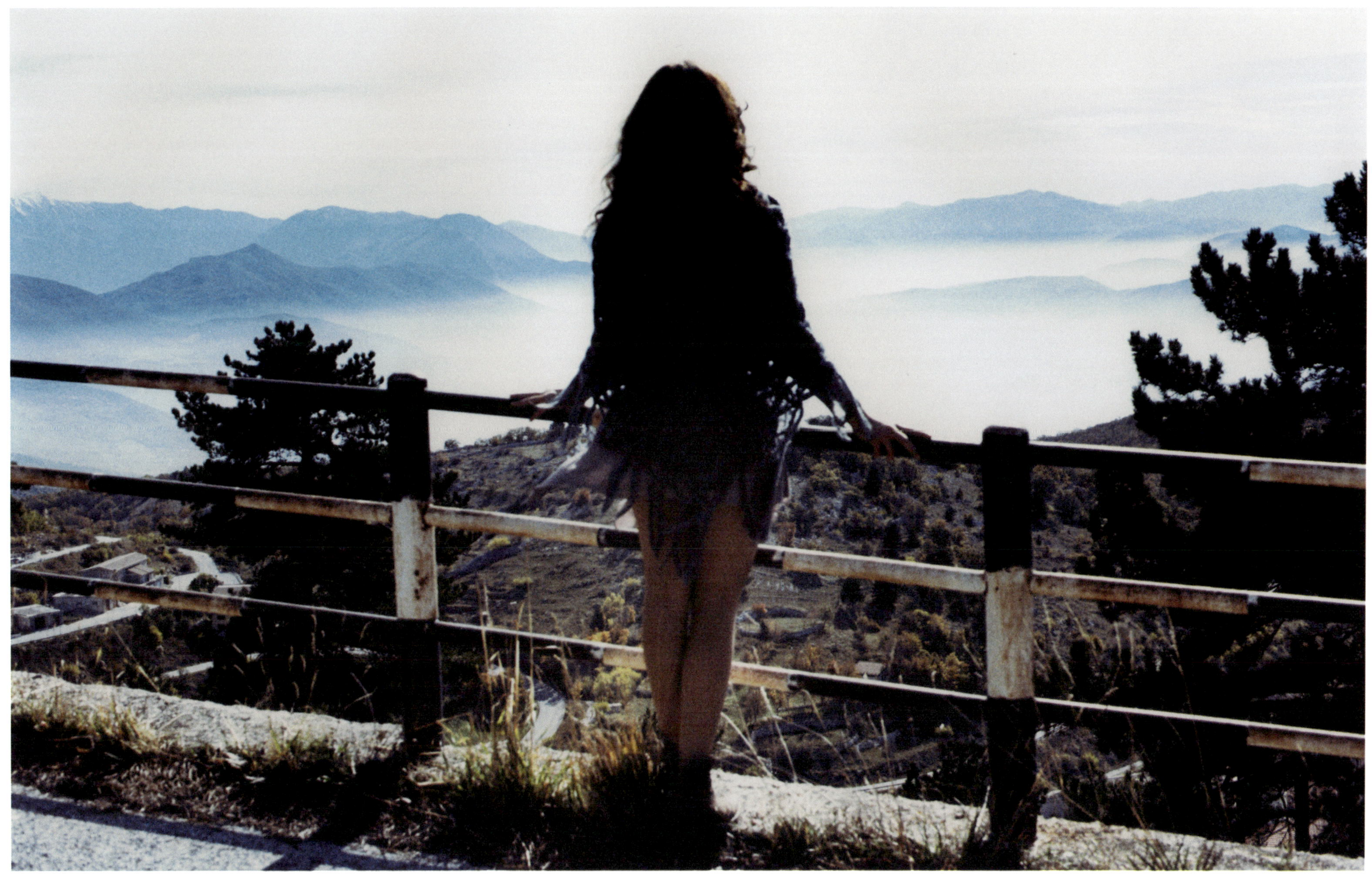

Violante looking out from a road just above Castel del Monte which is to our right.

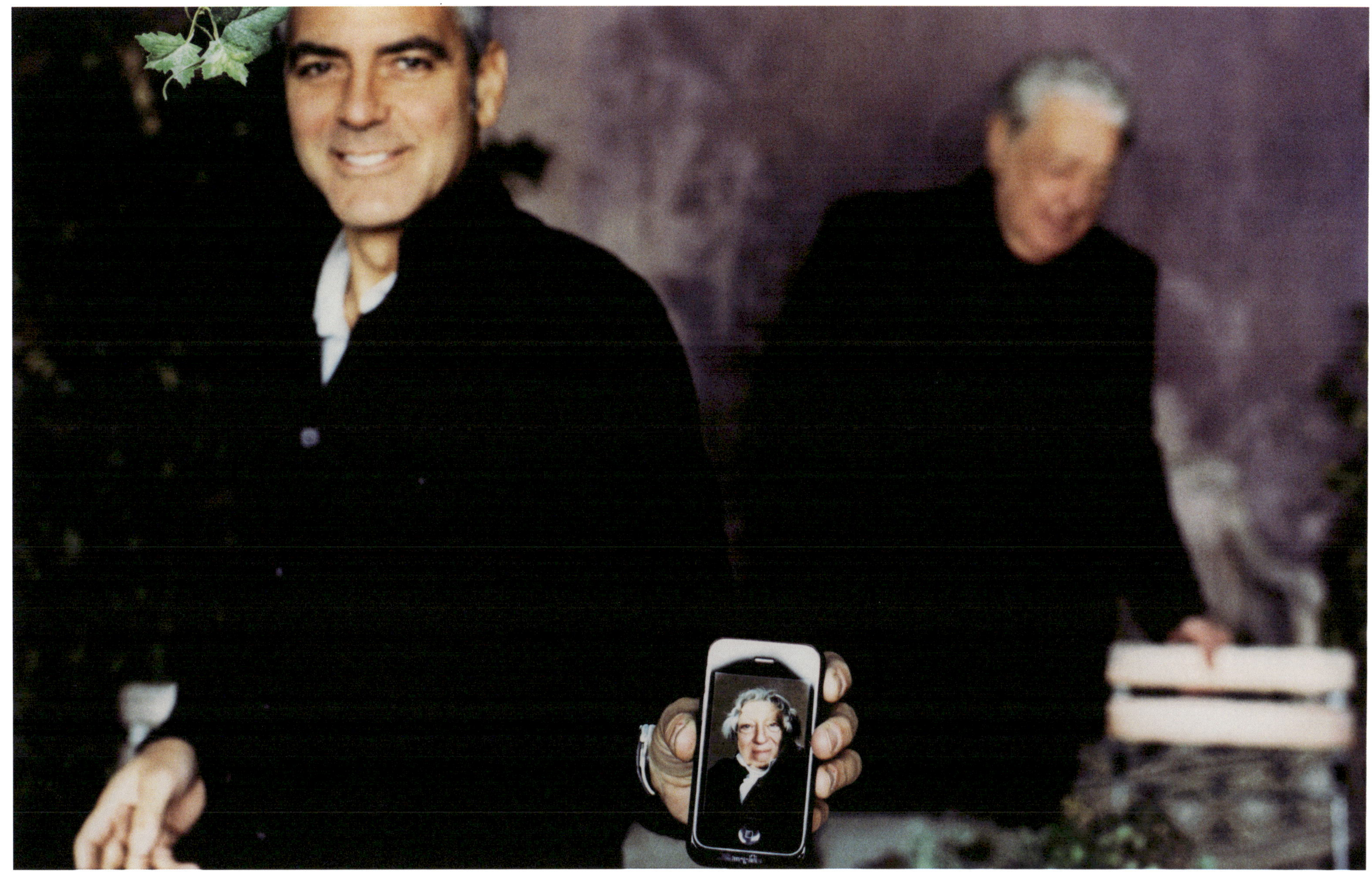

G's phone has an application that combines photos / portraits with a certain pre-set look. Paolo was the willing victim here on the set for the evening drink early on in the film.

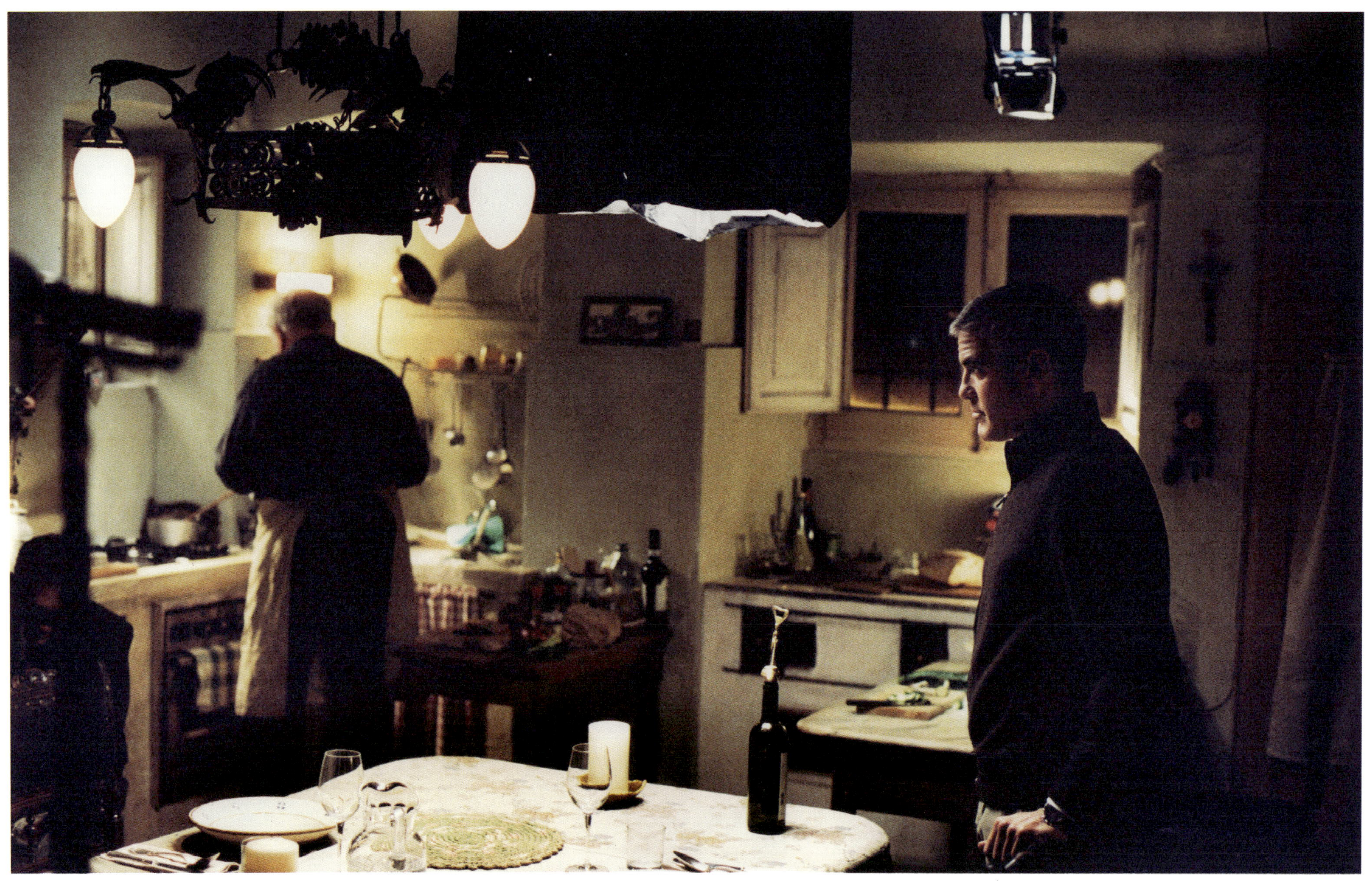

George + Paolo in the kitchen, listening to Madame Butterfly by Maria Callas.

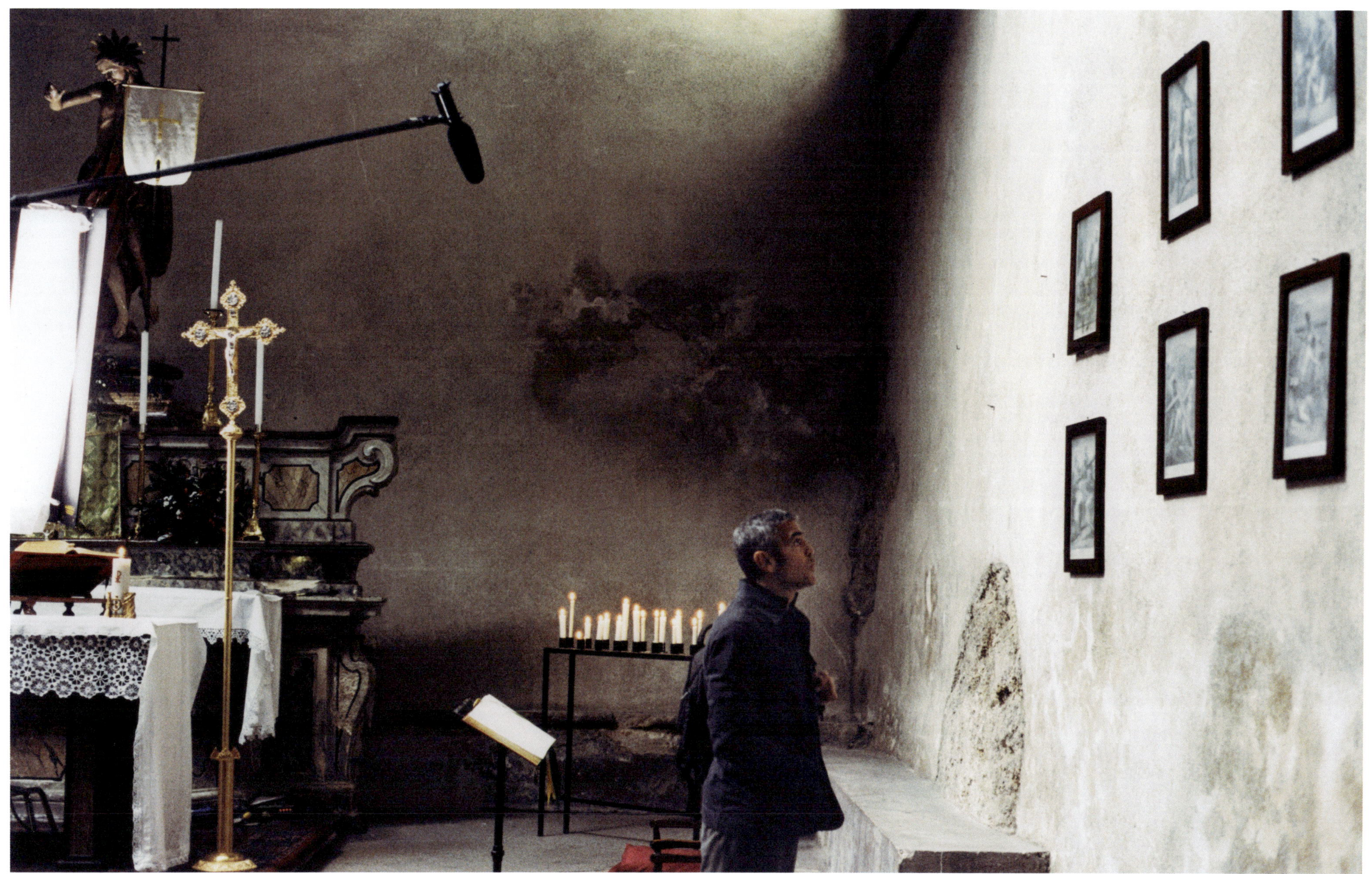

Still of a scene we never used with George looking at images of the various stations to the Cross in Benedetto's church. This church was in a town called Anversa, real beautiful small church.

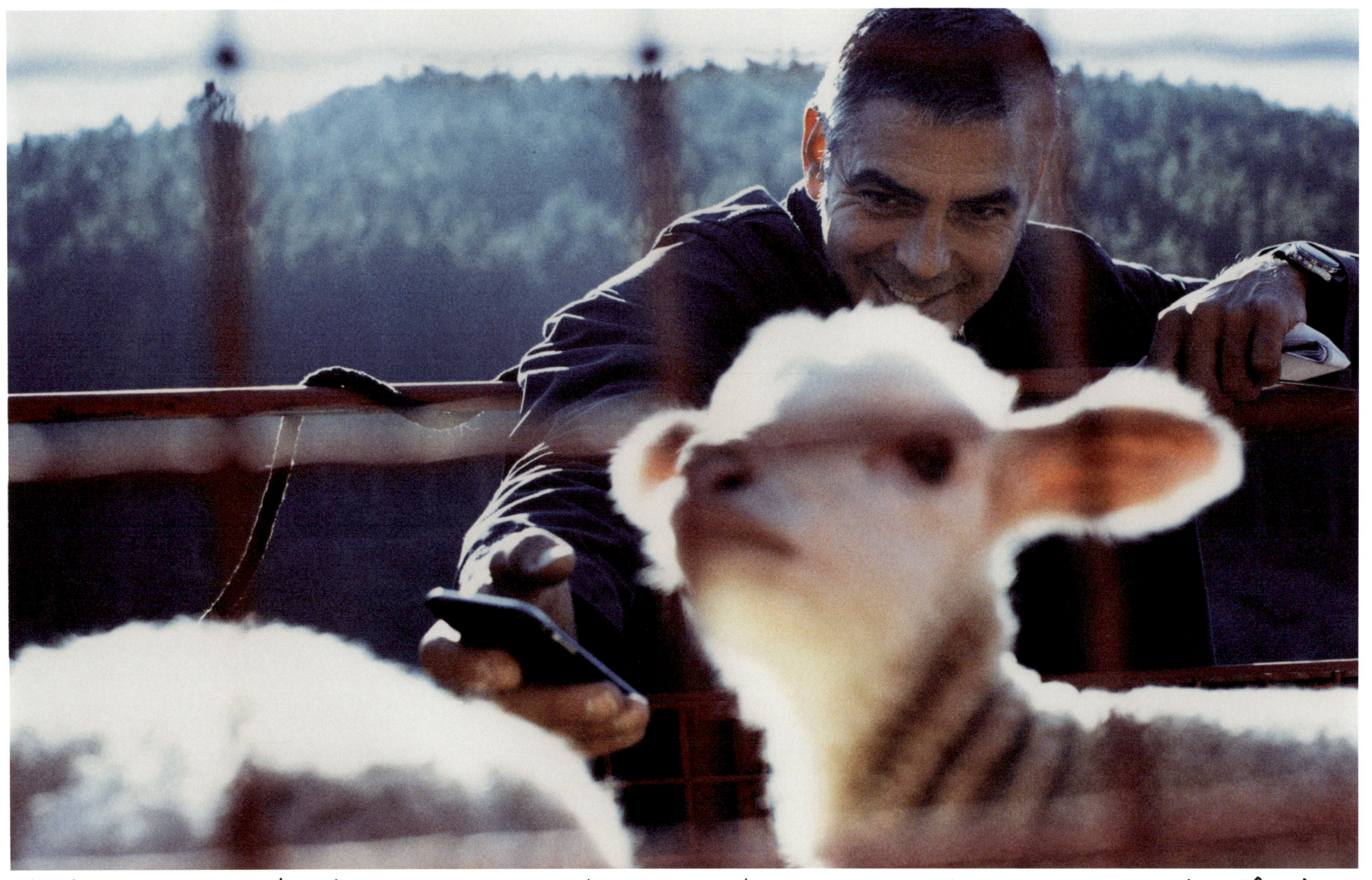

The lamb might not lie down on Broadway but could be on his way there as G records its bleating.

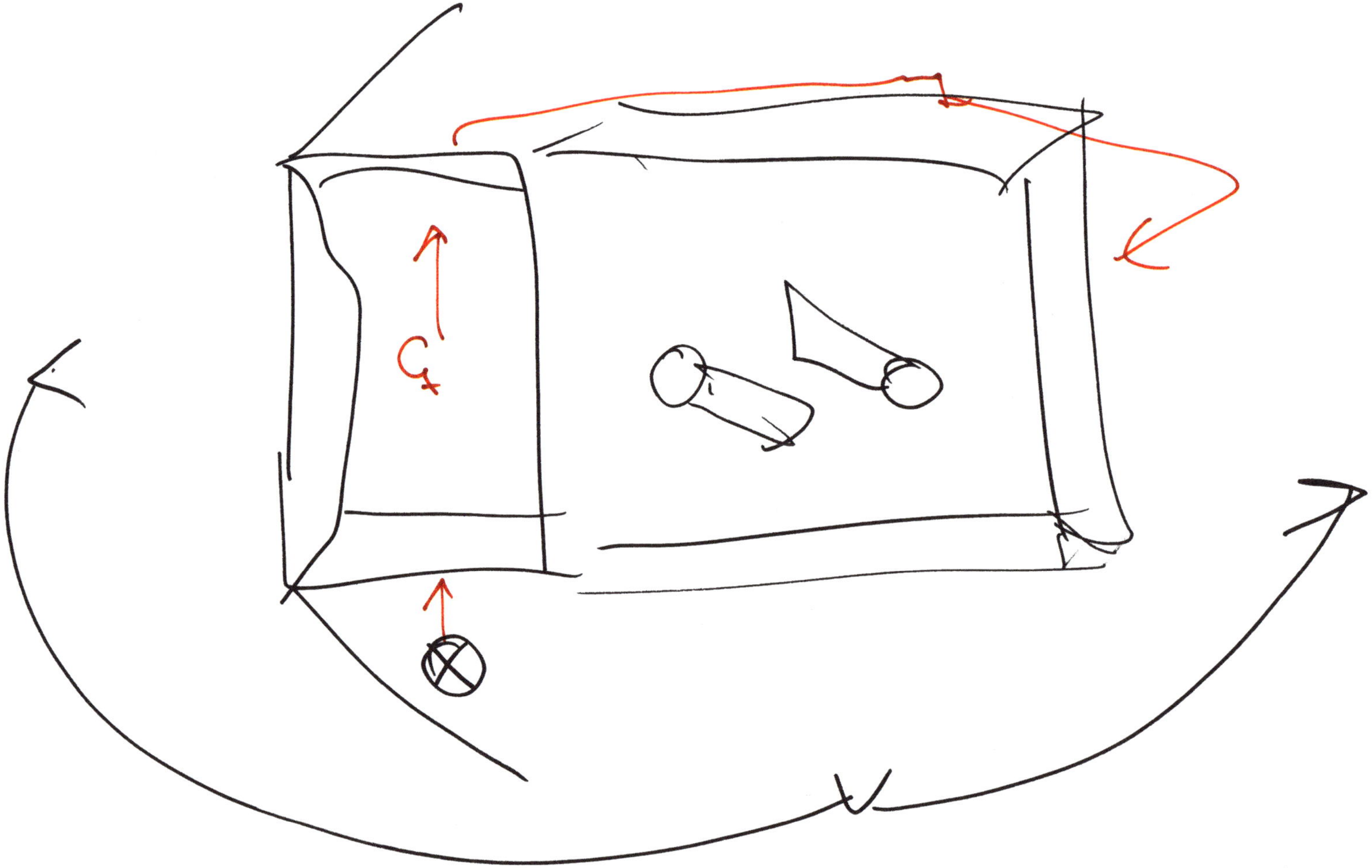

114

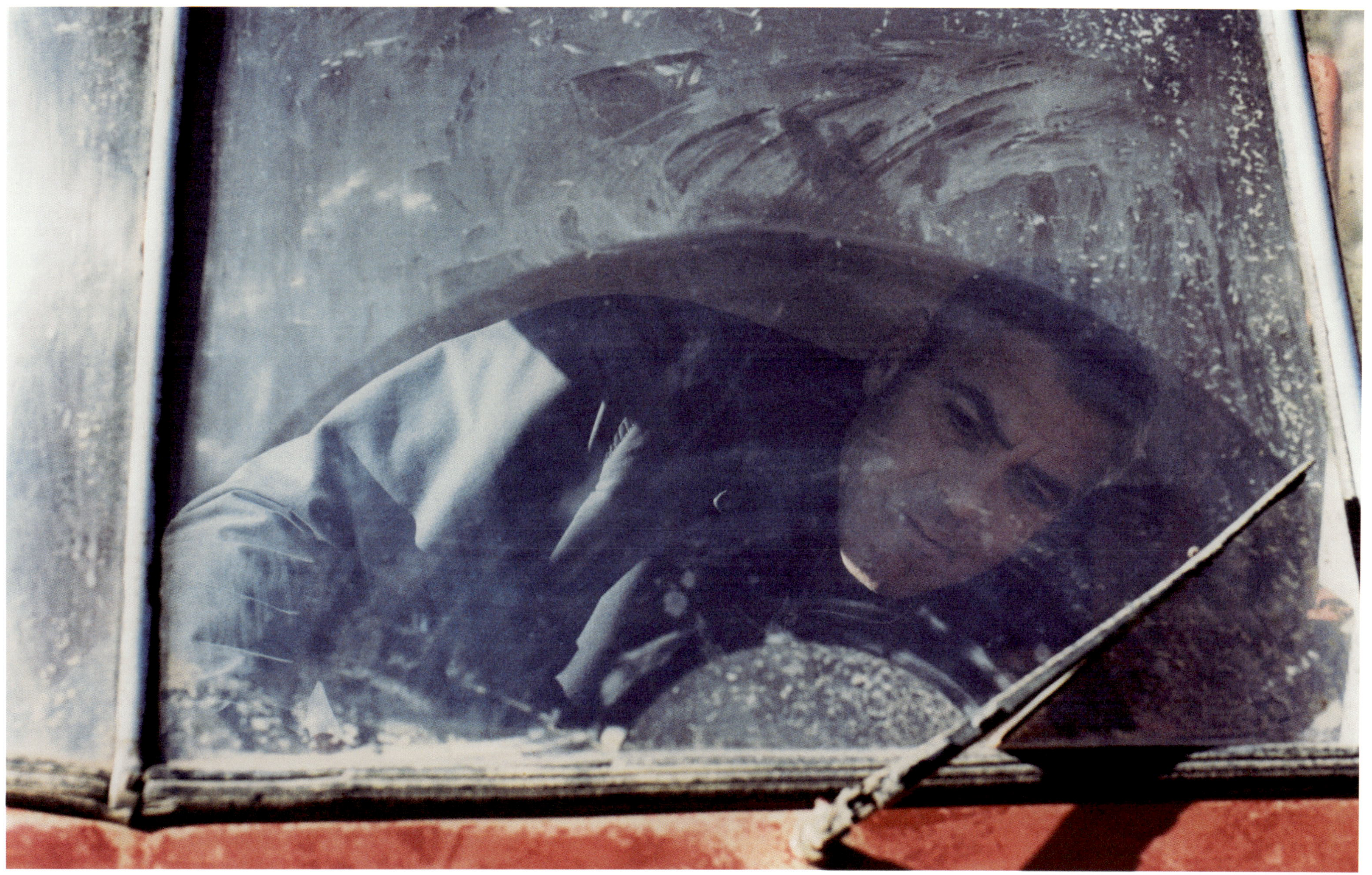

These small three-wheeled vehicles are called 'APE' – they are fun but not comfortable.

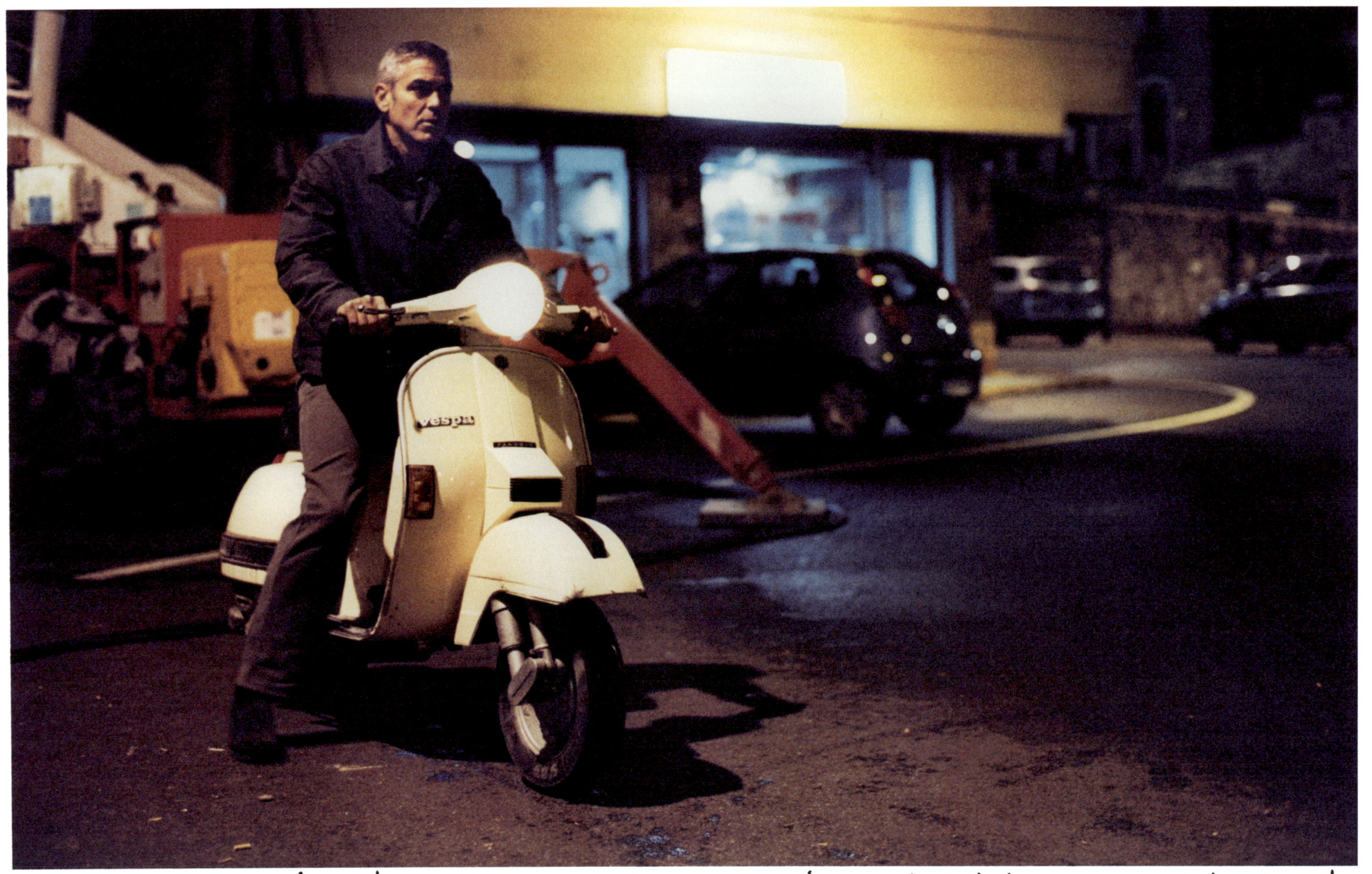

Cd Monte is a pretty deserted place for most of the year. I reckon 75% of the houses are empty bar 2 months in the summer, so George chasing a car on his scooter didn't really wake up anyone at night.

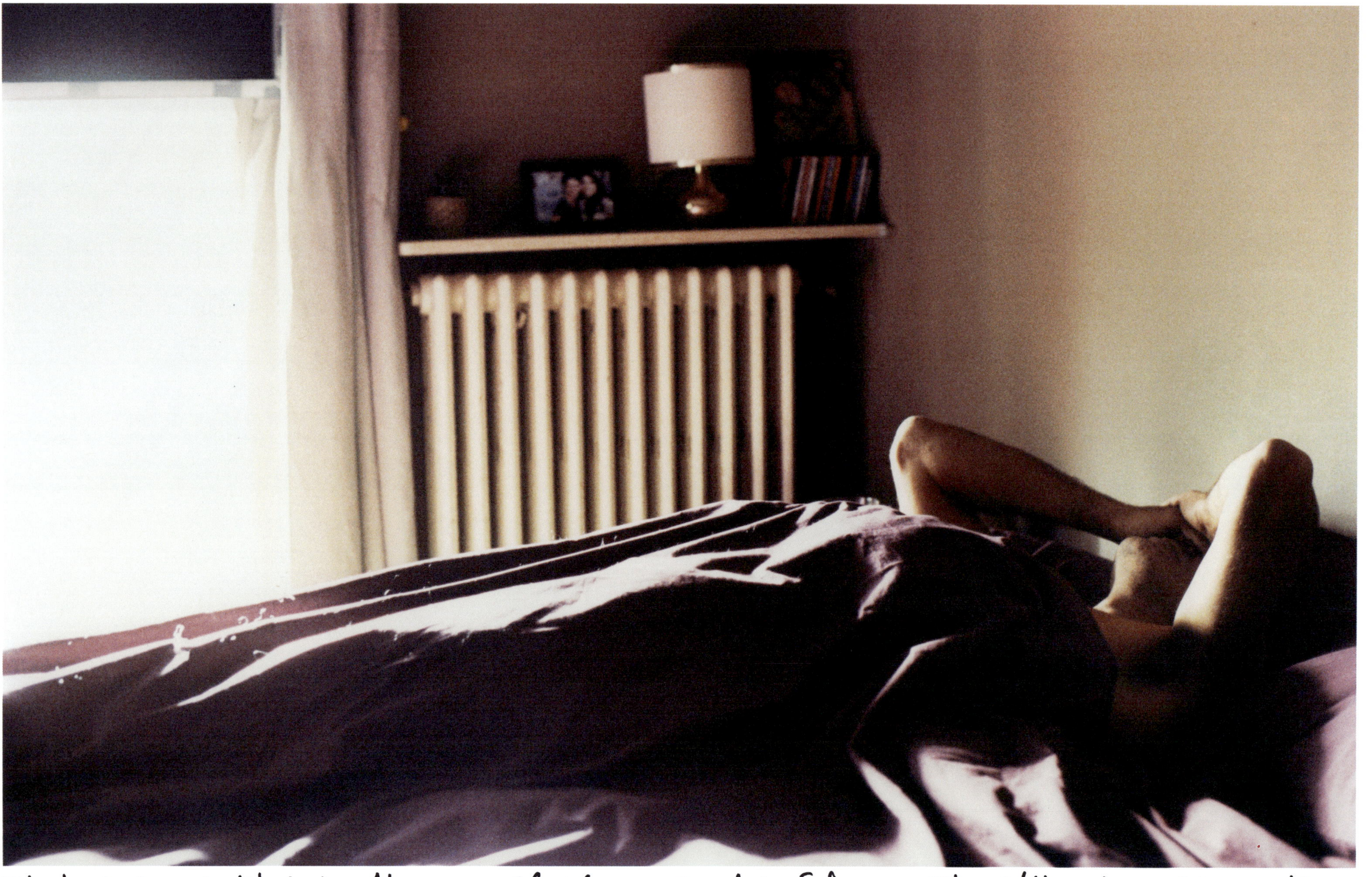

The last day of filming in Abruzzo: Clara's apartment in Sulmona. The setting for 2 scenes – the one above where George wakes up and discovers a gun in Clara's handbag, and the one opposite →

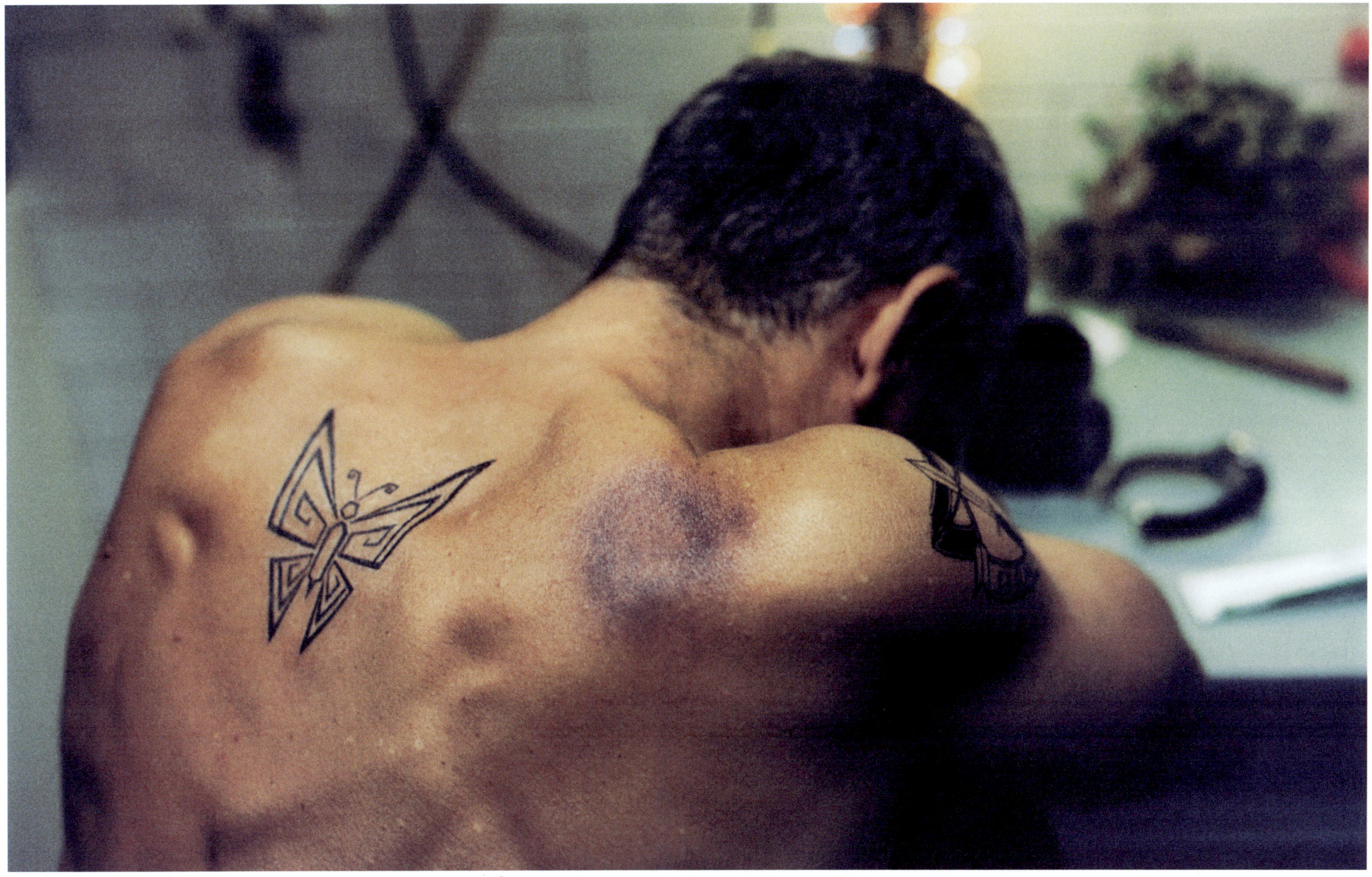

where Violante massages George's neck and shoulder. Originally planned as scene after he fell off his scooter, it now shows an intimacy after the dinner scene.

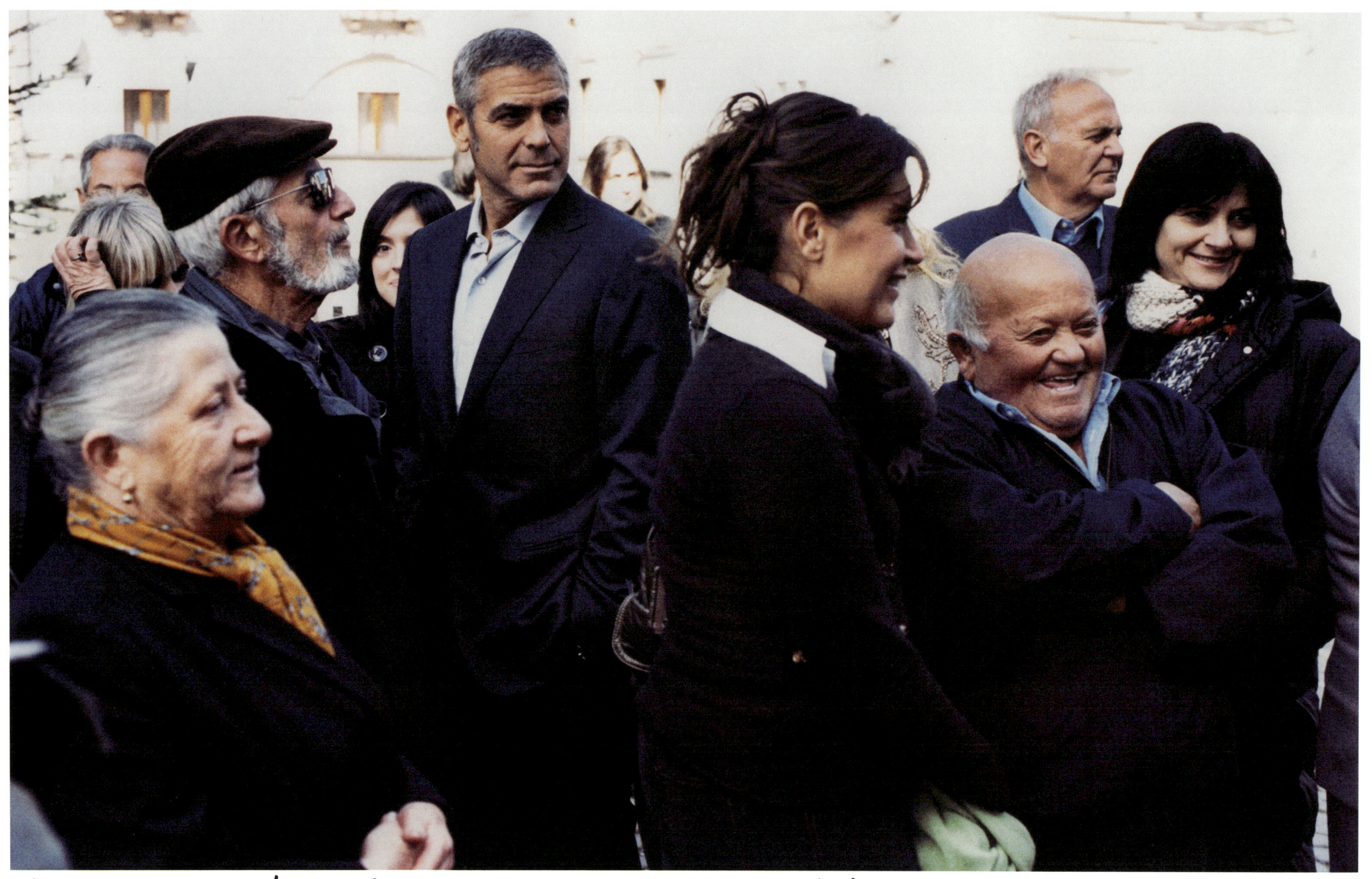

George towers above the indigenous people of Abruzzo at the procession we set up in Castel del Monte. Every village has its own kind of procession and the locals are fiercely protective of them.

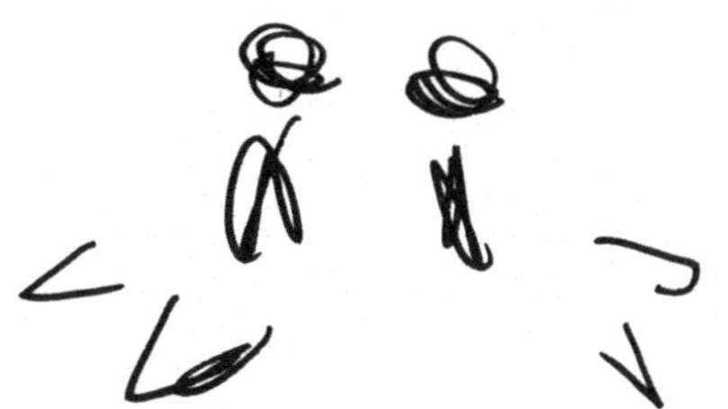

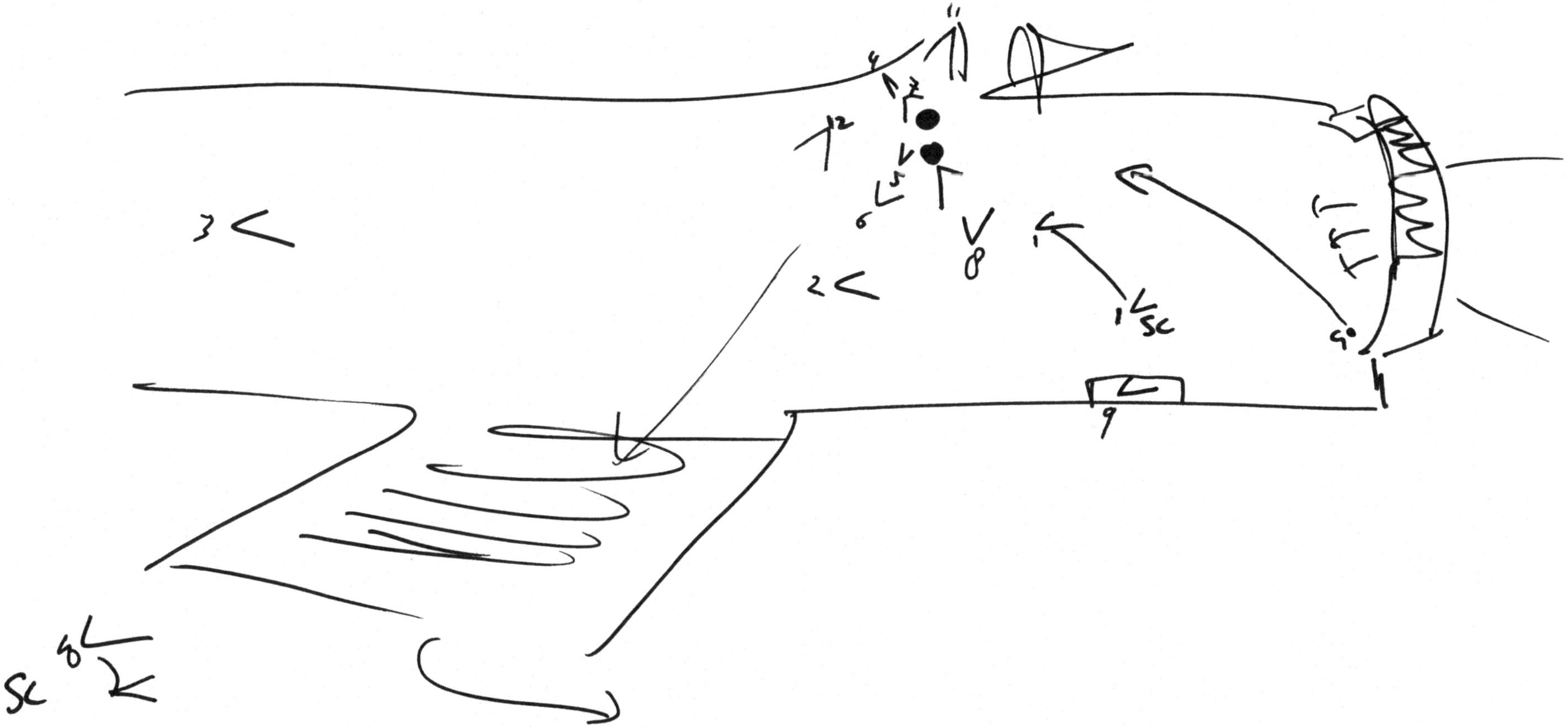

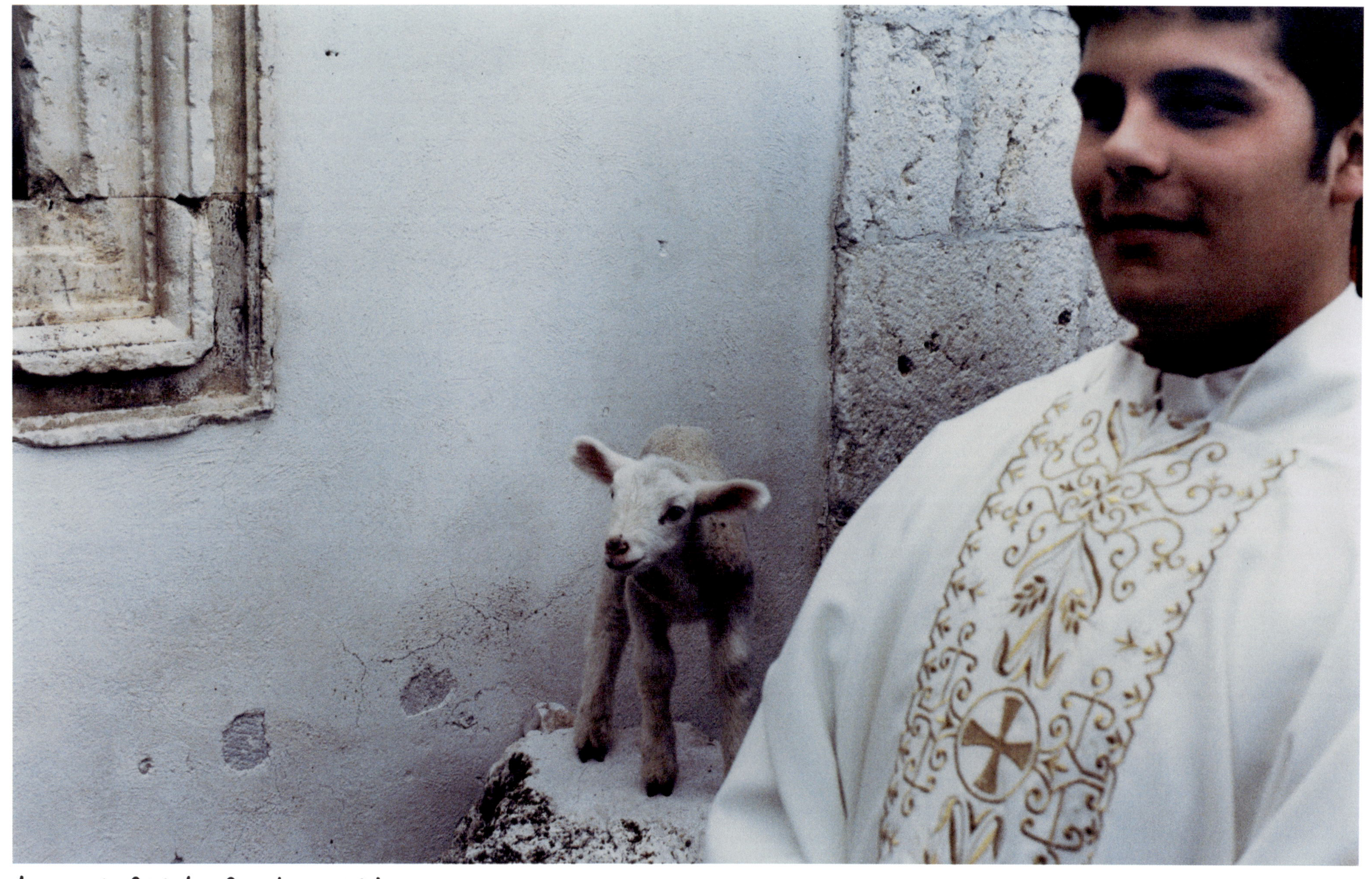

A sweet little lamb getting ready for the procession – one of 3 lamb related scenes. Offing big time.

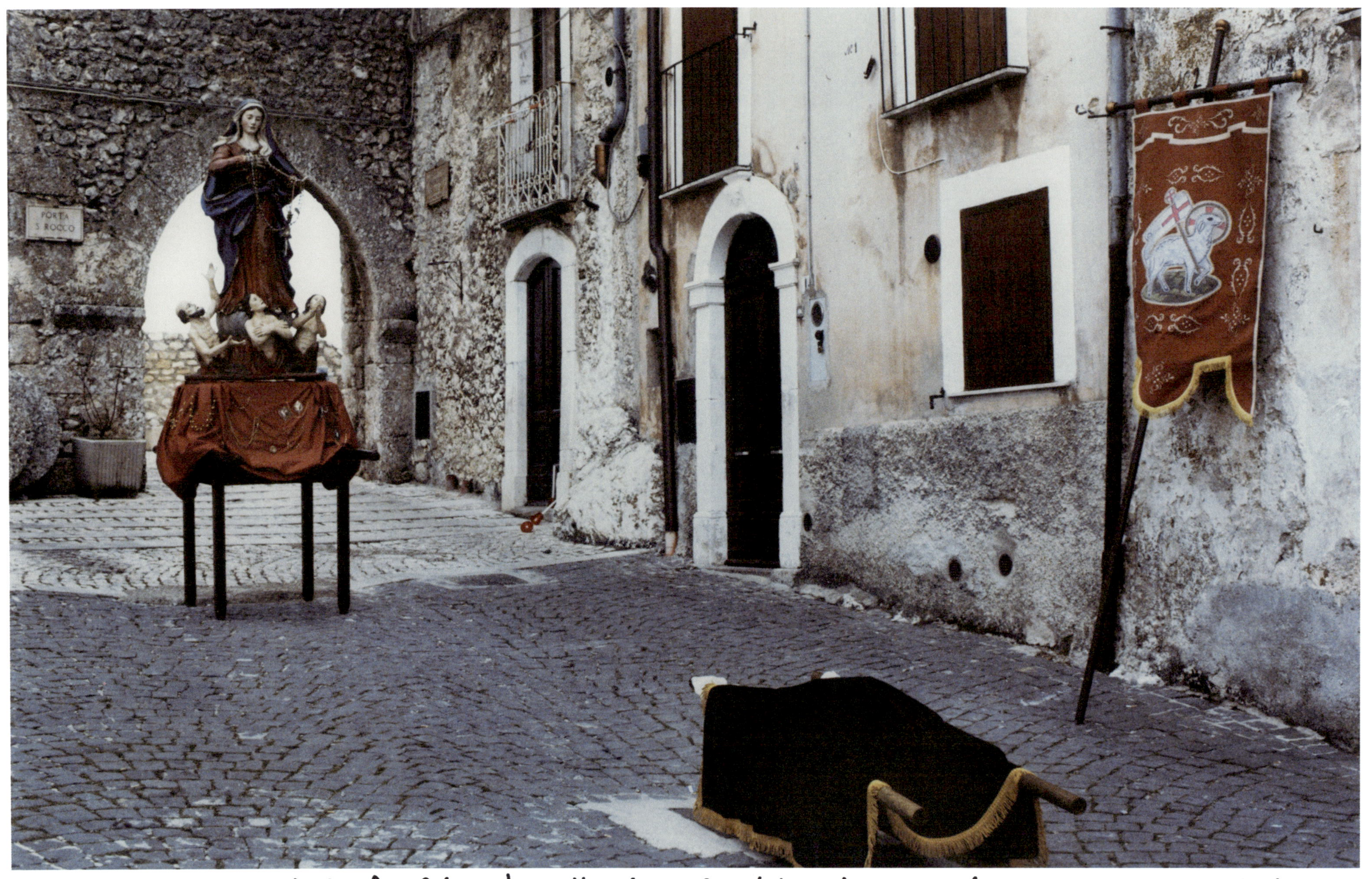

This is what the set looks like when there's a lunchbreak during the procession. Note the lamb↑.

125

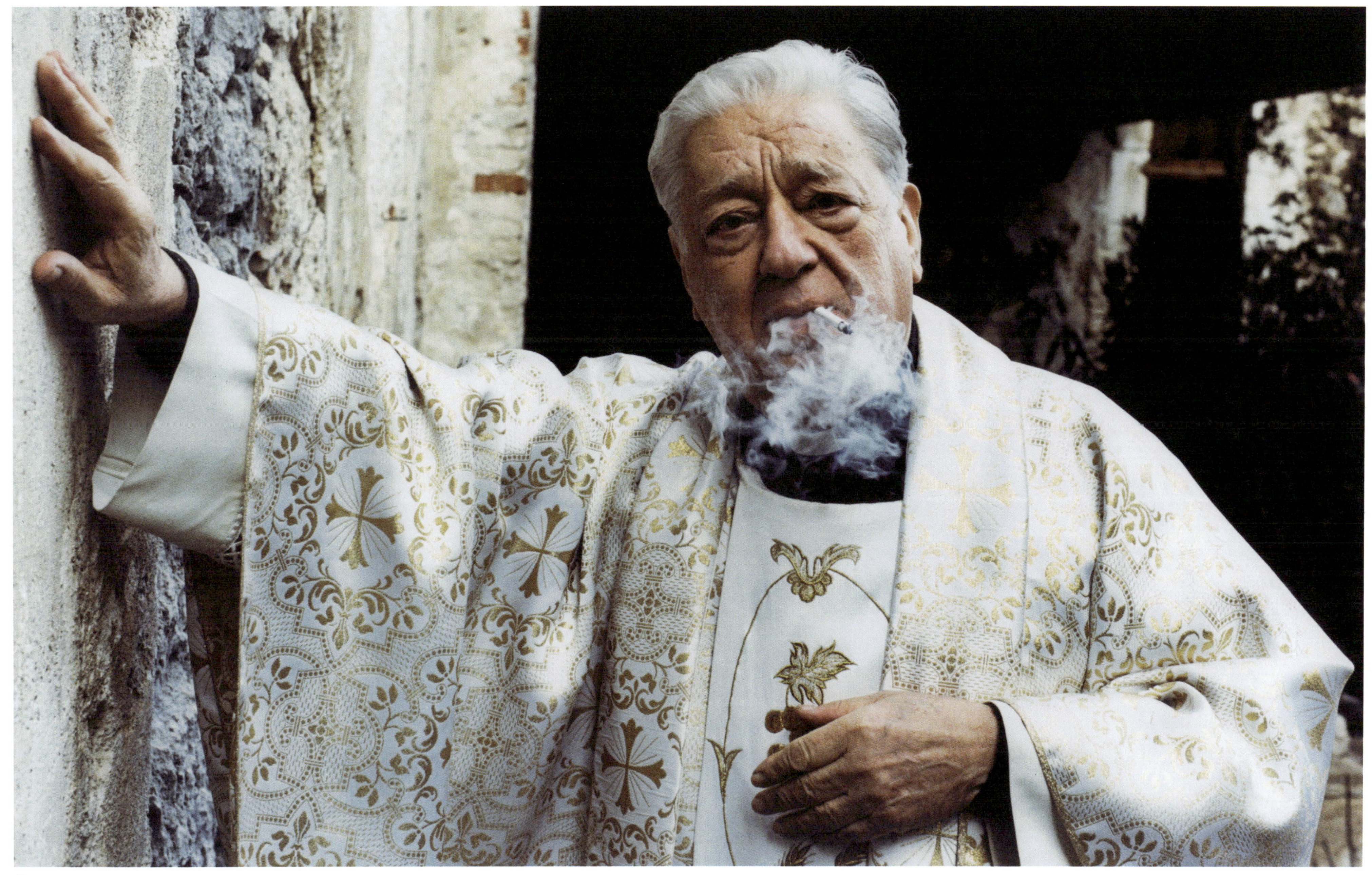

Paolo Bonacelli enjoys his lunchbreak too.

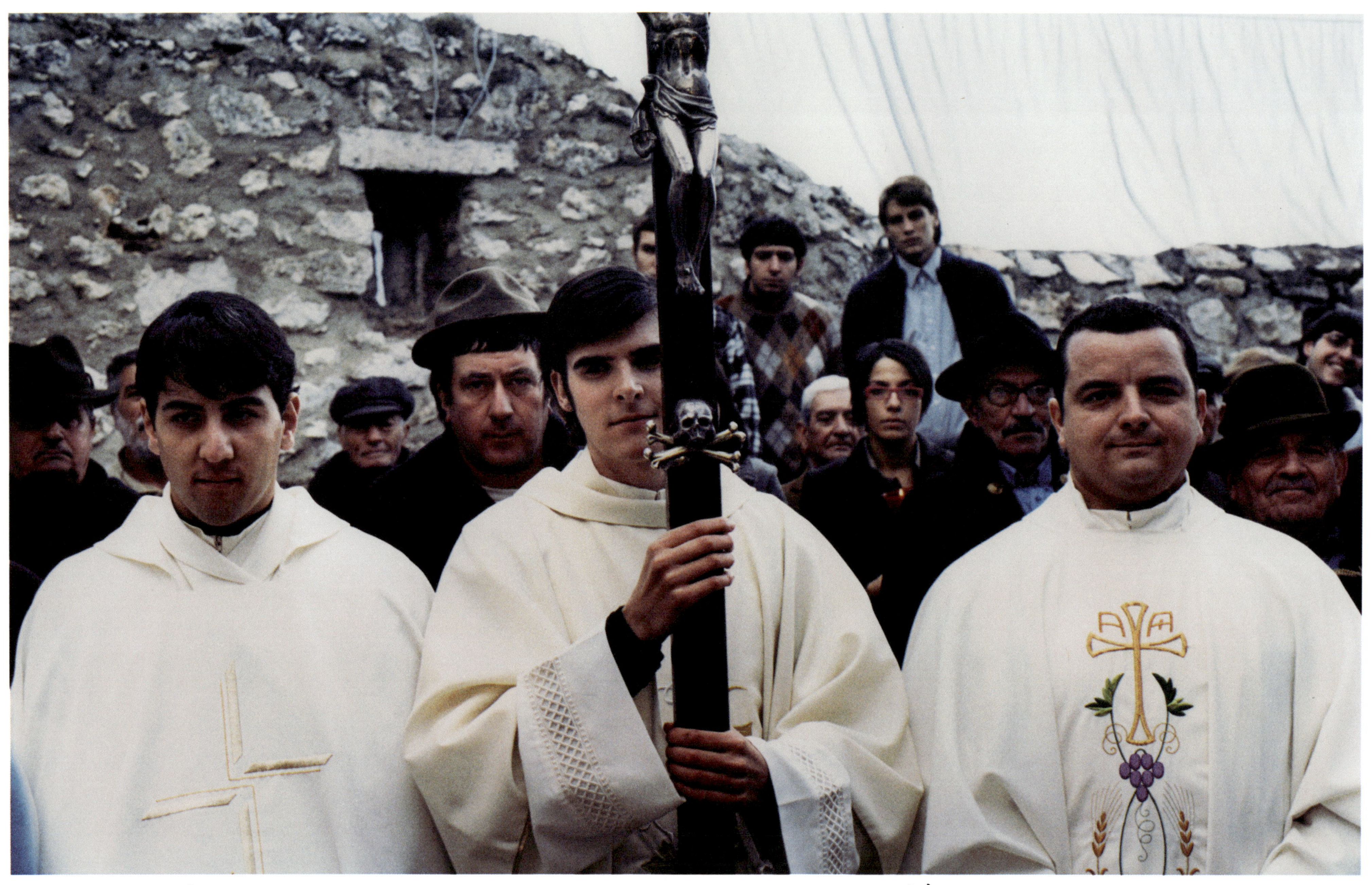

Wonderful faces in the crowd. The cross is not made for the film, i'm amazed by its imagery

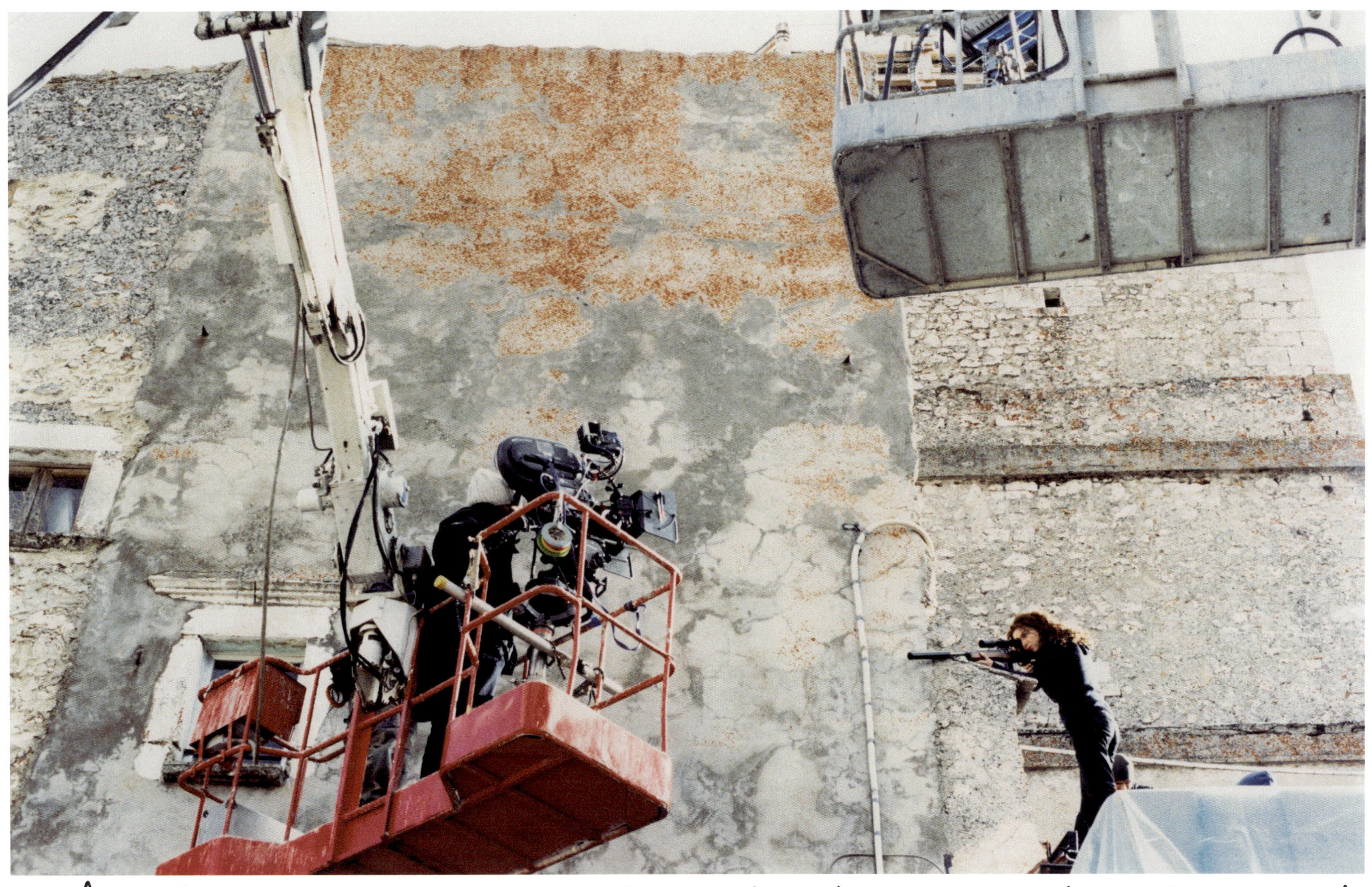

Thekla taking aim while on top of the church roof. It had snowed at night and was around

129

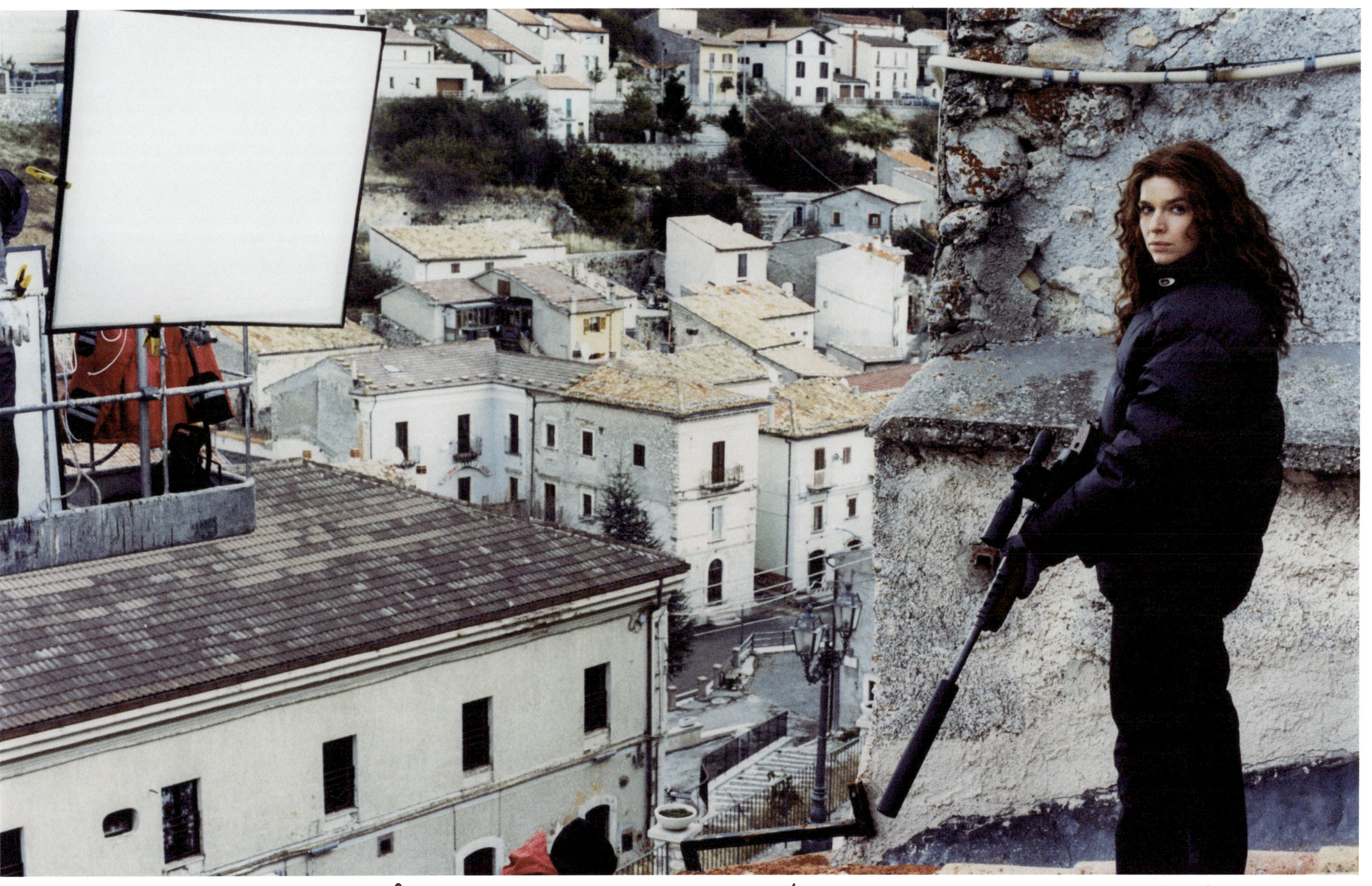

freezing during the day making it a very hard shoot when you're on a roof with nowhere to hide.

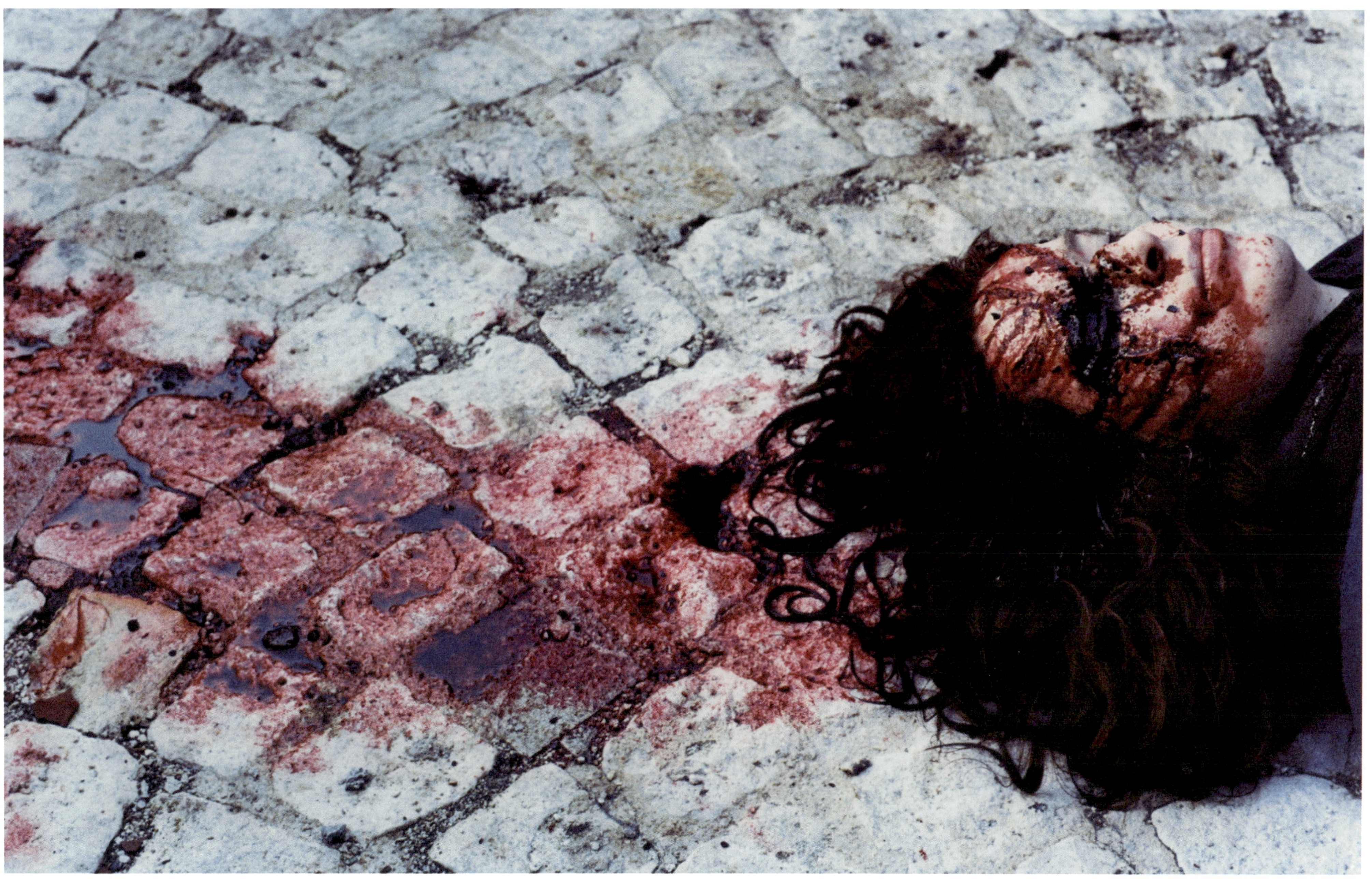

it is tough sometimes!

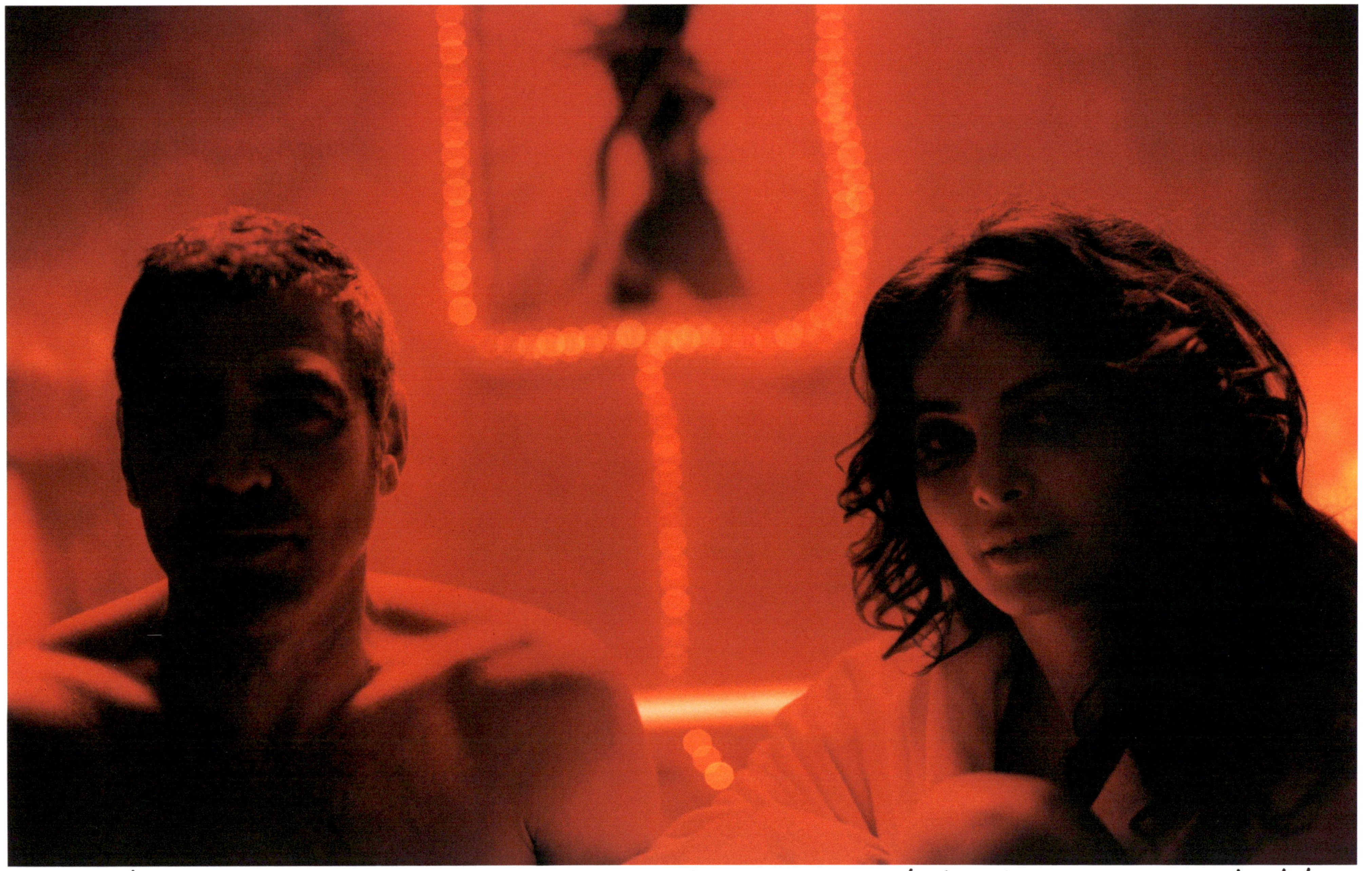

In the brothel there is a sexscene between Jack and Clara which i find very important to include in the film. It shows Jack's anger and frustration with himself when it comes to love

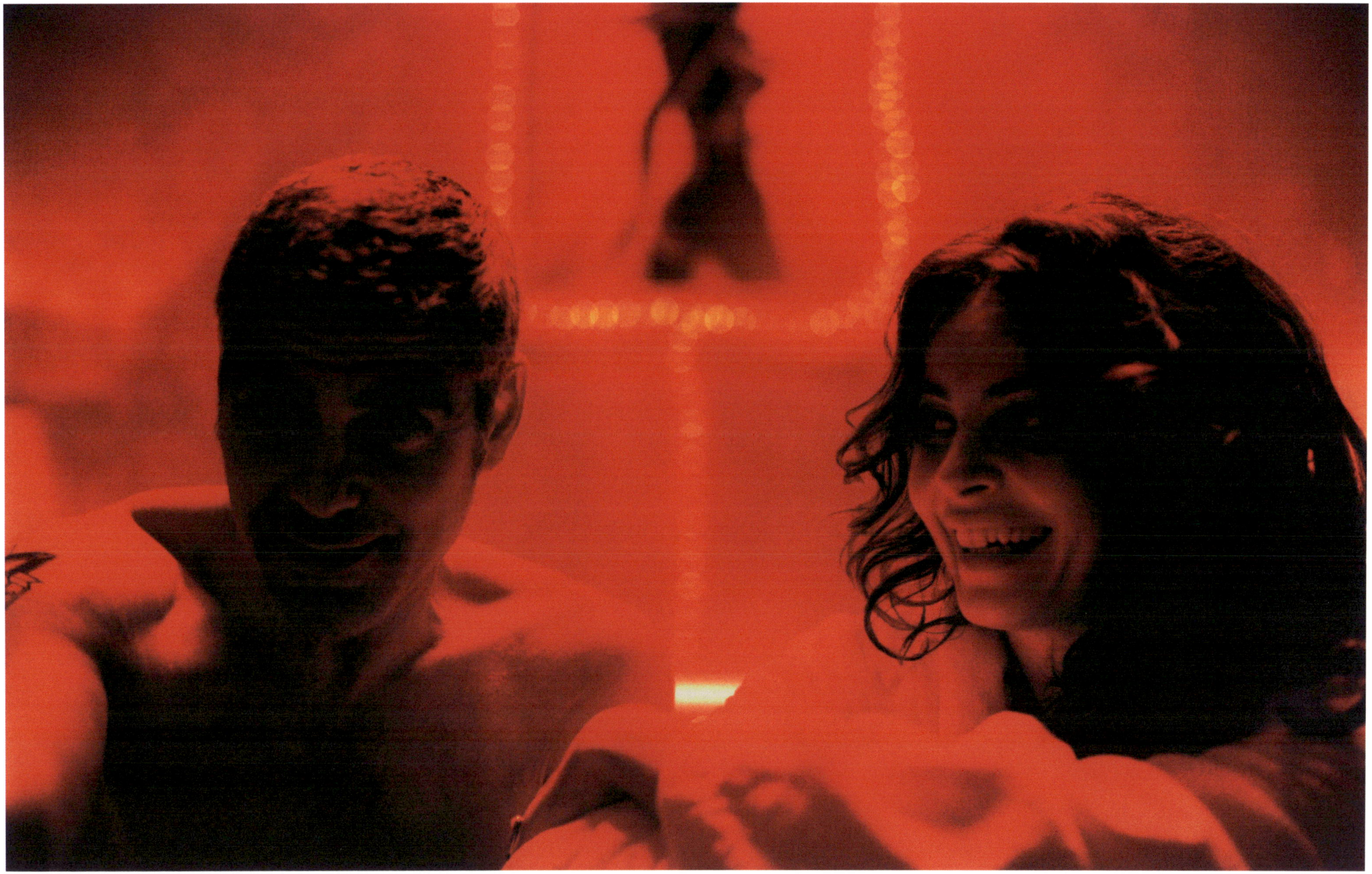

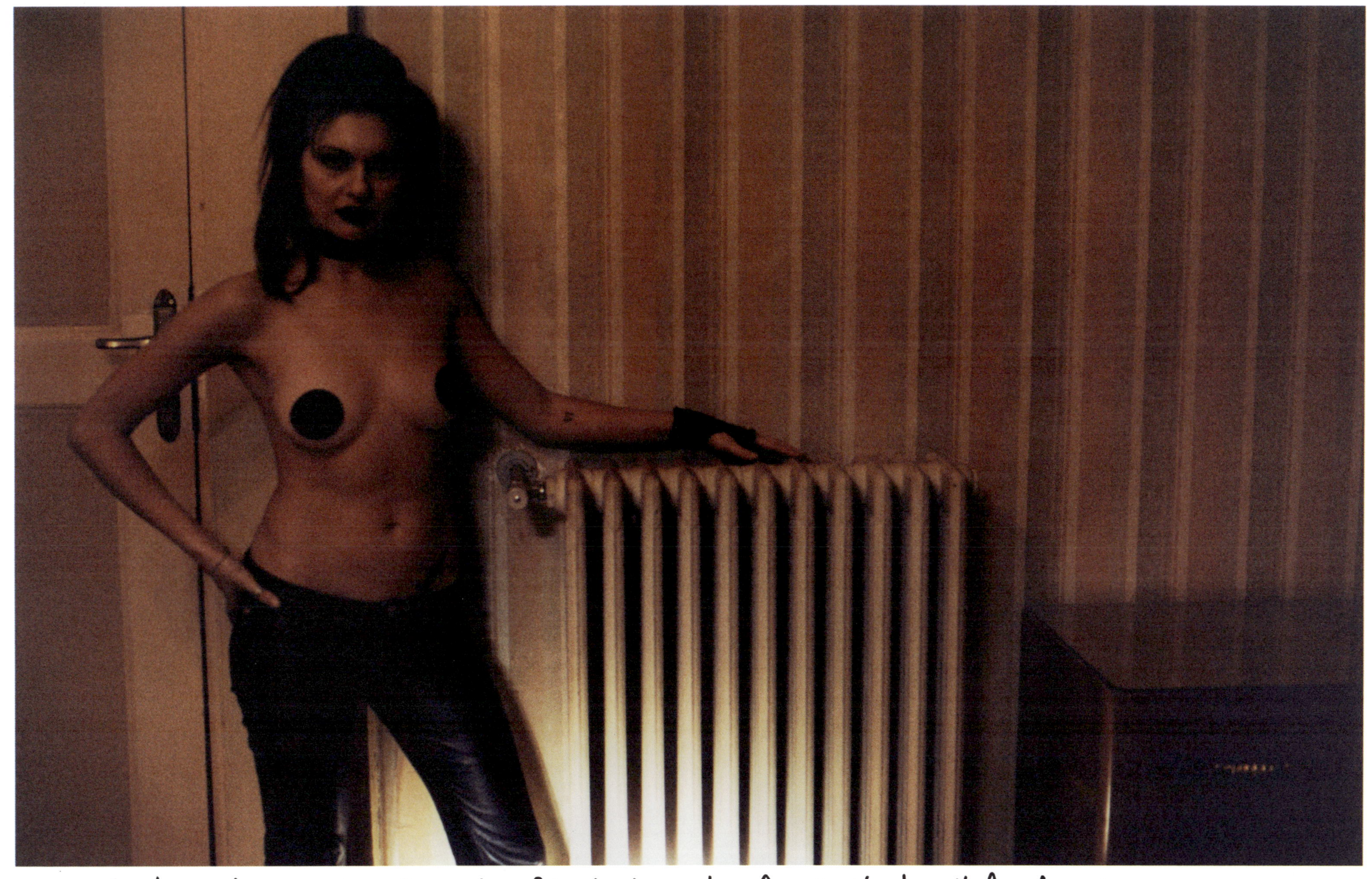

One of the actresses (Angelica Novak) playing a hooker in the brothel, keeping warm.

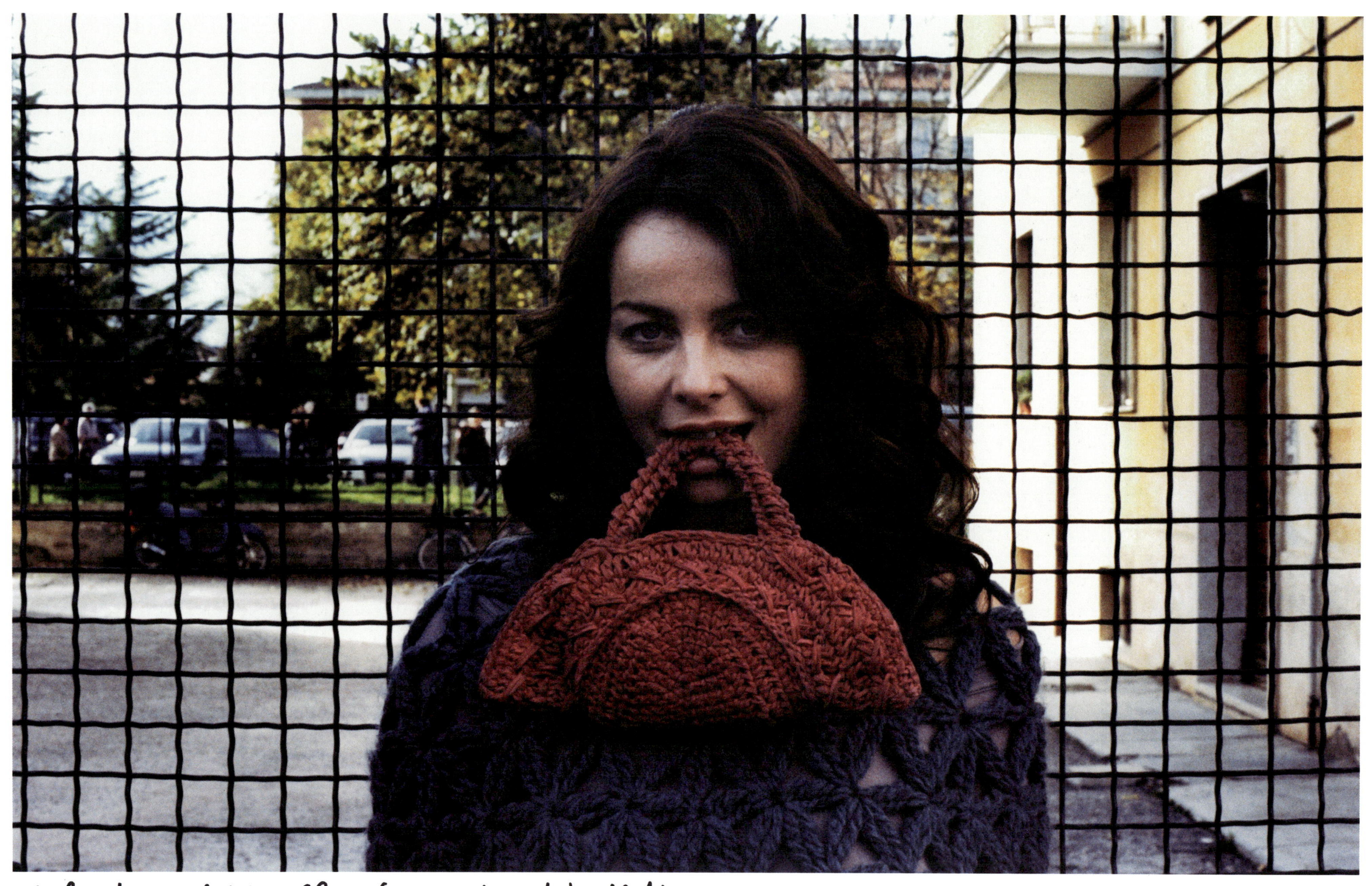

Violante outside Clara's apartment building.

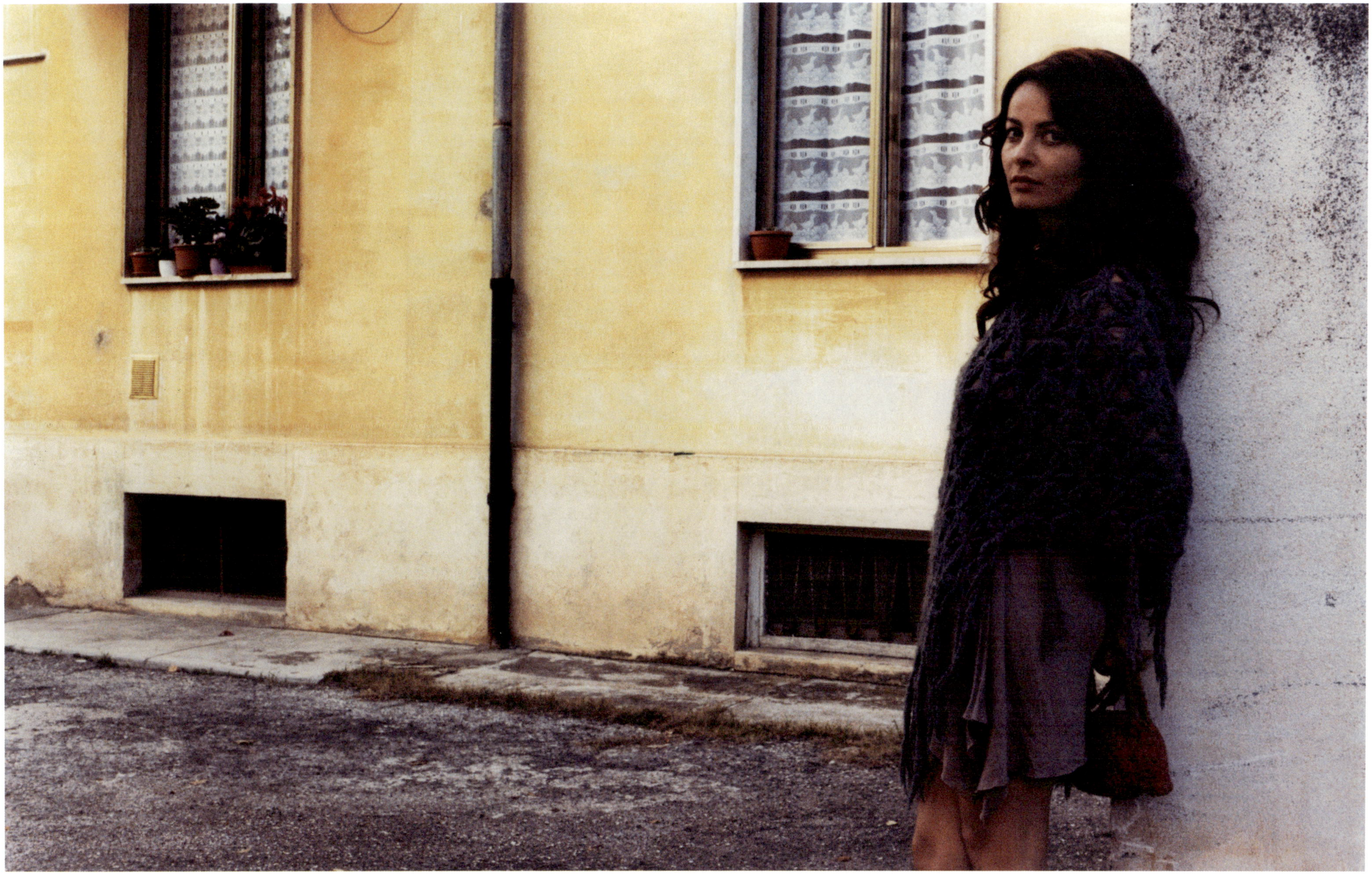

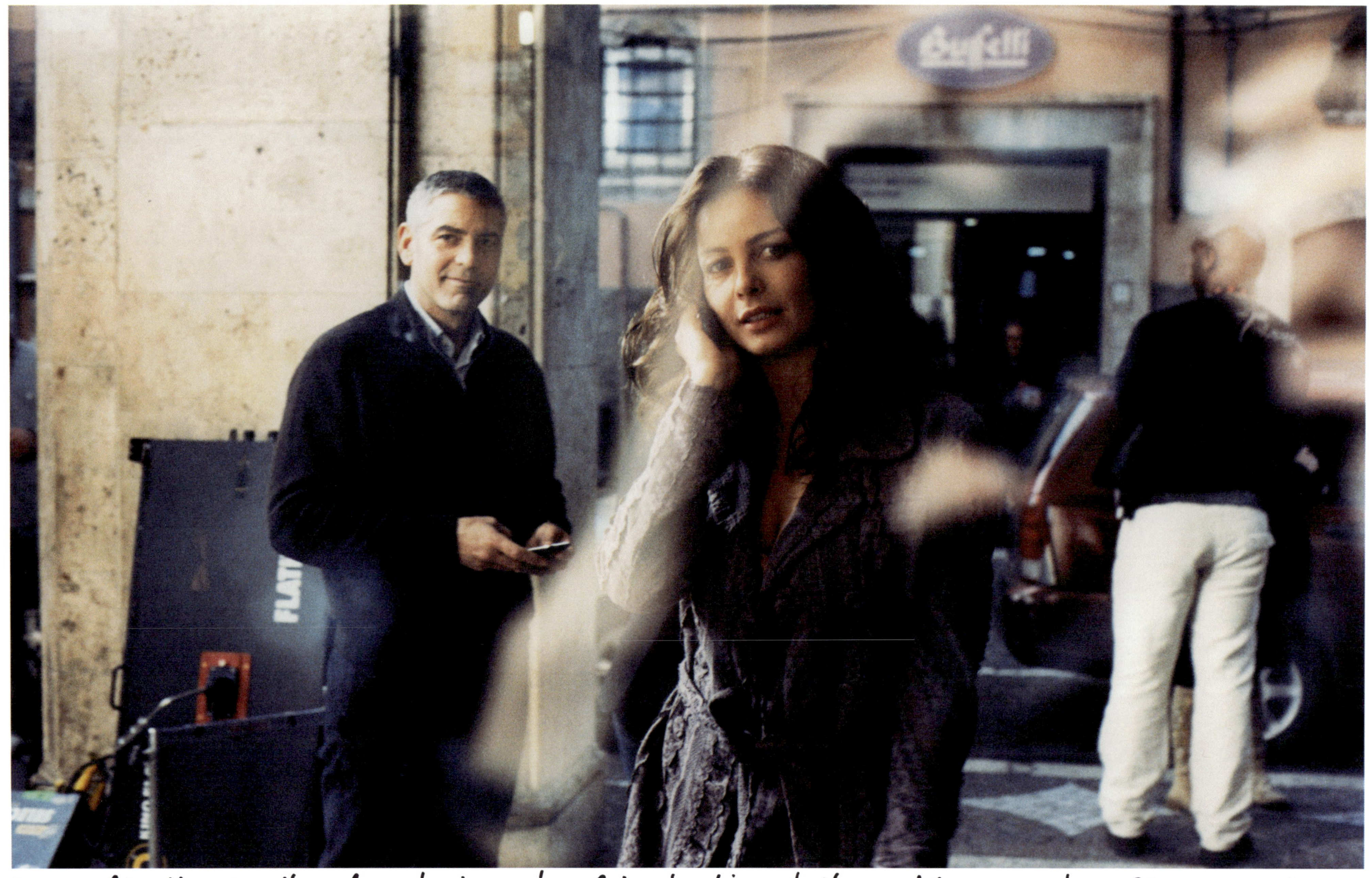

My reflection in the glass during a break in shooting of the café scene where Clara surprises Jack having a coffee and reading about prostitutes getting killed in the area.

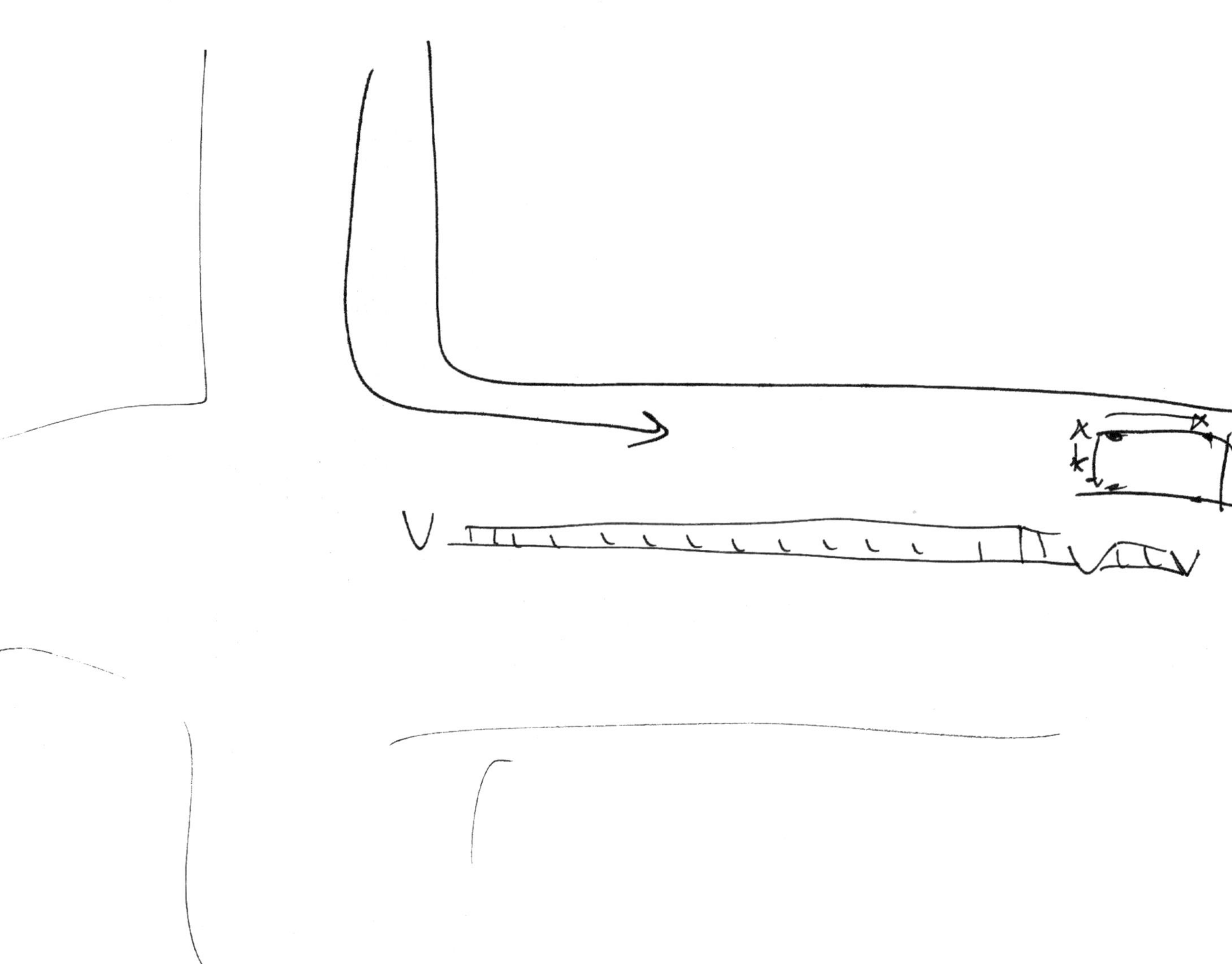

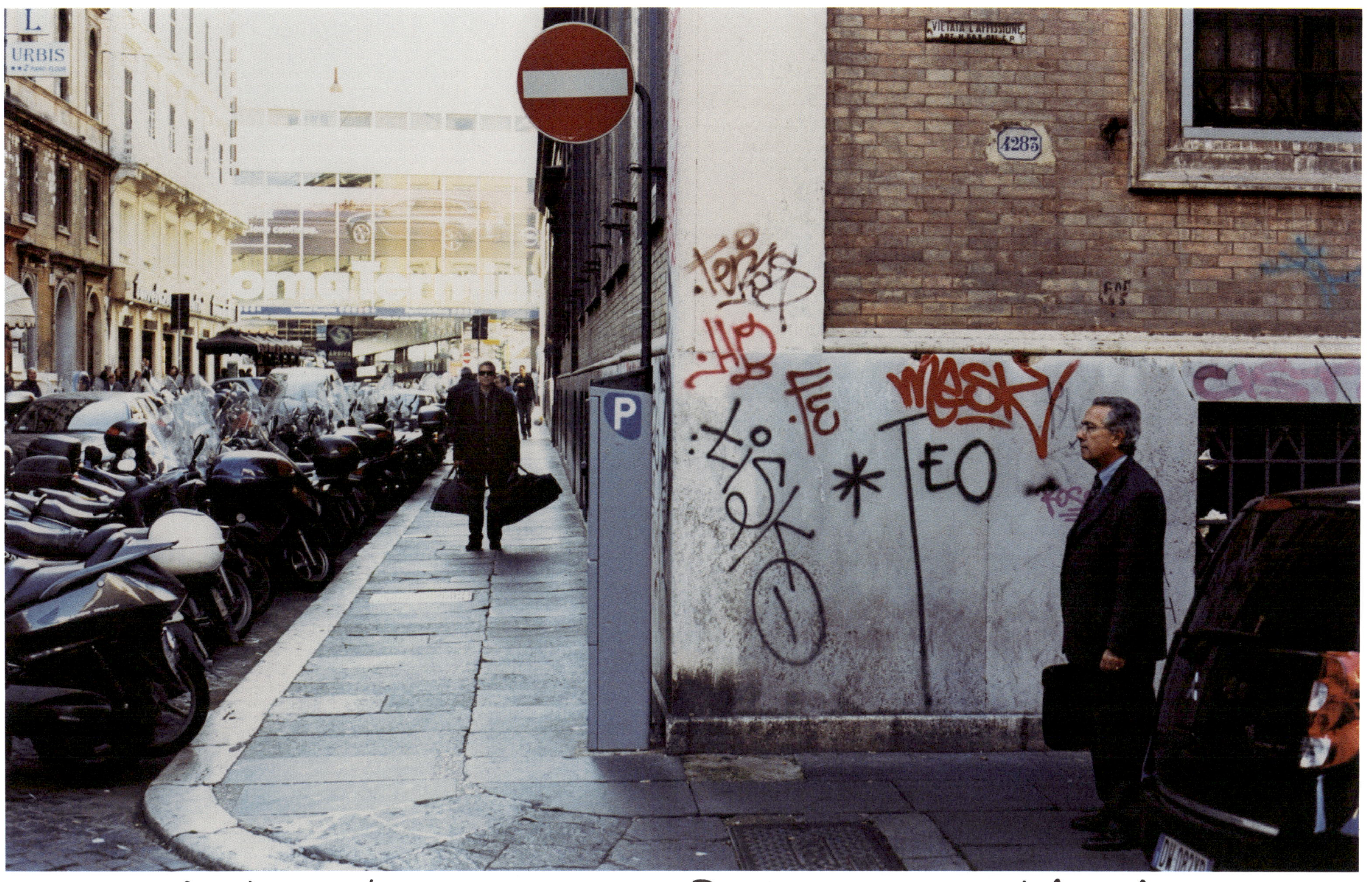

George walking towards his car in Rome with Termini Station seen behind him.

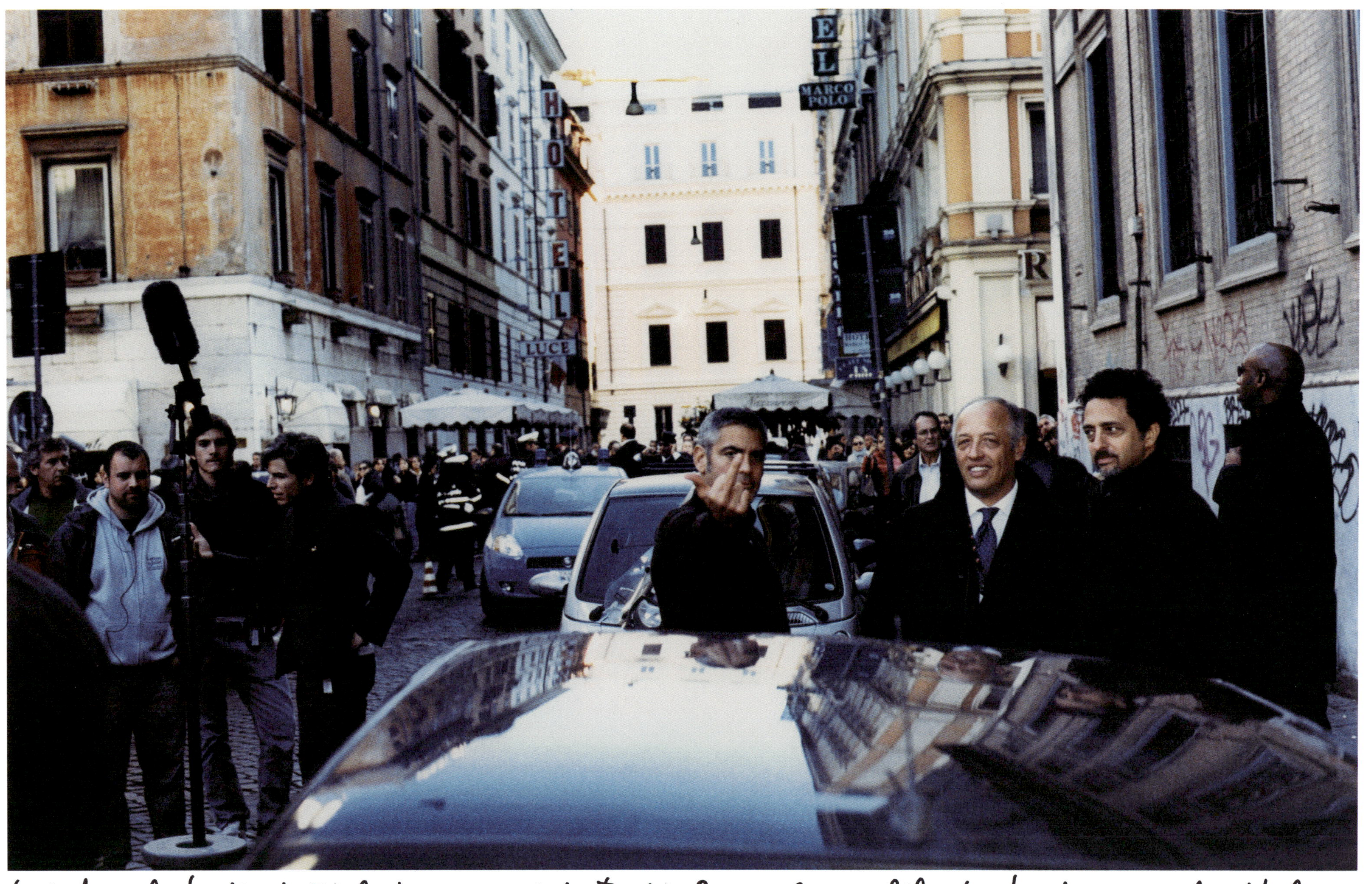

Last day of shooting in Italy in a crowded street in Rome. George likes to shoot 1 more day i believe is what he is indicating to me. To his left: Gio, most charming security man, and producer Grant Heslov.

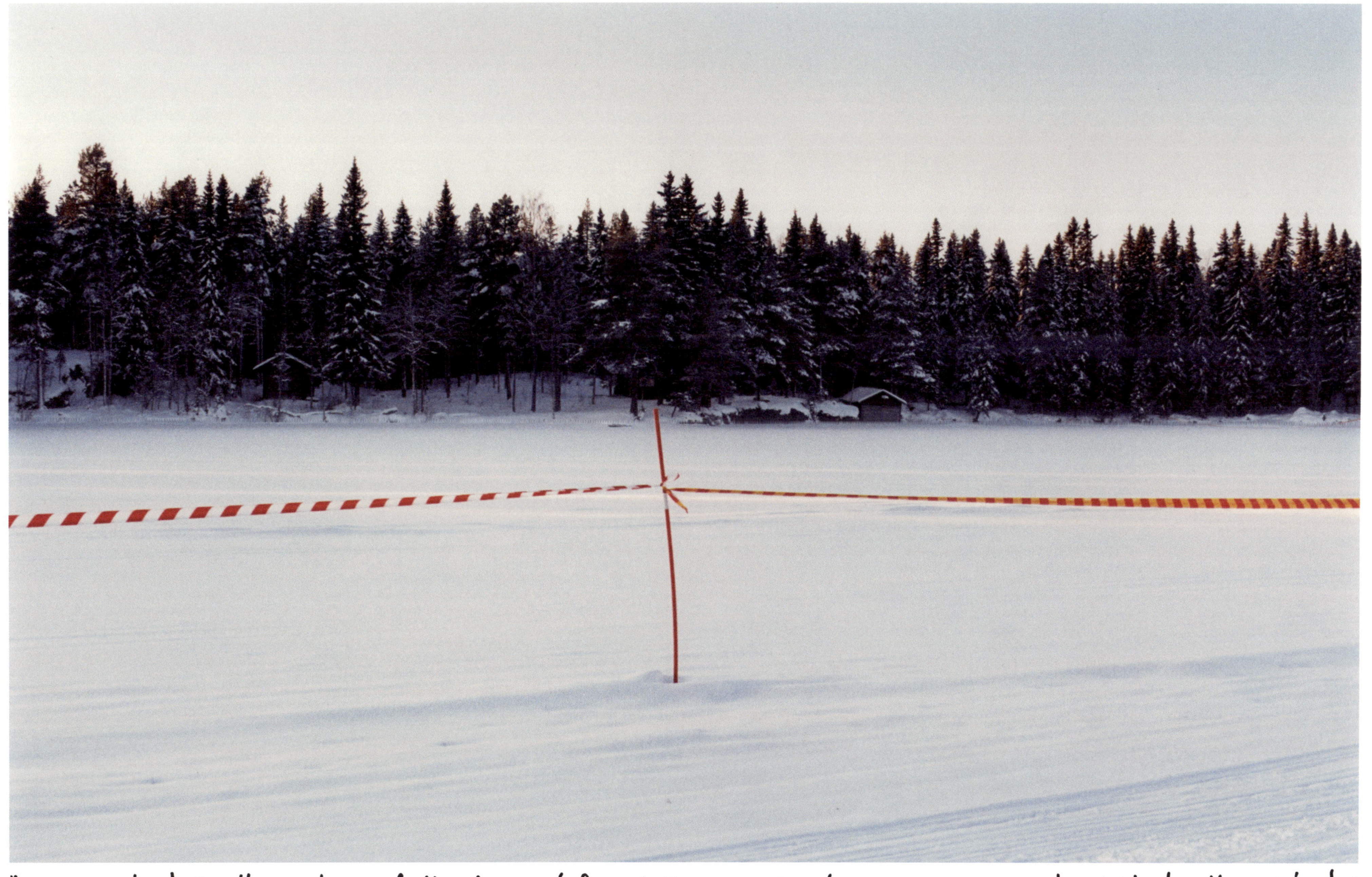

Measures to keep the surface of the frozen lake pristine are in place so we can shoot it for the opening shot of the movie. The location was roughly 30 minutes drive outside Östersund in the middle of Sweden.

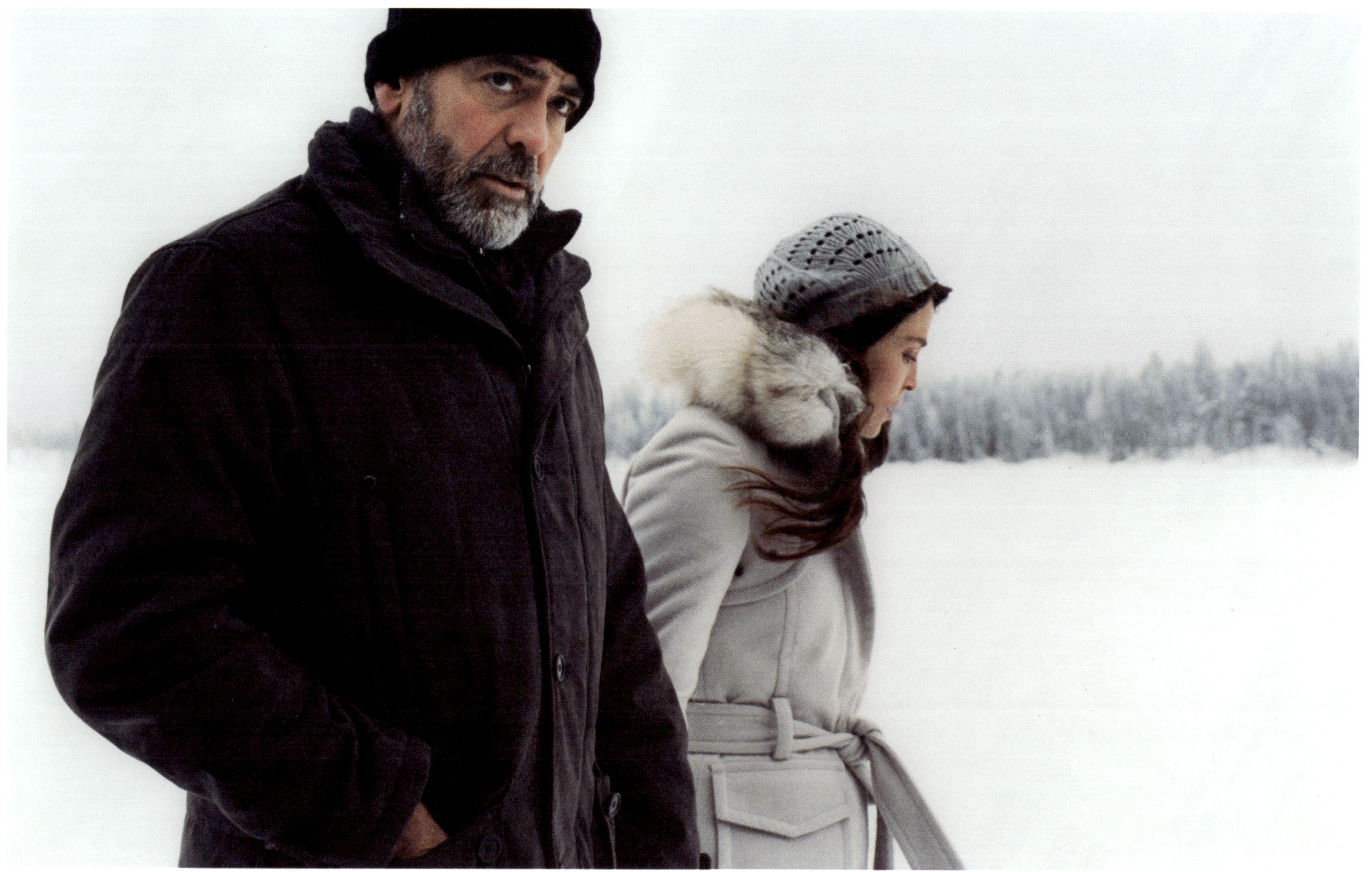

George and Irina walking over the lake at minus 20°C. It was tough on everyone but days were short.

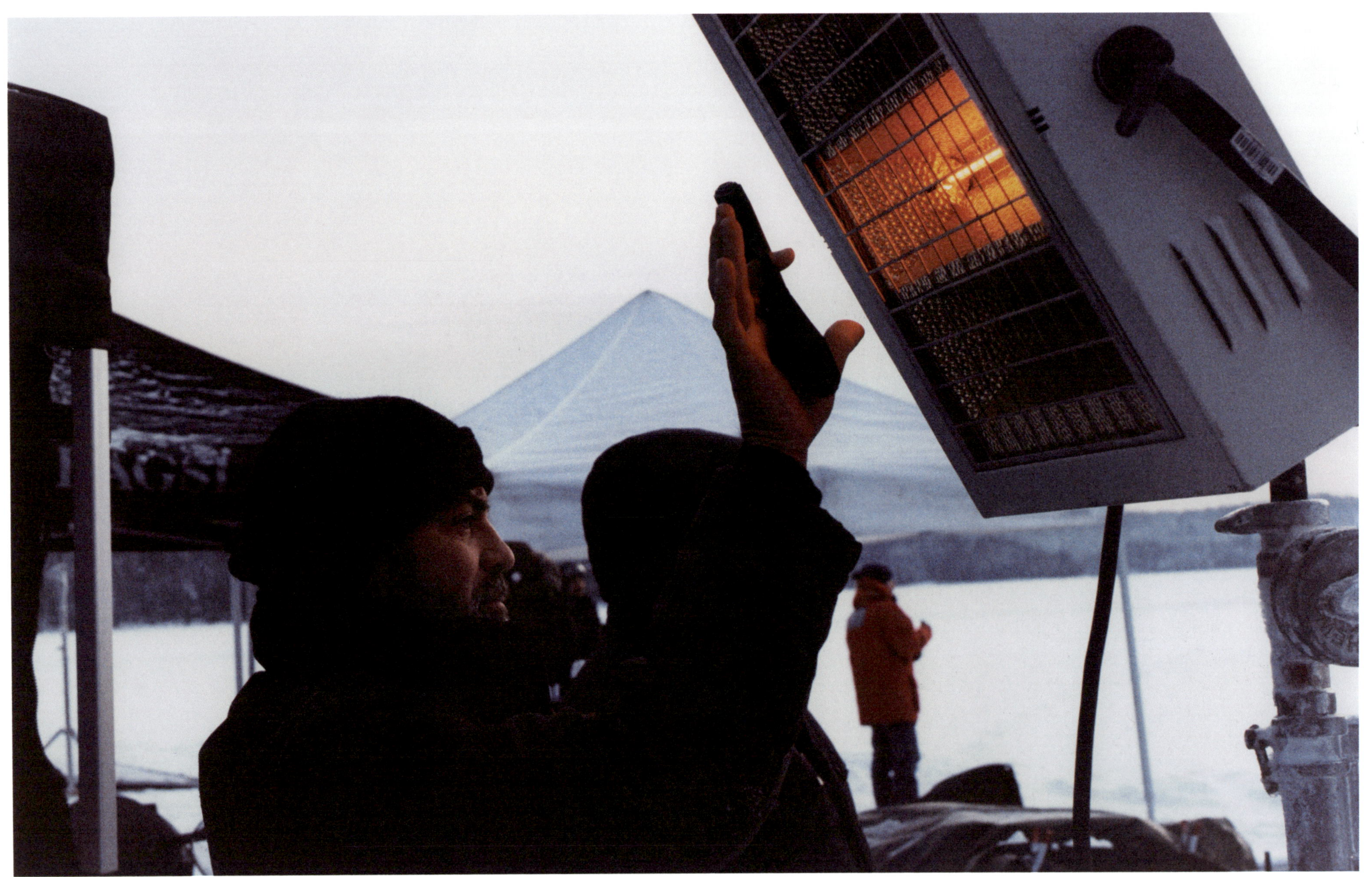

As an expert on the Beatles' Repertoire George knows better than most that Happiness is a warm Gun.

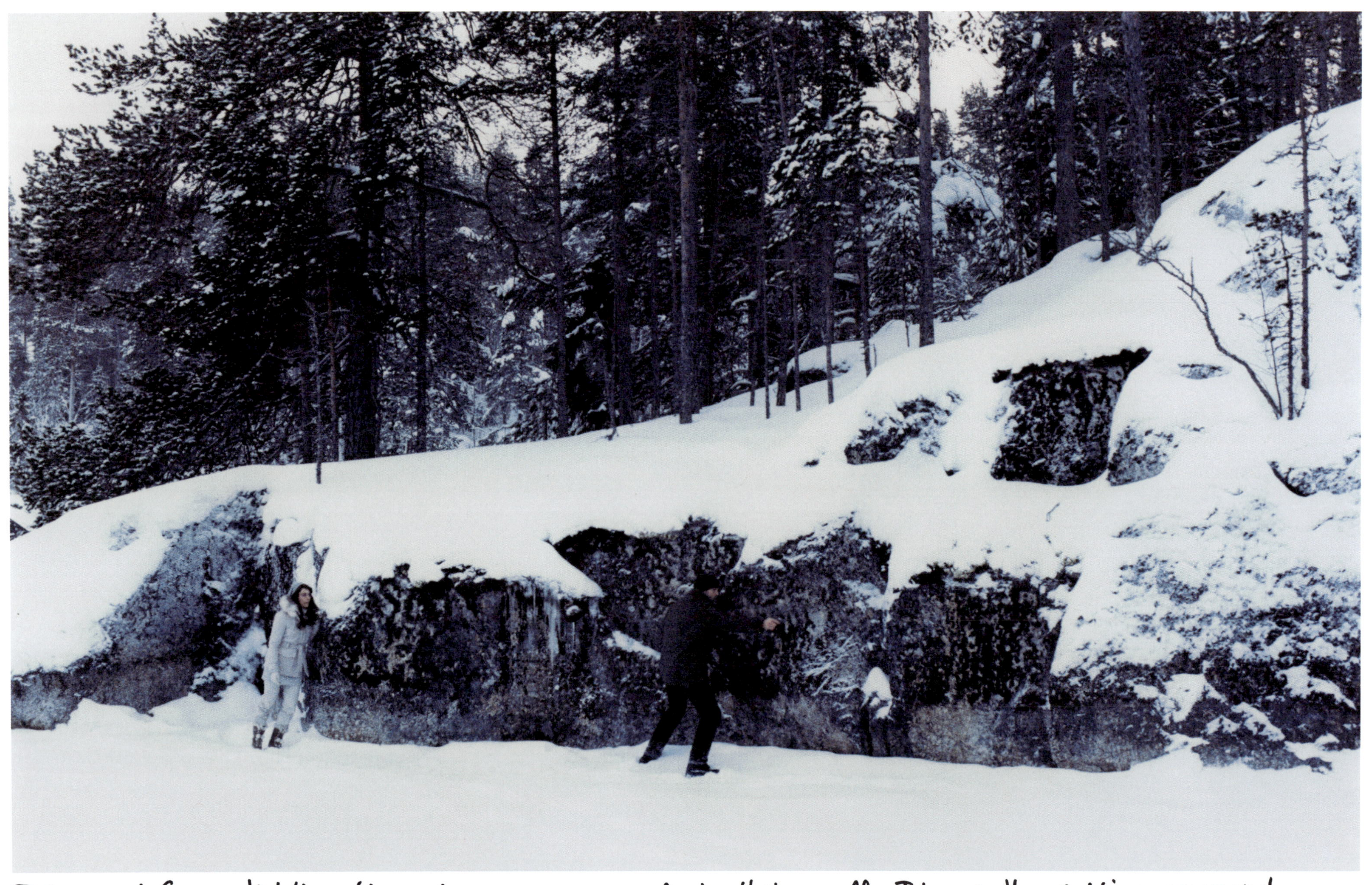

Irina and George fighting off a dangerous enemy during their walk. I loved the setting enormously.

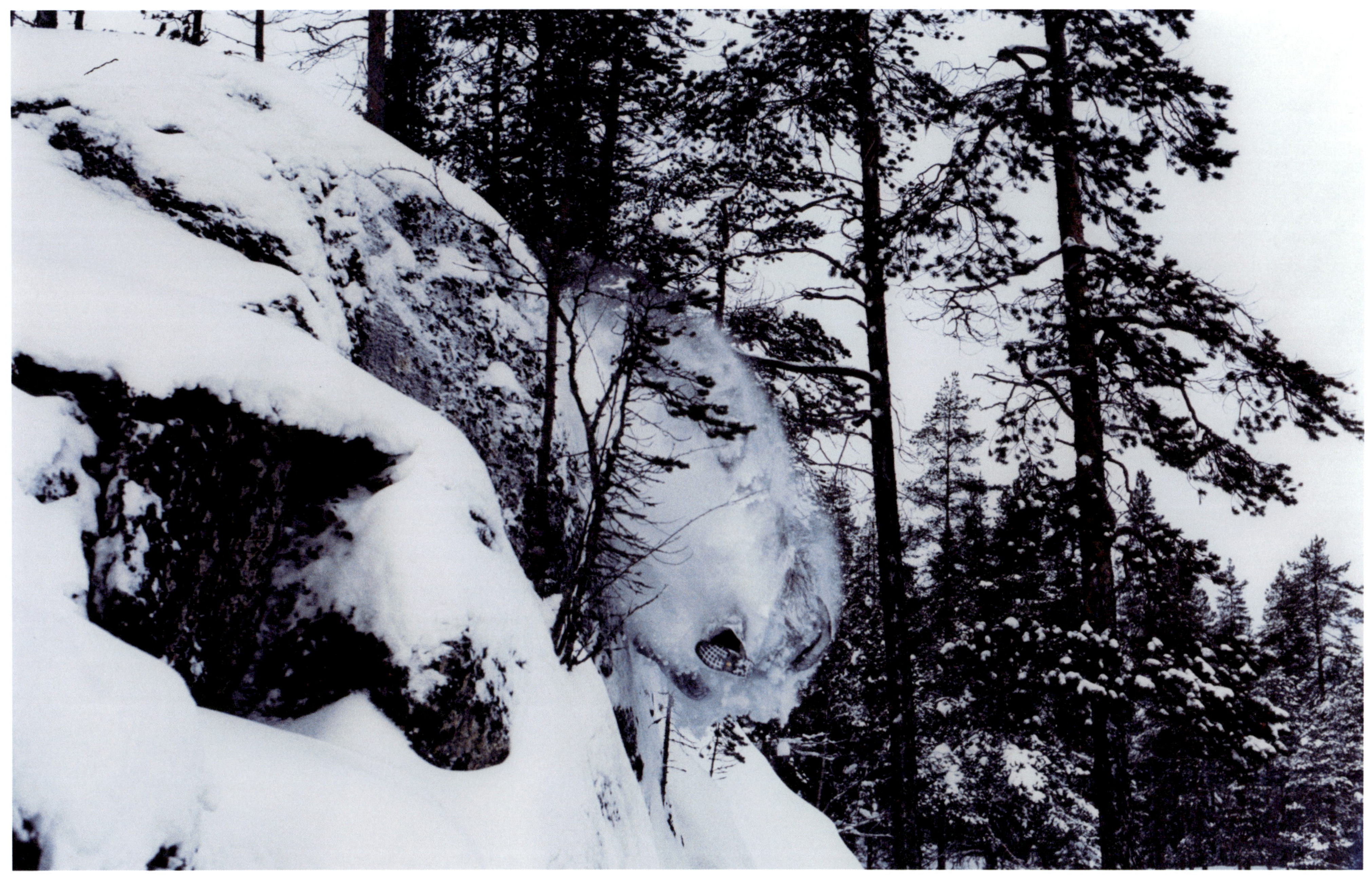

The enemy falling off the rocks. Snow makes everything look so beautiful and peaceful, and death serene.

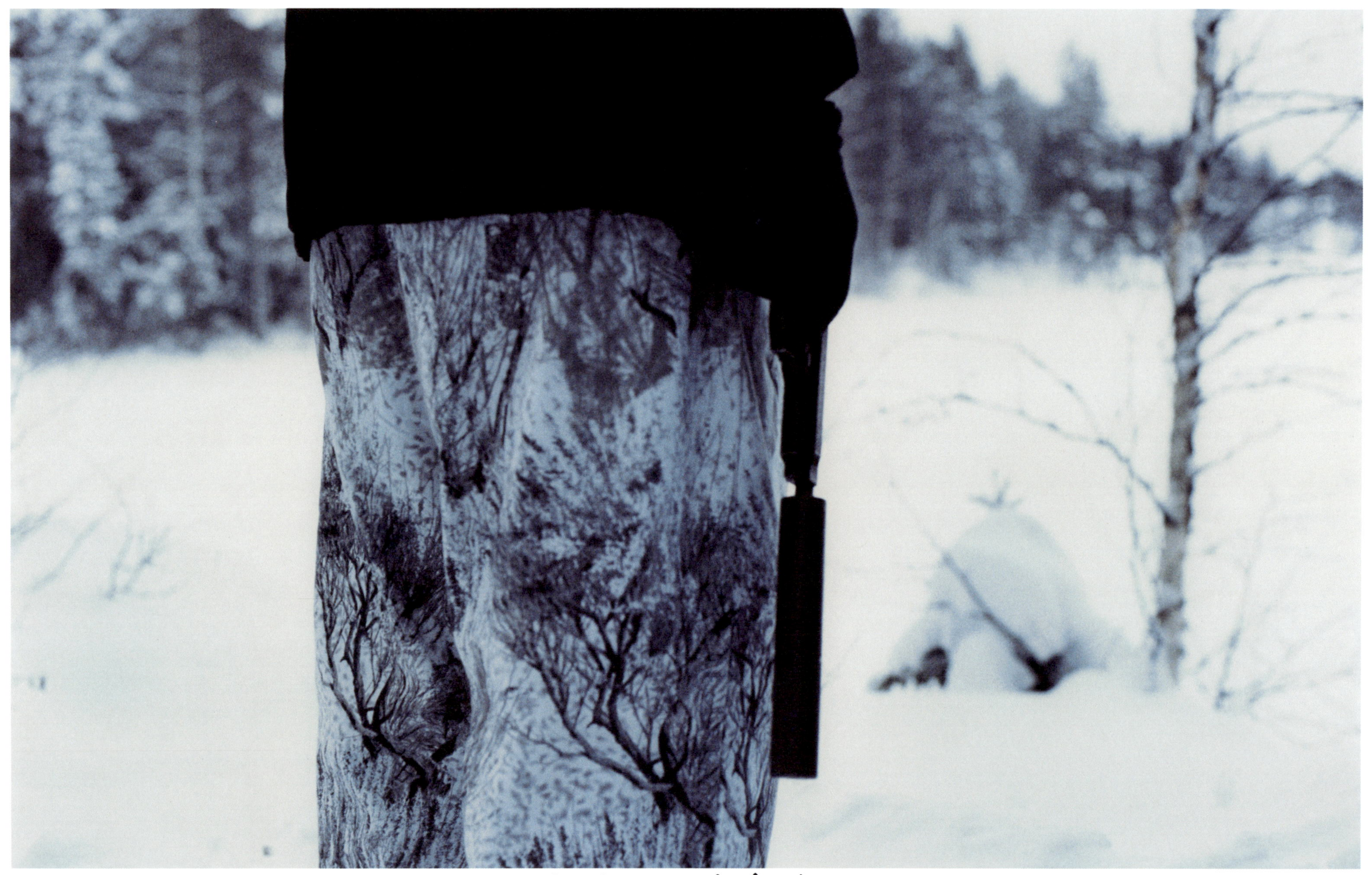

Björn Granath is a dangerous man - even his trousers look deadly. He plays the second Swedish 'hunter'.

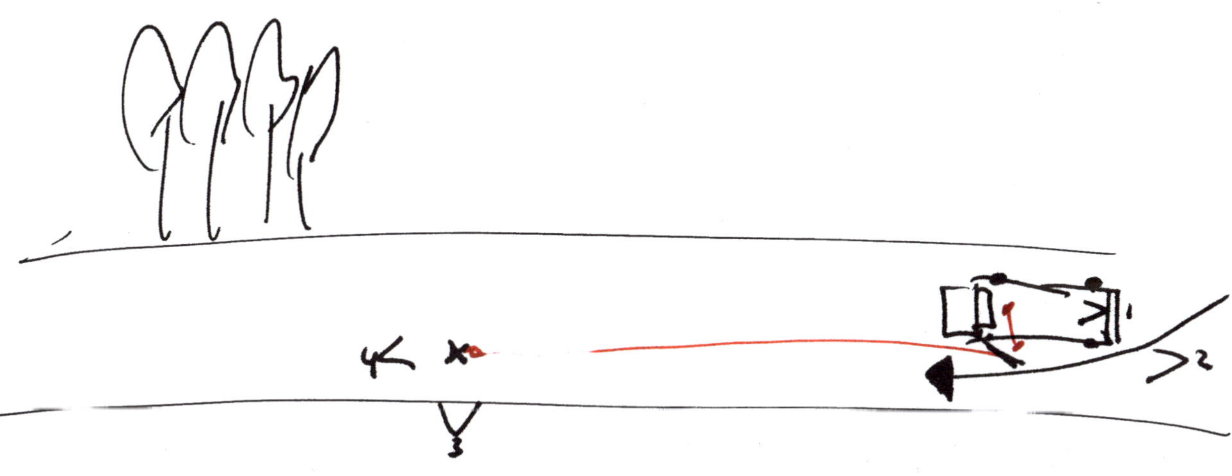

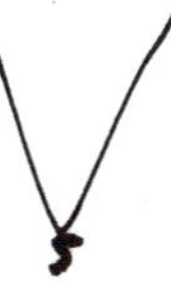

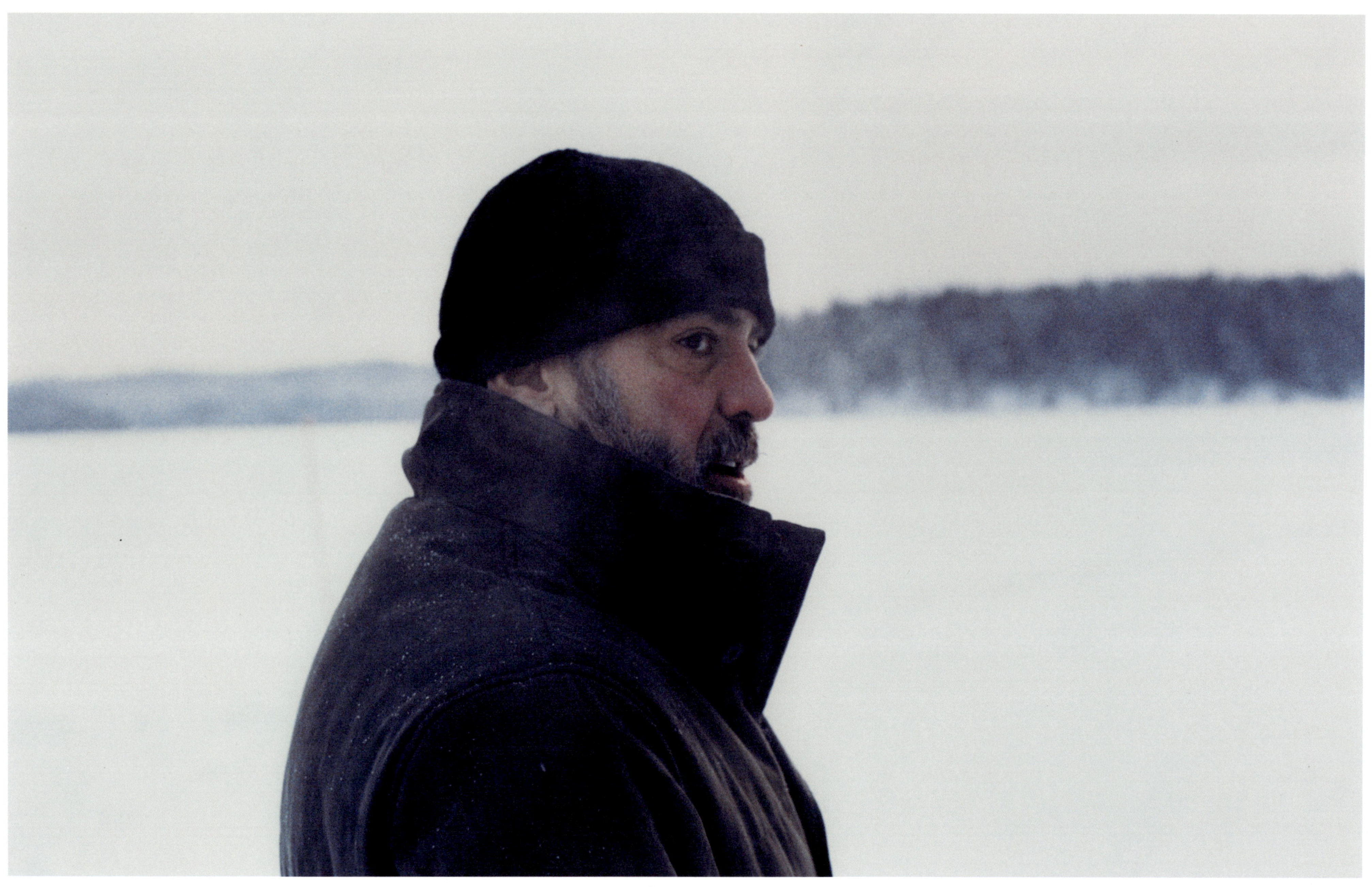

George

155

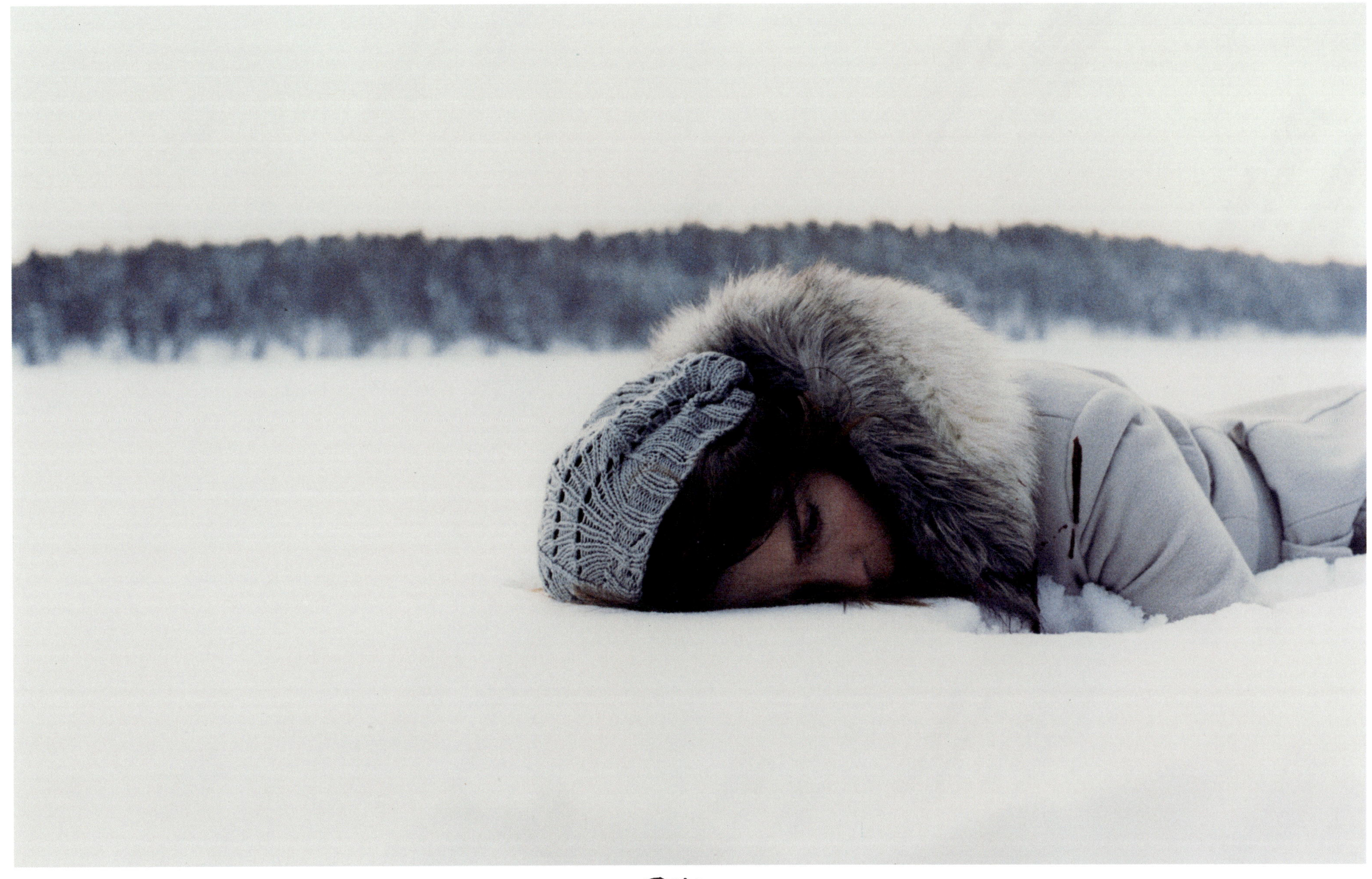

IRina

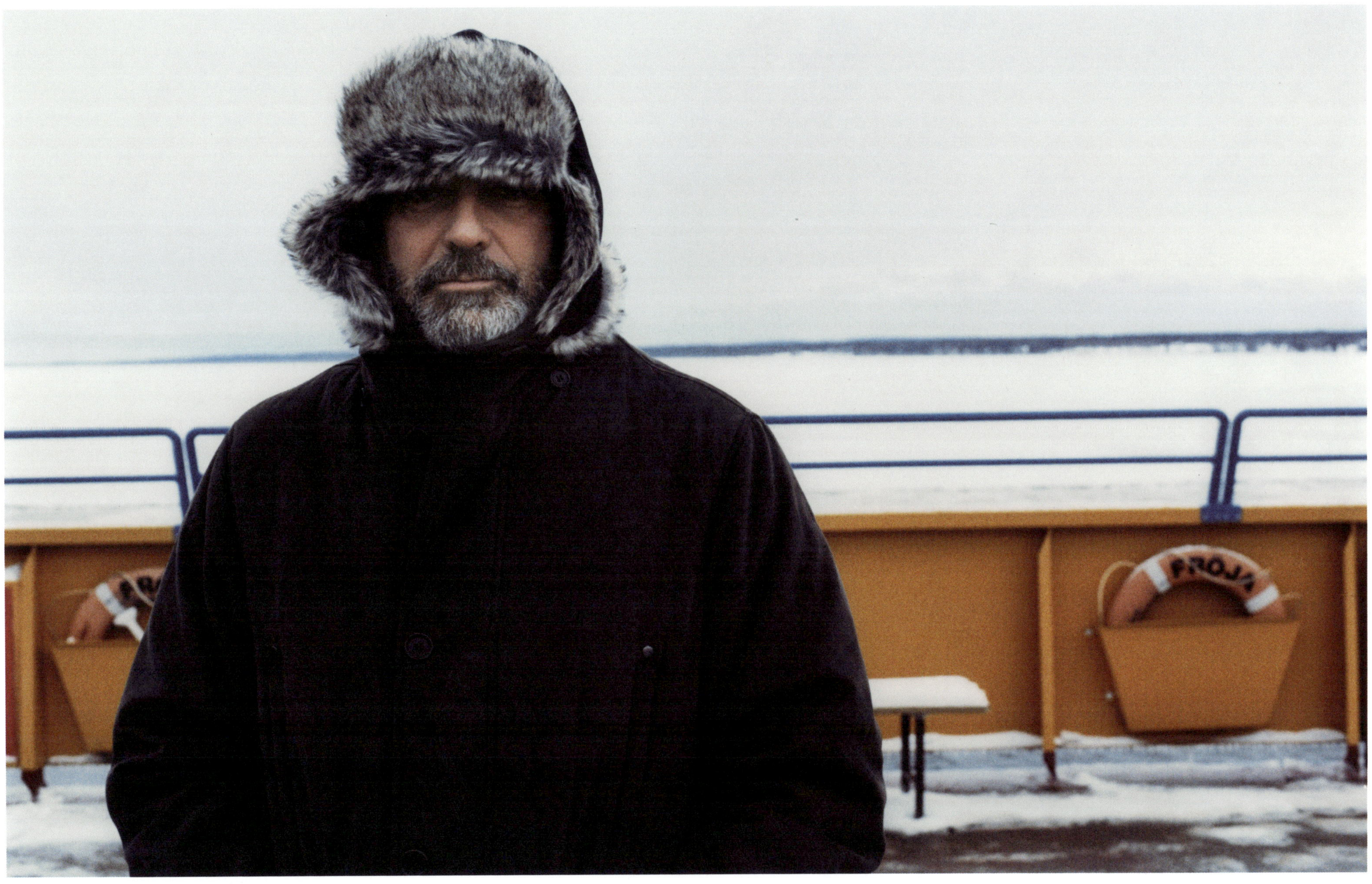

In between takes George tries to keep warm aboard the ferry, the start of his journey.

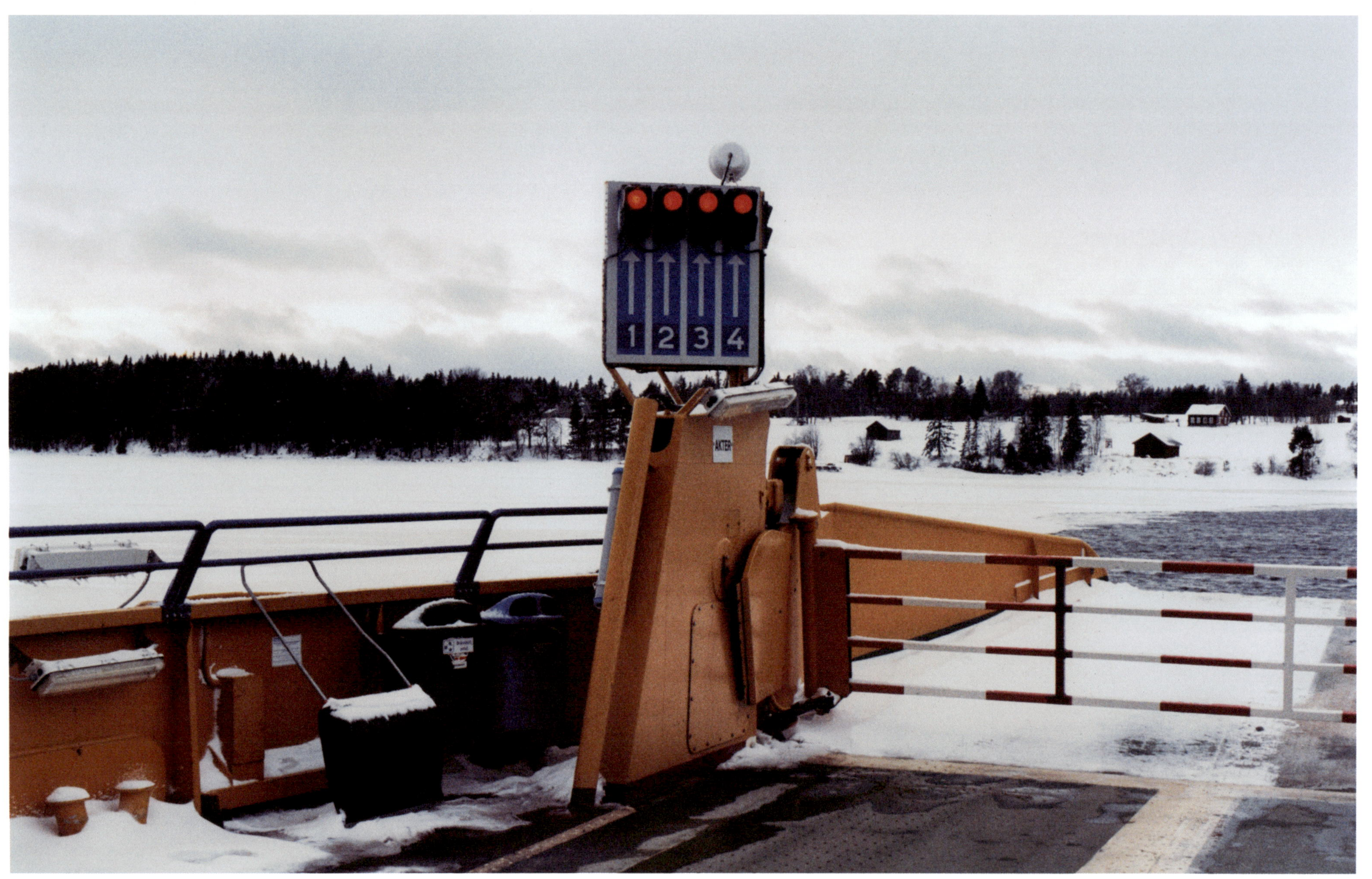

Symbolic last photo in the book.

158

CREDITS

Anne Carey is the main producer of the film. She had been trying for about 12 years to get a movie based on Martin Booth's novel made. Here she is contemplating the wisdom of letting me loose on this project whilst admiring the beauty of Campo Imperatore. She is a fantastic person and I'm very grateful to her for supporting me with The American. I needed it for sure.

Herbert Grönemeyer used to be an actor and is been telling me for at least 10 years that i should be making movies. So I forced him to act in CONTROL and asked him to do the score for this film. It's a magnificent score and below is Herbert during the recording at Abbey Road Studios. We are trying where possible to work together.

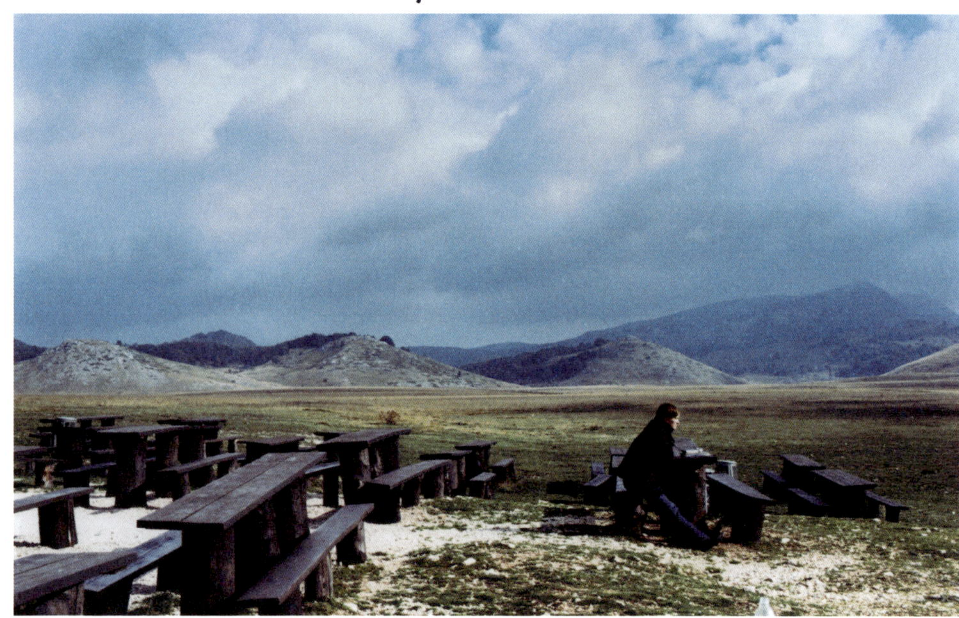

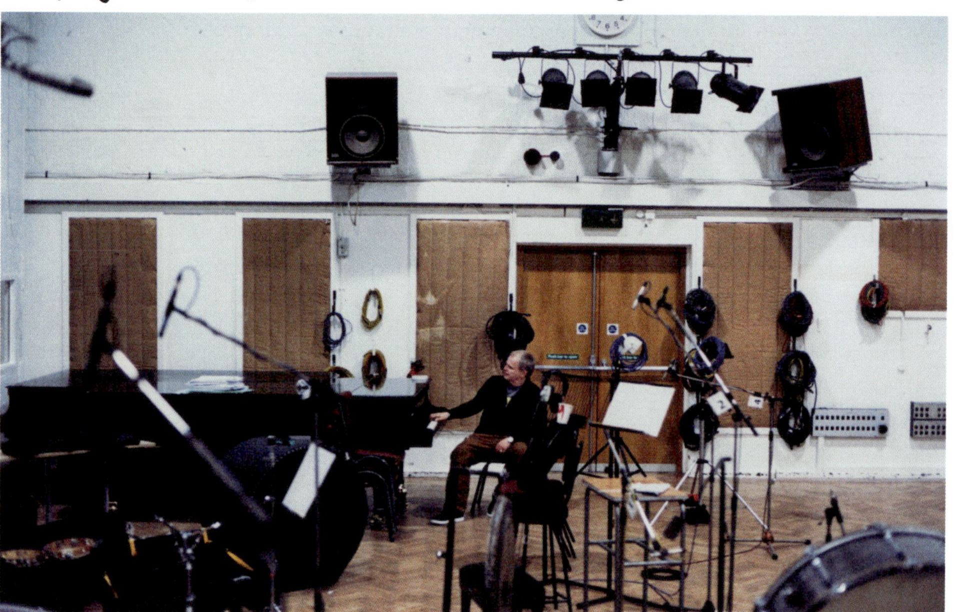

THANK YOU!

people of towns and villages we shot film + photos in, specially Calascio, Castel del Monte, Castelvecchio, Pacentro, Rome and Sulmona.

all the actors portrayed here as well as the crew and extras who appear nameless in this book.

the people who made this book possible, specifically James Schamus and John Lyons at Focus, Maha Dakhil and Steven Brookman at CAA, Jack Thomas and Duncan Heath at Independent Talent, and Lothar Schirmer.

Martin Ruhe is the eye-catching DP, camera man, of both CONTROL and THE AMERICAN. I like to think we compliment each other very well as he posesses qualities i lack. And i like to think vice versa too. We met a long time ago on a video shoot for Herbert G! It is all connected you understand!

George Clooney, man of many many talents, most of these displayed in this movie and we are richer for it. This Charming Man is not only a great Great actor, producer, raconteur, director, all round entertainer, Not on Our Watch initiator, but also a very gifted charicature drawer. The victim below is the director of The American.

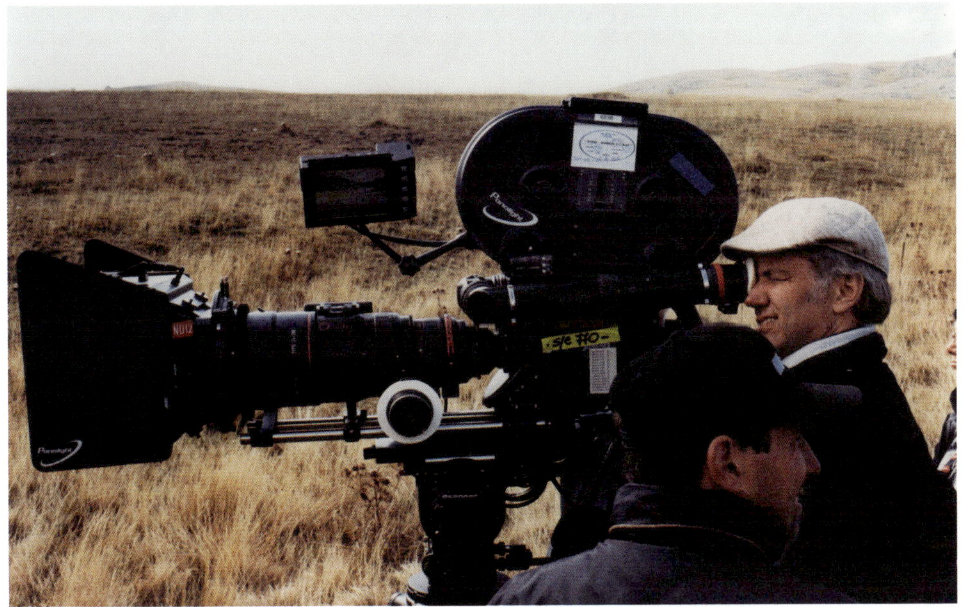

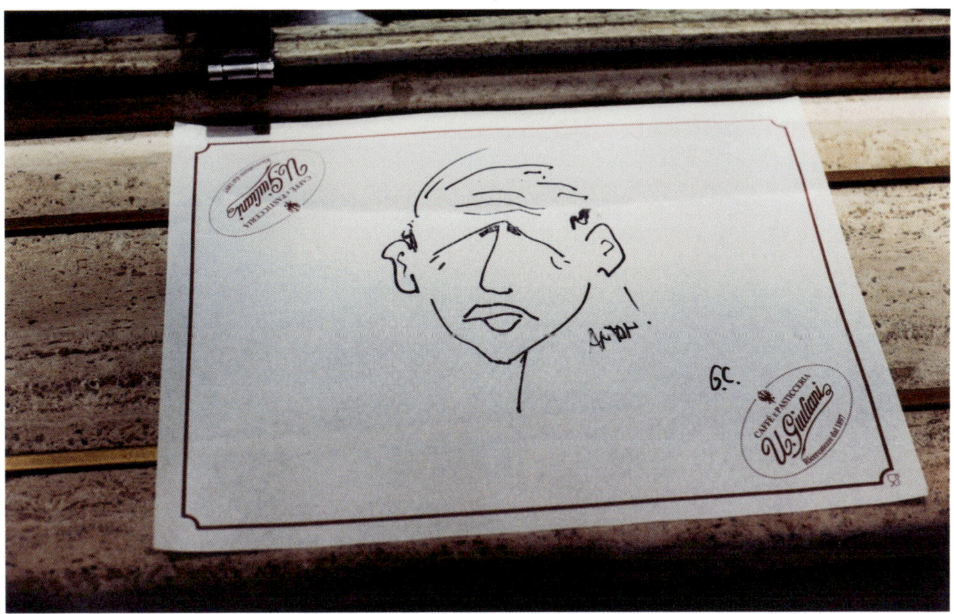

my friends and family who supported me during the process, yes you, aaf, stijn, thijs, peter b, herbert, alex, peter s, bart, bono, klaartje, nathalie, martijn, frans, bobby, jan-maarten, britt, lars, connie, jean-paul, ton, kathleen, harry, pierre, stoya.

monica axelsson, my righthand maverick.

brian dowling, master colour printer.

warren jackson for the design - again.

DESIGN BY WARREN JACKSON
PHOTOGRAPHY AND TEXT BY ANTON CORBIJN
PHOTOS PRINTED BY BRIAN DOWLING
ANTON CORBIJN LTD MANAGED BY MONICA AXELSSON

PRINTED AND BOUND BY EBS, VERONA
ISBN 978-3-8296-0476-5

A SCHIRMER/MOSEL PRODUCTION
WWW.SCHIRMER-MOSEL.COM/CORBIJN